FLOTILLA

FLOTILLA

Colin Walsh

Published in the United Kingdom by Granta Editions 2011.

25-27 High Street, Chesterton, Cambridge CB4 1ND, United Kingdom

Granta Editions is a wholly owned imprint of Book Production Consultants Ltd

A CIP catalogue record for this book is available from the British Library

ISBN 978-1-915662-93-4

Illustrator Emma Macleod-Johnstone
Cover design by Paul Barrett
Design and production in association with
Book Production Consultants Ltd, 25-27 High Street, Chesterton,
Cambridge CB4 1ND, United Kingdom
Printed in the United Kingdom

W. W. W.

Colin Walsh was born in Bootle in 1945, thus bringing an end to World War II. Educated at the end of a leather strap by Christian Brothers, he read psychology at Reading University, graduating with a lousy degree but gaining a first-grade wife, Sarah, by whom he has two sons. After spending three years as a professional actor, he proved that he had no talent at all and joined the *Spectator*, plummeting to a publishing career via Cambridge University Press. In 1973, he and his partner, Tony Littlechild, founded Book Production Consultants Plc from which they eke out a precarious but exciting living turning trees into books – and occasionally vice versa.

FLOTILLA is his eighth book and his first novel. He lives on, and periodically in, the River Cam, where he is working on his next book, the definitive novel about the Sixties, imaginatively entitled *SIXTIES*.

Contents

FLOTILLA – THE CAST

THE FLOTILLA SKIPPER

Ulysses X............. Ted Banks and Sally Carson

THE CREWS

Annus Mirabilis... The Hon. Crispin St Clair, his wife
Tara and children Lucien and Arabella

Becker................. Gerhard Felgruber and his daughter
Monika

The Bounty......... Steven and Amy Clawrer

De Profundis....... Jürgen König, his wife Elke and son
Arnold

Discovery............ Sidney and Clara Chippendale

Moby Dick.......... Jack Armitage, his wife Rosie and
children Sharon and Darren

Nemesis.............. Eric Warbelow, his wife Penny and
children Alan, Trudy and Mark

Siren................... Bernie and his three nurses Lorraine, Liz
and Julie

Thistle................ Hamish Gillicuddy, his wife Flora and
children Angus and Angie

THE SEA SERPENT

Angela Mia.......... Luigi Giannovi and his companion
Ariadne Xstanopoulis

THE CASTAWAY

Angela Mia (unauthorized)................ Oleg Grameshic Dhoni

THE POLICE FORCE

Chief of Police in Thessadikios......... Georgiou Komoulides

THE MILITARY MIGHT

NATO Headquarters for
Balkan Operations............................ General Samuel B. Hochhymer

His Aide.. Major Gabriel Swit

CHAPTER ONE

THE FLOTILLA ASSEMBLES. HAMISH TAKES A RIDE. SHARON BRINGS CORFU AIRPORT TO A HALT. ERIC IDENTIFIES THE OIKS. AMY LONGS FOR LOVE AMONG THE RUINS. GERHARD LONGS FOR LUST AMONG THE CREWS.

Mrs Rosie Armitage decided to try again. Very cautiously, she heaved up her eyelids like the slow-acting shutter of her long-ago Brownie.

There *was* a pecker at the porthole. Strictly speaking, it *wasn't* a porthole: she couldn't think of the exact nautical term. 'Fanlight' came to mind, but she couldn't imagine sailors talking jauntily about fanlights. They liked tougher-sounding words, mainbraces and hoisting and cleats; 'fanlight' suggested scrubbed steps and brass door-knockers.

Whatever it was, there was a pecker in it. She eyed it dispassionately as it bobbed up and down in perfect timing with the – the porthole. It made her think of synchronized swimming on telly, each movement so well rehearsed, so perfectly balanced.

I suppose, she thought, since the boats – the 'yachts' – are all roped together, we're all whatsit, *synchronized*, bobbing as one to the dictates of the waves. This Newtonian logic explained adequately why a pecker on one yacht could be synchronized to a porthole on another.

Mrs Rosie Armitage shuffled uncomfortably onto her back, seeking a patch of sweat that would have a temporary cooling effect. Her thigh rebounded off her husband's huge buttock with a slimy 'thuck'. Two adults sleeping in a V-formation took some getting used to. It required an element of cooperation. If four feet were to wiggle in the pointy end of the 'V', then the rest of the bits must dispose themselves about the cabin as best they could, give a bit, take a bit. Jack Armitage's bits, though, were large and demanding, requiring more than their fair share.

She sighed, not an unhappy sigh, but a sigh of resignation tinged with martyrdom. Yachting was not quite as – as *smart* as she had thought it would be. She hadn't given much thought to the toilet – the 'heads', they called it although the 'bottoms' might have been more appropriate – until she found that the storage tank was right under their bunk. Not even an open bottle of Ambre Solaire balanced precariously above her cabin light could dispel the distinctly unpleasant aroma that pervaded the cabin.

She flicked a glance to the left. 'It' was still there. Moments of great trauma are supposed to last only seconds yet there is time, she had read, to review your whole life. Perhaps only seconds had elapsed since she had set eyes on the pecker.

Mrs Rosie Armitage screamed. The yachts rocked violently as the pecker's owner fell overboard with shock. The Ambre Solaire upended itself, its perfumed oil pouring neatly into Jack's cavernous mouth.

The Ulysses Flotilla woke up.

*   *   *

The charter flight bearing the varied crews who would make up the flotilla had been relatively uneventful, at least compared to those which crated Brits to the Costa Brava. With barely an hour's delay, it had left Gatwick at 6 a.m., the majority of passengers being drunk only with lack of sleep.

There were the diehards, of course, solidly plastered as they made their way up the gangway from the wrong end of the plane to their seats where they spent the next three hours vomiting into their ghetto-blasters. For them, 'Cor–Phew' offered the delights of Benitses, of lobster–red flesh in impeccably elegant bovva boots, perhaps a little rumble with the locals, a few quick bangs with the totty on the next balcony and a Metaxa-induced sleep to the gentle strains of Motorhead.

The majority, though, stoically went through the routine of emergency procedure, dutifully dropped butter in their laps from their plastic trays and balefully listened to the howls of the spoilt brat whose enraged neighbour had finally done something awful with his spam in an effort to silence it.

As the plane disgorged its contents on the tarmac of Corfu Airport, the outgoing ranks of tanned holiday makers returning to England's cultured shores waved their worry beads from the balcony in derision at the white knees and harassed expressions of the incoming tourists. If the P.A.

system had been working, their cheerfulness would have abated at the news of a four-hour delay to their flight home.

Gathering around the two inert carousels beneath the broken telemonitors, the anxious array of motley passengers waited for their luggage and began sizing each other up, eyeing the labels on hand luggage to determine *who* was travelling with *which* company. To the relief of those with other labels, it was noted that the ghetto-blasters were labelled 'Simpsons'.

As yet unknown to each other, the crews of the ten yachts due to make up the flotilla of Ulysses Holidays formed part of the increasing congestion as more flights arrived. Suddenly a carousel jerked into life, elbows jabbed into ribs in an unmannerly jostling for position, and an incongruous pair of Alpine skis rattled into view before jamming the mechanism.

At the head of the carousel, his worried bearded face creased with consternation, squirmed the figure of 'Mr Neurotic', flanked by a thin, severe-faced wife and two shadows of children, both squeaking like hamsters. As he pulled tentatively at the jammed skis, his thin white legs clad in depressing shorts strained to keep balance, his sandals – the sort that the old SDP might have supplied by mail order – slithering on the greasy floor.

With a jerk, the reluctant carousel stuttered on its way bearing the flailing figure of Mr Neurotic like an upturned woodlouse on a circuitous tour of the baggage retrieval lounge. He completed half a loop to the silent amazement of the considerable crowd, before a hugely-plump arm stretched out and hooked him off in one upward sweep and landed him like an uncooked lobster.

"Zo, you cannot wait for starting your holiday, ja?" smiled 'Mr Hugely Fat', patting Mr Neurotic on the head like a pet Alsatian while the latter trembled with the sensation of sickness that fairground rides always induced in him.

The first flotilla contact had been made. Jürgen König, a hearty Bavarian, whose proudly rounded belly proclaimed fifty-odd years of unceasing consumption of metres of varied

Wurst, had saved Hamish Gillicuddy, the diminutive ecologically-concerned Scotsman, from delivery into the hands of three tattooed yobs eager to remove his Army and Navy surplus-to-requirements shorts.

*   *   *

The bubbling tarmac outside Terminals 1, 2 and 3 (impressively named but, in fact, the same terminal for any flight that cared to risk landing) supported three bubbly nurses plus Bernie, a pink Englishman with a startling resemblance to Tommy Cooper.

The crew of *Ulysses X* (as they turned out to be) was to remain an enigma throughout the next fortnight, an intense source of speculation. Which guardian of suppositories, anti-insect spray and kaolin-and-morphine shared with Bernie the double cabin in the bow of their immaculately clean yacht? There were obviously three candidates, each so generously proportioned that the keel of their yacht was some six inches lower than any other in the flotilla.

Bernie offered no answer, issuing orders to his three sirens with perfect equanimity, confident in his macho ability to sail a twenty-eight-foot yacht with a totally inexperienced crew. While all the other passengers awaited the arrival of their luggage with irritation and impatience, Bernie and his harem were already surrounded by an awesome collection of baggage which included a portable delivery unit, designed to allow a mother-to-be instant production of an infant under pristine hygienic conditions. Bernie was nothing if not thorough.

The Armitage family, flanked by most of the male airport staff under fifty, emerged into the heat blast and struggled with their assorted luggage over to the traffic island where Bernie sat comfortably on a fold-away bidet provided by his thoughtful entourage. There was, as yet, no sign of the coach which was to deliver them to the yachts waiting in the harbour of Mengalissi.

It was Miss Armitage, or rather the spangled miniskirt

which would not have provided sufficient cloth to make a suit for a fashion-conscious gerbil, which had caused the general alert among the Greek personnel. None of them attempted to help the delectable Sharon with her assortment of vanity cases, carrier bags and pink-and-white panda. There were collective groans of appreciation every time she bent down to retrieve one of her various baggages: the rounded cheeks of her pretty bottom, unsuccessfully restrained by a flash of white panties, were causing unaccountable delays to incoming circling planes. The fight which had broken out in the radar-control tower for possession of the airport's only pair of binoculars was now causing air-traffic logjams in Gatwick.

Jack Armitage, whose daughter's charms were the cause of constant bother in Bradford, was feeling irritable, angry and hungry.

"Get a move on, will yer," he snarled at the sulky Sharon as panda hit the tarmac for a third time. "I told yer not ter bring that bloody stupid whatsit on a boatin' 'oliday."

He glared balefully at the appreciative audience.

"Don't bloody 'elp, will yer?" he bawled, his blood pressure rising a few more degrees at a ripple of applause from the male fans.

"Shud up, Jack," murmured Rosie, wishing she'd remembered to change out of her slippers before getting off the plane. Her feet swelled up something awful. Behind her slunk Darren, his tight leather gear causing sweat rivulets to gather uncomfortably in his crotch. He had the suspicion that the red dye of his Mohican was cruising down the back of his neck, ruining the slogan 'LEEDZ FANZ GOT GREAT GLANZ' on the back of his designer-ripped T-shirt. It was difficult to swagger in front of the foreign bastards when both arms were filled with your mother's duvet, brought as protection against cold nights at sea.

"Allo, then," said Jack, more or less affably, to the enthroned Bernie as the Armitages collectively dumped their loads. "Ye're with the flertilla lot, are yer?"

There was a general round of introductions and sweaty

handshakes, while Darren feverishly searched for his mirror shades in his mother's beach bag. Sharon's high heels teetered around each nurse, her doll-blue eyes smiling a friendly greeting while her doll-blank mind dismissed the opposition.

"Gawd, it's bleedin' 'ot, ain't it though," said Jack, wiping melting Brylcream from his forehead with a Kleenex. A piece of the tissue parted under the soaking and remained stuck above his eyes, like a greying quiff attached to what remained of a 1950s Teddy-boy's haircut.

"Yacht?" answered Bernie. "They're not here. Got a bit of a way to go yet, when the coach arrives."

"Not YACHT," suddenly yelled Lorraine, the plumpest and, in her opinion, the most luscious of the nurses. "He said HOT."

She turned conspiratorially to Jack. "He's a bit Mutt and Jeff," she explained, in what was supposed to be a whisper yet drowned the noise of an approaching jet.

"Oh aye," responded the startled Jack, "let's 'ope we won't need any bleedin' foghorns then!"

Three nurses glared at the weak witticism.

"We don't make jokes about people's disabilities," remonstrated Julie, the youngest and, in her opinion, the most desirable of the nurses.

"Anyway, he's a real sailor and can do anything on a boat," added Liz, the most short-sighted and, in her opinion, the most lovable of the nurses.

There was an uncomfortable silence until they became aware that the group was being 'Hallo'd' by a small, dapper-looking figure in a navy-blue military shirt, matching shorts and white socks, each pulled to exactly the same height below the knee.

Two blond-haired youths, both annoyingly taller than their father by several inches, flanked their mother who looked, despite the heat and confusion, relatively serene and cheerful. Alan and Mark inherited both their height and their blondness from Penny, as did their sister, Trudy, whose prettiness was almost disguised by a curious out-of-date presentation. Not *old fashioned:* out of date.

A pony tail that was *too* pony-tailed, *too* little girlish, a dress that was, well, too much of a dress. She certainly wasn't wearing 'gear'. You looked at Trudy and suddenly you heard Connie Francis singing *Lipstick on Your Collar* and felt Pat Boone crooning down your neck.

Trudy was wholesome. Trudy was wholesome *and* feminine *and* didn't do the things *boys* did. Because her Dad warned her – often.

Eric was a neat little man, everything in its rightful place, spectacles, testicles, wallet and watch. Standing in the baking sun on the edge of the broken pavement, his tight, compact body was poised ready for action, his alert black eyes scanning the horizon for Indians.

He was at odds with the Nineties. Today's world – mainly the world perceived through television – sickened him. Its morals, its fashions, its tastes, its values. And next birthday, he was the big five-oh, 50. He couldn't believe it: he didn't *feel* fifty – he didn't even know what fifty felt like.

But he knew it was *middle* middle age, he knew he was now more memories than hopes. That was an increasingly crushing knowledge which, combined with his fetish for all aspects of healthy living and need for a sense of order, produced a diminutive neurotic.

The plane journey had got him through Chapter One of his holiday reading, *Facing Your Fifties,* leaving him more worried than ever. In twenty years' time he would be one of the few people alive who could remember most of the words of Lonnie Donegan's *Does Your Chewing Gum Lose its Flavour on the Bedpost Overnight.*

"I can't see a coach," he said stressfully, "There isn't a coach in sight."

Penny smiled reassuringly.

"They're waving back, that must be our group. Why don't we just go over and wait with them?"

"Well, they could be anyone sitting in the middle of the road. That courier said there would be a coach outside."

"I'm sure there *will* be," comforted Penny, marshalling

the children. "They look like – like yachting people. I'm sure that's them."

"Oh, by the vay, my name is Gerhard, Gerhard Felgruber."

With one pull on the string, the Warbelow family turned in unison towards the utterer of Teutonic vowels. Gerhard raised his rather racy leather stetson.

"I think you are being with the flotilla, *nicht wahr?*" smiled the tanned German, his sinister silvery eyes flickering over the group.

Alan, the eldest and most forthcoming of the Warbelow children, agreed.

"Er, yes, we are. We're looking for the coach. I think those people over there are waiting for it."

Gerhard gestured to what appeared to be a youngish female standing next to him. It was difficult to tell: she wore a long flowing robe that concealed the outline of her body, her face in the shade of a large floppy hat that fell to her eyes.

"Oh," said Gerhard, "that is good. By the vay, this is my daughter, Monika."

The hat made a floppy movement of greeting: from somewhere underneath it a low vibrant voice muttered an indistinct acknowledgement.

Eric took over the introductions, unconsciously clicking his sports shoes together at each name, some dim memory of old black-and-white movies motivating this need for protocol.

"Trudi," said Felgruber with a good 'trrr' roll. Although his English was undeniably accented, he eschewed the 'zss' so beloved by actors playing Nazi interrogators, leaving 'wss' as his main problem. "Ja, ve have the same name in our language."

His eyes scanned Trudy appraisingly, bringing a winsome flush to her peachy cheeks and alarm bells into Daddy's eyes.

"Yes, but it's with a 'y'," said Eric pedantically.

"Please?" queried Old Sinister Eyes.

"Yours is with an 'i'," answered Eric, an edgy belligerent note coming into his voice. "You Germans spell it with an 'i'."

He made it sound typical of Germans.

"Vith an eye?"

Gerhard was bewildered and beginning to dislike this aggressive-sounding Englishman.

"Vot am I doing with my eye?"

"Oh, for God's sake, I'm just pointing out..."

Penny interrupted before any more heat was added to the sun.

"We spell 'Trudy' with a final 'y' in English, not with an 'i' as you do in Germany," she said smilingly.

"Ah, now I understand. Trrrud–ee. So. But how did you – ah – guess that ve are Germans?"

Penny was saved the embarrassment of replying by a stentorian holler from Jack Armitage.

"Oi, you lot over there! You with the flertilla? Coach is 'ere!"

"Oh my God," moaned Eric. "Oiks!"

"Ja," shouted Gerhard, "Thank you. Ve come."

Grabbing their assorted luggage, the Anglo-Germanic Alliance toiled to the coach stop where the Armitages seemed transfixed at the sight of Lorraine's generous rear squeezing through the coach entrance.

"Gawd blimey," breathed Jack, "she'll never get that lot into a cabin. Bloody boat'll capsize!"

Gerhard removed his stetson with a Teutonic flourish.

"May I make an introduction of myself? I am Gerhard Felgruber and this is my daughter, Monika. And," he said, pleased to show how quickly people took to him, "Eric here says that you are the Oiks."

The hand replacing his hat hovered in mid-air as he noted the stricken faces of the group around him. Dimly aware of some sort of *faux pas*, he slowly lowered the stetson into place.

"I think, perhaps, you are not the Oiks. Maybe," he murmured, looking up at Bernie's face peering from an open window on the coach, "maybe you are an Oik?"

Bernie's expression did not reflect the camaraderie you would expect to find in a holiday party. Though his hearing was not acute, you had to be stone deaf not to hear a foreigner bawling 'Oik' at you.

Gerhard turned to the pop-eyed Eric for rescue.

"Ah, I think, perhaps, I have not correctly understood. I – thought, ah, that you had seen your friends ven you said 'Mein Gott, the Oiks'..."

Eric looked as though rigor mortis had taken a firm hold. Once again, Penny came to the rescue.

"No, no," she said, going for an Oscar, "he said '*Yoicks*'. It's an expression we have, like – er – like '*Tally Ho!*' It means 'let's get going', doesn't it, Eric?"

"Yoicks," assented Eric, in a strangled voice. "Tally Ho."

The Armitages eyed him grimly.

"Well," sniffed Rosie, "I thought this was a boatin' 'oliday, not a bloomin' 'unt."

Jack looked as though 'hunt' was not the word he had in mind. He turned to his family.

"Come on," he snorted, "get the stuff on board before 'ole Jorrocks 'ere gets 'is bloody whip out. An' don't show 'im yer panda," he warned Sharon, "else 'is bleedin' 'ounds'll rip it ter bits."

Difficulty with language was merely the first problem to hit the flotilla.

*   *   *

It was another hour before the coach was ready to depart. By that time, all but two of the missing flotilla crews had been rooted out of various buses with mysterious destinations, most of their baggage had been recovered and Sharon had rewarded the fans gathered around the coach by giving them a tantalizing flash of her pert pink-nippled breasts as she changed her tank top for a becoming yellow halter, tied at the neck. The coach sped away with a grinding of gears, tumultuous applause and cat calls from the appreciative audience.

As it threaded its way along dusty-white roads lined with prickly cacti and half-completed villas, sleep gradually

11

overcame most of the exhausted travellers, despite the awful racket the thoughtful driver provided for his passengers on the badly-tuned radio.

The Gillicuddys lolled together in a sad-looking mess, like evacuees torn from their roots. Behind them were the Königs, Jürgen occupying most of two seats, his wife, Elke, sprawled lovingly in deep sleep across his wobbling belly as though clinging to a raft at sea. Their son Arnold stared unseeingly at the scenery, still unable to cope with the fact that the love of his life, a lustrous-eyed Italian, Stephania, had given him the bird for a rich old *Schweinhund* in her home town. He had reluctantly joined his parents TO FORGET but the deep sighs that spiralled up from his painful chest every other minute were not the symptoms of a chronic asthmatic but of a man who knew the cupidity of women.

The Armitage party sat as far away as possible from the Warbelows, Jack – still with a piece of Kleenex clinging to his forehead like a persistent piece of fungus – refusing to forgive the suspected insult in true holiday spirit. Darren's head had fallen against the window while he dozed uncomfortably, spreading a peculiar layer of grease and red dye over the glass as though his head was leaking.

Behind the Armitages sat a couple of late arrivals, American newly-weds. Steven – he wouldn't answer to 'Steve' – was a thin, dour, thirtyish man, black haired and black-browed. He had not returned any proffered greetings save for a glare and a grunt. His eyes were glued to a glossy length of smooth thigh protruding from the seat in front where Sharon's lithe body made a warm cocoon for her panda – a fact noticed by his wife who appeared at least twenty years his senior.

Amy Clawrer wasn't sure if she was in seventh heaven or sixth hell. Twice divorced, Steven was to be third time lucky but this honeymoon in the Greek Islands was off to a bad start. Though Amy was of a volatile disposition, which had frequently led to the launching through the air of a bottle of Southern Comfort at a previous husband's head, on the whole she maintained a reasonable calm.

But Steven was something else. The personification of moroseness, he found fault with everything – the climate, the Greeks, and her piled–up hairdo which she had thought was rather in the 'classical' style. (At what point the Greeks had undergone the change from blond Gods and Goddesses to Mediterranean blackness was a mystery she couldn't fathom. When she'd had a bit part in *Hercules Unchained* back in the Fifties, she'd worn a yellow wig that precisely matched the complicated braid presently piled on her head. Maybe Hollywood had been a bit off beam.)

She was, however, prepared to give Greece a go, it being the cradle of civilization and all that. From the moment she stepped off the plane, she had felt surrounded by legend, myth and heroic deeds. Even now, after such a fatiguing start, she was on the lookout for signs of Ancient Civilization. Looking at the bus driver, she thought she could faintly discern the look of a Trojan – or perhaps a Spartan – about his chewing profile. He could be, just possibly, descended from Achilles or Hector or one of those guys who had been featured in those *Hercules* movies. The coach had already passed simply dozens of places selling all those Greek vases which presumably had been dredged up out of the sea. She could hardly wait for her 'Stevie' – he hated her calling him 'Stevie' but it sounded sort of cosy – to dive to the ocean floor and bring her up a vase or two.

Bernie, his neck comfortably cradled in a blow-up pillow, slept with the serene look of a King Solomon serviced by three attentive Shebas. Lorraine, Julie and Liz were seated strategically around him, taking turns to swat any Greek mosquito eager to taste Bernie's blood. This over-kill was quite unnecessary: Bernie was so full of anti-malaria shots that the merest sip by an unwary mosquito would have brought about its demise.

Along the back seat of the coach reclined the enigmatic figure of Monika Felgruber, with only a hand protruding dramatically from the draped robes and enveloping hat to indicate that a body was concealed within. Her father sat in the corner, his stetson tipped sufficiently over his eyes to conceal their constant roaming and speculation. This would be a disappointing flotilla if Gerhard failed to find romance.

The sweat-sodden passengers arrived, two hours later, at the port of Mengalissi where, it was hoped, the two missing crews would be joining them – with luck, before the end of the holiday. Among the assorted craft moored to the quay were the ten shroud-tinkling Ulysses yachts, bobbing gently on the glistening, sun-glinting sea.

Their patience rewarded, seven crews stumbled down the coach steps onto the quayside. It seemed almost impossible to believe that, two weeks later, they would all be one happy family.

Almost . . .

CHAPTER TWO

ROSIE RECEIVES ANOTHER SHOCK. THE SKIPPER'S BRIEFING. THE CREWS GET TO KNOW EACH OTHER, FOR BETTER OR FOR WORSE. THE FLOTILLA NEARLY GETS UNDERWAY. JACK NEARLY GETS UNDER THE FLOTILLA.

Ted Banks had nearly completed his first morning exercise when Rosie Armitage's scream literally rocked the flotilla.

"Wuuurghhh" groaned Ted as he reached orgasm.

"Croooohhh" moaned Sally as she climaxed.

They were a perfect couple.

Ulysses Ltd could not have found a more appropriate couple to chaperone the flotilla crews. For a skipper, even Ted's name sounded reliable, the sort of name you added 'Good old...' to, when reminiscing with the photo album.

If Ted had a drawback, and not many would have been willing to come forward and say it straight to his good-natured, sort-of-wholesome face, it was being too enthusiastic, over keen. He embraced life with an ardent fervour, much in the same way as he had just embraced Sally. He went the whole hog – in the right mood, he could *eat* the whole hog.

It was hard to determine his age; perhaps forty-something but, with his boyish delight in everything around him, he could be ten years younger. Sally was easier to appraise: a lovely, sweet-faced thirty, long black hair, dimpled cheeks and with such neat jet-black eyebrows over smiling, dark-lashed eyes that any artist would have made them slightly blurry so as not to appear too amateurish in their reproduction.

Ted always started the day as he meant to go on, making love with vigour and dedication. And sometimes, Sally thought a little wistfully, like a gymnastic work-out. If there had been room for a trapeze in their rather cramped double-berth, he would have swung from it. He had a time schedule for every manoeuvre, when they should change position, how much attention to be given to each bit. It was always perfect. Perfection. Predictable perfection. Sally would have liked, just once, to have slightly missed out, a little bit of dissatisfaction, something to aim for next time. Ted's aim, though, was infallibly on target.

"J-a-a-a-c-k!" screamed Rosie, so loudly that Ted wondered if Sally's moan of ecstasy had echoed around the flotilla.

"It's someone on one of ours," said Sally anxiously, quicker on the uptake than her muscled fiancé.

Ted opened the cabin skylight and poked out an enquiring head.

"Yuh got problems over there?" he shouted, his Aussie accent making 'the–yar' echo around the bay.

Tousled heads were appearing from similar openings down the row of yachts, like targets on a hoop-la stall.

Jack's head swivelled round in Ted's direction, a glove puppet operated from below by Rosie. The Armitage yacht was tied up at the opposite end of the row to Ted's, just about within hailing distance.

Jack hailed.

"There's a – yurghh – there's a bloody – ruugh – there's a bloody pervert running round exposin' 'imself," bellowed Jack's head, little streams of Ambre Solaire running from the miniature oil well of his mouth.

"Crikey," answered Ted, "that's a bit rough."

A heave of his finely–tuned biceps took him through the skylight onto the white deck, already warmed by the sun. With a series of athletic bounds, leaps and dodges, he passed from one end of the moored yachts to the other, until he reached the Armitages'.

Jack had retreated below, a vigorous pumping suggesting that he was attempting to gurgle suntan oil down the heads.

Rosie's head replaced Jack's at deck level, just as Ted bounded on board.

"Oh Jesus, Mary and Joseph," she screeched, "Jack, Jack, there's another one!"

Ted regarded her blankly then spun on his heel to the sound of Sally's urgent voice.

"Your trunks," she shouted, waving a garment in the air, "Ted, your trunks!"

"Strike a light," he gasped, peering at his naked nether regions with dismay.

"Abyssinia," was all he could summon up on the spur of the moment before he executed a perfect backflip over the bow.

*   *   *

By midday, the crews of the Ulysses flotilla were assembled at the café opposite the quay, nervously and attentively awaiting Ted's briefing under the sunshades. Jürgen König, whose digestive system was more complicated than most, there being so much of it, took advantage of the occasional clatter of mopeds and scooters to release a steady output of odiferous farts. With a true Brit bias the English commented on the inability of foreigners to sort out their drainage system. There was a general shifting of seats, leaving the König family, long since immune and impervious to *Vati*'s irrigation channels, feeling that the war was still a recent memory for the English. This, despite the fact that they had deliberately chosen egg and bacon from the menu to express their kindred spirit.

The two missing crews had arrived in the early hours of the morning, after being deposited at first in the wrong port and taking their places, amid much bewilderment, on board two yachts chartered from a dashing Italian entrepreneur. The owner, Luigi Giannovi, had unravelled the troubled situation with great charm, taking the opportunity to point out how such problems were often encountered with English companies and were generally resolved by Italians. He had a vested interest in discrediting Ulysses Ltd: Mengalissi, a bay much favoured for mooring flotillas, was full and would allow no further berths without present allocations becoming vacant. Unless something nasty happened to Ulysses Ltd – and Luigi could be pretty nasty – his yachts would have to remain at their present desolate location and his dream of organizing his own flotilla would remain solidly aground.

Luigi had persuaded Stavros, the ice-block seller, to pack his open truck with the near-hysterical travellers and their belongings and to deliver them, damp and dispirited, to Mengalissi. This was accomplished, naturally, by the application to Stavros's palm of large quantities of drachmas collected from the travellers...with only a modest percentage as Luigi's commission. As the fatigued passengers, four

18

adults and two children, bumped and bruised their way to their awaiting berths, the cynical thought did occur to them that they had been conned right from the airport and that Luigi regularly hijacked other flotillas' crews. To be the victims of a pirate before they had even set sail was depressing.

After barely a couple of hours' sleep to refresh them, the two sets of new arrivals were now slumped somewhat dazedly under their respective umbrellas, with their sole interest in the proceedings confined to the next opportunity of falling unconscious.

Ted's equanimity and prestige was restored largely through Sally's diplomacy and by a bottle of Retsina for each of the stunned crews after the unfortunate displays of nudity – the other offender had been Gerhard who still could not believe that the English were so prudish as to take offence at the sight of what he secretly and affectionately referred to as his *Zeppelin*. Ted once again happily faced his companions at sea for the next fortnight.

"Well," he said, "you all feelin' kosher now?"

There was no response to this incomprehensible question so Ted ploughed on, a picture of rude health and exasperating cheerfulness.

"It's real dapper to see you all in holiday mood," he chimed, confusing them further with his curious mixture of adopted homely slang, "I'm sure we're all going to pucker together into an amazingly blithe team!"

"Sweet Jesus, Amy, I can't understand a word this guy is sayin'," snorted Steven loudly to his elaborately coiffured bride, who regarded Ted with a mixture of mystification for his language and admiration for his biceps. The flotilla skipper reminded her of an extra in *Hercules Hits Back* with whom she had investigated Greek legends back in the Fifties.

"He can't help it, honey," she said appeasingly to her exasperated paramour, "he's only Australian."

Ted's soul was as sensitive as his A1 hearing.

"It's great we've got such a mixed bunch on board. Lessee, we've got Brits, an' English, an' Jer– Germans, an' even Yanks!" he enthused, shooting a wicked glance in Steven's direction.

"As you've twigged, me and Sally here are from Down Under though we've – "

"Down under what?" yapped Steven crossly.

One of the late arrivals spluttered into life. A round, totally bald squinty-eyed man in his fifties, he was known to his few friends as Old Pompous Arse. OPA knew the answers to everything, had advice for everyone. He was seated now, clad only in his trunks, like a hairy Buddha – there was enough hair growing from his shoulders to make two fashionable pony-tails – ready to pontificate.

"Well, you wouldn't know in America," lectured Sidney Chippendale, in a surprisingly squeaky voice, "because the Australian continent is not, as it were, on the other side of the world to you. But to the English, and," he smiled ingratiatingly at the Gillicuddys, "to you Europeans, Australia is literally underneath us. If you were to bore a hole..."

"I'm bored with this asshole," came from Darren in an almost audible whisper.

"Shudup," said Rosie, "and watch yer language. Sharon, don't lounge like that, ye're showin' everything you've got."

But Sharon was oblivious, lost to the throbbing of Bros in her earphones. With her chair tipped back, that glorious oil–smoothed body was fetchingly displayed, fetching the poor one–eyed waiter to the Armitage table with alarming frequency, his good eye gliding over kissable breasts down to the beckoning valley between her legs.

Sally came to the aid of her man.

"This is our second season in the Ionian," she smiled reassuringly, "and you're the third flotilla that Ted has skippered."

"Ah so," joked the witty Gerhard who liked to make his presence felt from the outset,"but it is not the third time lucky, ja?"

Ted looked startled.

"Hey, well, Ulysses maybe shouldn't have mentioned that.

I mean, there's always teething troubles. And most of them got their money back once they'd got out of Albania..."

Sally's interruption was timely.

"Oh, yes, that's right, I remember. The – er – Oedipus Flotilla, not one of ours fortunately, yes, there *was* a navigational error, it's very easy to stray into Albanian waters."

Timid Hamish Gillicuddy looked alarmed.

"Albania? Was that – I read something about that in *The Scotsman*. Surely they weren't the ones who were put in prison and had to be exchanged for tractors or something?"

To the German ears, what he actually said, though his Scots accent wasn't that broad, was something like 'Albania? Hootna reedathatayeanthanoo, etc'. Sidney, on the other hand, had assumed the Gillicuddys to be at least foreign, small and dark-haired as they were. In fact, with their collective greyish appearance and drab summer outfits, they could even have been Albanian.

Despite it being a fine, clear and sun-warmed day, the atmosphere was becoming unsettled.

Bernie Houghton, flanked by his three perspiring nurses who had carefully positioned themselves to give him the maximum shade available, came to the rescue.

"Well, Skip, here we all are, the best crews in the Med. Alright," he looked momentarily irritated by OPA's muttered correction, "in the Ionian. When do we get the show on the road?"

"That's talkin'," said the relieved Ted, "that's the input the old lugholes want to hear. Now, I think you've maybe all met along with each other and just know you're all goin' to be mates so I'll just introduce the – er – late arrivals who didn't make it 'til sparrowfart."

"Dawn," clarified Sally, noting the bewildered looks.

"Er, now, lessee." Ted consulted his manifesto. "We've got the – er – Honcrips – no, Honcrisps, that's, er, Sinclair, Tar– Tara, Luchin and Arabia? You looked a bit rooted when you turned up but I bet ye're feelin' chipper now, eh?"

The St Clairs felt anything but chipper. Looking

collectively pale and drawn, they were seated as far away as possible from the others, thereby contributing to the family's general air of depression.

"Look here, apart from getting our names wrong," said a thin, sharp-nosed man clad elegantly in a safari suit, "you've also got this charter biz wrong. We are *not* part of any jolly old flotilla. We have chartered a yacht from Ulysses Ltd in order to sail two weeks' bareboat."

"Gawd 'elp us," squawked Jack, "more bleedin' nudists. An' 'im with kids an' that."

"Can't be done, old sport," answered Ted. "We don't do bareboat. No insurance for independent sailing, see, and the owners won't have it. Must have been some mistake with yer bookin', Sinclair. Don't you get worryin' your noodle, though. You'll really enjoy paddlin' yer canoe along with the rest of us."

Lady St Clair, a disdainful but spirited-looking lady with a clipped snap of a mouth, spoke up with some asperity.

"My husband's name is Crispin. Crispin St Clair. I assume your 'Honcrisp' refers to my husband's title, the Honourable Crispin St Clair. My Christian name is Tara, not Tar – Tara, nor Tarara, nor yet Tararaboomdeay. It's not very difficult to grasp, even for Australians. And," she indicated her two pre-teen children, "these are Lucien and Arabella."

There was an embarrassed shuffling of chairs while this announcement sank in.

Darren Armitage, who was having trouble coping with the melting grease in his Mohican, thought the time opportune to impress Trudy with his globe-trotting experience. Though he wouldn't have been seen dead with her on the terraces at Elland Road, there was something about Trudy Warbelow that appealed to him. Despite her red-and-white check dress and head band, which made her look like a promotion for a wholesome Fifties Doris Day movie, if you looked hard at the top of her dress – and Darren did look hard – you could make out a couple of bumps, one pushing out a red square, the other a white.

"We stayed at an 'otel once called The Arabella, didn't we Dad? It were in Benidorm, remember? We were taken to the wrong one and you said every bleedin' 'otel in Spain was called bleedin' Arabella an' the kharsi broke off when Mum sat on it..."

"I already told you watch yer language," admonished Rosie, comfortably chewing a bacon rind from Jack's plate. She wore a bright, shiny shellsuit that looked as though it was made from aluminium foil. It provided a comfortable internal temperature of 100 degrees centigrade.

"Right then. Got it. Right." Ted proceeded with determination. A leader has to be a leader. "Well, now, er – Crisp, look, no worries. You've got a boat, everything's all tucker, what's the problem, eh, Crisp?"

"One problem, my *dear* fellow," gritted Crispin hotly, "is being called Crisp. I object to being called 'Crisp', absolutely. I do not wish to be called 'Crisp'. My schooldays are long since over."

There was a chortle from Jack.

"Eh, I bet you got them all. I knew a bloke called, what was it Rosie, I told yer, oh aye, Murphy. We called him 'Taters' and 'Spud'ole', not to 'is face, like, bloody big Irish git, got chucked out for rammin' a bin over the 'ead of that teacher, what was 'is name, Rosie –"

"It's no fun being called nicknames," said Eric Warbelow seriously. "Particularly if you're a bit – on the short side. It torments you. I remember, I had a very painful boil, it was when I wore shorts at school, and just because you could see the plaster they called me 'Sore-below'. It diminishes your self-confidence."

He subsided into glum recollection.

A grey Flora Gillicuddy chimed in.

"Children should be taught to be kind and considerate above all else. If there was more respect for the individual we wouldn't have pollution and bad housing and – and smoking," she added with a glare at Steven Clawrer who had just lit a cigar.

The Gillicuddys added smugness to their greyness.

Sally felt that the script had gone wrong.

"Well let's all make the best of it, shall we?" she said lightly. "It's always a little difficult getting the names right at first. I'm sure we'll come to a satisfactory arrangement, Mr – er – Sir St Clair. Just so long as we keep in touch, we don't *have* to sail everywhere together."

She turned to the remaining unidentified couple, Old Pompous Arse and his wife.

"Mr and Mrs Sidney Chippendale, isn't it? Well, that's a name we've all heard of, haven't we? Body Beautiful, and all that..."

She finished rather lamely, eyeing the combined body fat of the Chippendales in front of her and comparing them in her mind to the rippling torsos of their more famous namesakes.

Sidney didn't seem to mind, perhaps because he'd never heard of those embodiments of some female fantasies.

"Chippers! Everyone calls me Chippers! Nicknames do *not* worry me. I don't have such a high value of myself that I can't take a bit of familiarity. I'm a chip off the old block!"

There were polite smiles.

"That's chipper," said Eric, trying it out.

"Chips and Crisps," added Jack nastily.

"Oh, ah, ja, Old Pommes-frites," said Gerhard, going heavily international.

"Chip off the old blubber," suggested Steven maliciously, puffing cigar smoke over the Gillicuddys.

Sidney glared at the American.

"There is, of course, a limit if you come from a *polite* society."

Sally went on hastily.

"And it's Clara, isn't it, er – Mrs Chippendale?"

Clara Chippendale would have replied if her mouth hadn't been crammed with hot stuffed tomato. Clara Chippendale *was* a stuffed tomato, an enormous mound of rosy–coloured flesh whose bulk made Chippers seem slim, like the plain girl who chooses to make friends with an ugly girl to enhance her own looks by comparison. Rubens would have loved Clara, her dollops of fleshy tyres would have filled acres of canvas.

Chippers saw with Rubens's eye and lusted over what he saw. All those handfuls of voluptuous wobble were his, he always seemed to discover a spare acre or two to excite him anew. True, their double berth cabin was unable to accommodate them both at the same time, but a complicated shifting of the spare bunks made it possible for them to cling in loving embrace amidships. The plimsoll line of their yacht was even lower than Bernie and his harem's.

"Wurrrgh," assented Clara happily, shifting her blubber to give the onlookers the full benefit of her more than generous figure clad in what looked like a rubber romper outfit.

"Good Gawd Almighty!" breathed Jack. It had never before occurred to him that Rosie might be anorexic and he ran a hand over her nearest dimpled knee to reassure himself.

"That is some woman," hissed Bernie whose predilection for weighty ladies had, up to now, seemed more than catered for by his three nurses.

The Gillicuddys, who at their healthiest looked like a family advert for Oxfam, gave a familial shudder.

A barely-smothered fart from Jürgen brought the transfixed Ted back to the briefing. He produced a chart of the Ionian and called the meeting to order.

"Our first day is quite a long sail to Sivota, here, on the Greek mainland."

"Excuse me," squeaked Sidney Chippendale, "but I think you've got the chart upside down. Or are we hoping to make Turkey in one day?"

He looked around with a self-satisfied smile.

"Cripes!" exclaimed Ted, "Ye're a sharp lot. No nongs here! Just passed yer first test with flyin' colours!"

A witness to the sudden exchange of glances among his audience might have been forgiven for assuming a team spirit was developing at an early stage. A mutual sense of foreboding was probably nearer the truth.

But the sun was shining, the magnolias were magnoling

and the sea sparkled its invitation, encouraging a holiday spirit of bonhomie which would not be denied.

With timely interruptions from Sally, Ted managed to get through the briefing without causing too much undue alarm. It became apparent from the questions asked that experience among the crews varied from those who considered themselves capable of doing a Chichester round-the-world – like the St Clairs and the Felgrubers (though Monika uttered not a word and maintained her pose of languid mystery) – and those for whom a rowing boat on the Serpentine was the equivalent of a mystery tour on the *Titanic*.

The Armitages were the sole representatives of the latter category. Jack's small windfall from the pools – Darren still hadn't got over the shock of his father marking a home match for Leeds as a loser – was buying them 'the holiday of a lifetime', though whose lifetime was yet to be seen.

Never one for false modesty concerning his talents, Jack had described his previous experience on the booking form as 'nothing floating that he couldn't handle', which in a way, was true. Sailing was another matter. He had, after all, gone out fishing with his mates off the coast at Scunthorpe one Bank Holiday. The resulting confusion among Britain's shipping lanes, and Jack's subsequent disembarkation seventy miles south accompanied by a lifeboat crew, did nothing to diminish his sense of accomplishment. Single-handed, he had saved his mates' lives. That was *not* the considered opinion of his mates who made a point of never seeing him again, but Jack's sea-faring spirit went undaunted. As for Rosie, if Jack wanted a holiday on a boat, that was what they were going to do.

And they were doing it. With provisions now stowed on board, diesel in the tank, a rough idea of where they were heading and Ted and Sally Banks acting like faithful shepherd dogs, the crews prepared to cast off.

Radios bleeped and whined, each crew choosing their own call-sign for recognition by the rest of the flotilla.

The Gillicuddys were the first out.

"*Thistle* to Leader," called Flora in efficient Scottish

tones. "We're underway. Over."

"Leader to Whistle, Over," called back Ted, at a loss. "Identify yourselves, Whistle."

"Not Whistle, *Thistle!*" snapped Flora crossly. "We're the Gillicuddys. *Ulysses III*. Our call sign is..." crackle, crackle, crackle, went the radio, "..istle!"

"Seems to me these Scots buggers are all the same," came back Ted's voice, attentively noted by all the crews. "Calling themselves Gristle, I mean, strike me, why Gristle for God's sake? Seems a bit kinky when yer ponder on it..."

There was an abrupt click as Ted was cut off then Sally's voice took over the airwaves.

"Leader to *Thistle*. We read you. Ted hadn't seen the list of call-signs, but I think he's got it now." There was a sharp crack, like someone being hit with a log book. "Have a good day. Over."

"Thank you, Leader," hissed Flora, "and for your information, it is not 'Scots buggers' but 'Scottish buggers' if we are to be buggers at all. Over and Out."

And the Gillicuddys swept out to the high seas in high dudgeon.

The quayside had burst into a clamour of activity, engines burbling, locker lids slamming, ropes slithering, heads flushing, sheets rattling. Contradictory orders went unheeded, smothered oaths accompanied frantic rubbing as heads hit unaccustomed obstacles, cries of exasperation sneaked up on deck from those who had forgotten to buy toilet rolls.

On board *Moby Dick* – the Armitages had pooled their collective knowledge of seafaring stories and remembered seeing the film on the previous Sunday afternoon – Jack was feeling distinctly nautical.

Engine turning over nicely, he stood at the helm wearing a natty little cap that he thought went nicely with his Hawaian shirt.

"You ready, Mother?" he asked Rosie who stood uncertainly forward, hand nervously clutching the rail. She, too, had slipped into something she considered rather dishy, a black one-piece similar, she thought, to one worn by a model in a well-thumbed Pirrelli calendar she had found under Jack's side of the bed. Michelin might have been more appropriate but Jack liked it and that's what counted.

"Stand by to – er – cast orf, Darren," shouted Jack the Cap'n.

"You bastard!" shrieked Sharon who was sitting bolt upright on the forward deck. Having spread her towel in readiness for a spot of sunbathing as her contribution to the preparations, she had lain back and spread herself to the devastation of the waiter who had nipped upstairs for a last one-eyed ogle of that sumptuous flesh. While he collapsed on his rumpled bed to relieve his profoundly disturbed feelings, Sharon's gaze had swept up to the top of the mast.

There, suspended from his little pink and white neck, hung Snubsy, the only panda in the Ionian looking as though it was about to throw up.

"Get 'im down," shrieked Sharon, shaking delectably all over. "You stupid moron, Darren, get 'im down!"

It is the duty of a skipper to remain calm.

"We'll get the bloody thing down later," said the skipper, remaining calm. "You silly sod, Darren, you'll get that panda down once we're out this 'ere 'arbour. Now, CAST ORF!"

The silly sod untied the mooring rope.

"Well?" roared Cap'n Jack.

"Well what?" replied the disgruntled mate.

" 'Ave yer untied that rope bit? 'Ow d'yer think I can see from 'ere? ye're supposed to shout sumthin', like 'aye, aye, skipper'."

"That's bleedin' soft," shouted Darren, "I'm not sayin' that. Anyway, it's loose."

Jack breathed hard. A few days at sea, maybe, and he'd turn his son into a sea-dog like himself.

"Chocks away, then," he bellowed inappropriately and pushed the engine throttle into gear.

The yacht leapt forward and hit the quay, tumbling the mate on to a bollard and Rosie on to her daughter.

The Honourable Crispin St Clair, who had been observing the crew of *Moby Dick* with deep apprehension, not the least because his yacht was still lashed to Jack's, spoke up.

"Might I suggest, old chap," he said icily, "that you disengage your engine. Then your craft will stop trying to mate with the quayside. Furthermore, you might observe that we are – 'tied together' is the most apt expression I can at present think of, though I am absolutely delighted it is not in holy matrimony – and it might prove frightfully useful to undo the ropes before you sink the flotilla."

"Oh, aye," replied Jack good-naturedly, having nearly understood the clearly-enunciated accent. "Good idea, that, Crisp. Rosie, can yer undo those blinkin' knots there?"

With Darren safely back on board, his Mohican streaked with oil and his temper streaked with passion, the crew of the good ship *Moby Dick* prepared once again to exit.

" 'Ave yer done the radioing bit?" asked Rosie, anxious to make amends before the interested spectators now lining the remaining decks of the flotilla. "Go on, Sharon, do sumthin' fer yer father."

"I'm not doin' anythin 'til I get Snubsy back," said the outraged Sharon, lying down on her stomach. She smoothed handfuls of oil over the exposed cheeks of her enticing bottom. An agonized wail came from the upstairs window of the quayside café, followed by the squeak of rusting bedsprings. Old One-Eye was at it again.

"Tart!" snorted Darren.

"You watch yer language, Darren. I'll do it, Jack."

Rosie gingerly descended the steps into the cabin. She picked up the handset with trepidation and pressed it to her lips.

"Ello, 'ello, – er – Ted, are yer receivin' at your end?"

Ted, who had been hoping to do just that with Sally once the crews had departed, gallantly tuned in.

"I take it that's you, Rosie. How yer diddlin' up there? Seems like you've got one or two problems."

"Oh, no," said Rosie with a hasty glance at her proud Jack, "We're diddlin' nicely thank you. Er – we're goin' out now, to sea, like. Are yer receivin' me?" Vague memories of Forces' Requests stirred in her mind.

"Right on, then, Rosie. Yer don't have to keep on asking me if I'm receiving you. Just say 'Over' when you've finished the verbals. An' don't ferget yer call-sign. What is it again?"

Rosie grew flustered.

"Dick. Moby's Dick. Not Moby's – MOBY – *Moby Dick*! OVER!" she shrieked.

"Over and Out," ended the Leader and allowed his mind and hands to wander as Sally mounted the ladder to the deck. She never made it.

All mooring lines cast loose, *Moby Dick* edged her way backwards into the bay, Jack grimly hanging on to the helm. The yacht cut a curious zig-zagging path as the helm swung sharply left then right, the skipper somewhat foxed by the complications of manoeuvring in reverse. Eventually the bow nosed clear of the quay, the stern bumping all the other craft as the boat turned, sending the spectators hurriedly about their own business.

With a grunt of relief, Jack judged that he was clear to go forward, pushed the throttle lever and was rewarded by a sudden thrust from the engine as the prop pushed twenty-eight feet of white yacht into the bay.

He squinted out to the harbour mouth, turning the helm with a professional pride. This was the life. This was Jack Armitage, at the helm of his own yacht, sailing these Greek seas and heading for adventure. He searched his memory for a suitable shanty to hum and settled for *I do Like to be Beside the Seaside*.

Strangely, although he felt sure he was steering in the right direction for the sea, *Moby Dick* seemed to disagree. While the skipper wanted to go straight ahead, his charge was, *quite definitely*, turning in an arc, back towards the quayside.

"Dad," yelled the trusty mate, "why are we headin' for the other boats?"

"Sumthin's the matter with this tiller thing. She keeps turnin', I can't stop the blasted thing. Wish I just had a steerin' wheel, this thing's plain stoopid."

He cut the engine, then swung it into reverse in the hope of straightening up. The yacht flung itself to stern and turned sharply to face the flotilla. Frantically, Jack plunged the throttle forward, desperately trying to steer *Moby Dick* away from the moored yachts. The engine was not particularly robust but five knots per hour seems quite a pace when you're set to ram some eight yachts not more than one hundred yards away.

The radio spluttered into life.

"For God's sake, cut your engine," screamed the excited voice of Eric Warbelow. "CUT YOUR ENGINE!"

"I think he means turn yer engine off," squealed Rosie, "Stop the engine, Jack!"

Obediently, the skipper cut the throttle and the diesel roar subsided. *Moby Dick* ploughed on under her own momentum, choosing accurately the very middle of the row of yachts, ramming very much in her shrouds.

Darren, ever the loving son, took his first swim of the day with a neatly executed dive while Sharon lay obliviously tuned in to Simply Red. Fifty yards, thirty yards and the flotilla was emptied of its crews, with the sole courageous exception of *Ulysses X*, its occupants seemingly otherwise engaged. Ted, too, was continuing under his own momentum.

Jack had never given serious thought to his will before but now, with Rosie wrapped around him like an undulating set of truck tyres, it crossed his mind that, after years of work on the factory floor and careful adherence to Union rules, his undeserving son Darren was likely to inherit the lot.

A sudden TWANG disrupted this unpleasant chain of thought. *Moby Dick*'s bow bucked into the air, less than five yards from the nearest stern, slapped back into the water, then slewed into a graceful arc away from the flotilla.

Steven Clawrer, whose leap onto the quayside had landed him on an unpleasant mound of fish entrails, spoke for the group.

"YOU BENIGHTED ASSHOLE," he yelled with little

sign of the cordial Anglo-American relationship, "YOU FUCKIN' MANIACAL SNAKE IN THE GRASS!"

There are sneerers who claim the American drawl results in a blurring of words but, true or not, this did not apply to Steven. His words were as clear as flying ice chips.

Jack felt righteously offended. He had, it was plain, saved the flotilla from a catastrophe.

"You shut yer mouth, Yank," he retorted. "This 'ere boat 'as got some blinkin' fault. If it were'nt fer me..."

Sidney Chippendale brought logic to the heated situation.

"You're still anchored. You didn't pull your anchor up. You forgot your anchor. You've got your stern anchor down. You're swinging on the end of your ANCHOR chain."

Even Jack perceived there was some human error to blame for their erratic course.

"I'm with yer," he hollered, "I must 'ave forgot to pull the bloomin' anchor up. Good point, Sid."

However good the text books, experience is the true mentor at sea. Jack had learned his first lesson in seamanship. So, indeed, had Rosie – *NOT* to go to sea with Jack.

"All set?" enquired a sweating Ted, emerging on to his deck. "No problems, eh? Everybody happy?"

From the café, the smell of meatballs and rosemary drifted across the flotilla. Resignedly, the crews of the Ulysses Flotilla headed for lunch. It was not yet noon but already it seemed like a long day.

CHAPTER THREE

The morning after the night before. Eric has a hangover and a sense of failure. While the caves are explored, Luigi fishes for trouble. Liz takes a dip. The St Clairs to the rescue. News of submerged rocks and sunburnt objects.

Eric Warbelow should have been a happy man. The crew of *Nemesis* – a slightly gloomy code-name but one which fitted neatly Eric's preoccupation with the onset of the BIG FIFTY – was beyond criticism.

Penny had tidied and cleaned below decks and the kettle was burbling pleasantly in preparation for Eric's second cup of liquidized Ginseng.

A light breeze kept the mainsail agreeably taut while Mark and Alan, both clad in white shorts and already honey-coloured, unfurled the jib, neither too much nor too little.

Trudy, sitting in the stern next to her father, a towel across her shoulders to protect her unblemished skin from the intense sun rays, was painting a dainty watercolour of the surrounding sea, not an exacting task since there was nothing to see but sea. Not even another sail in sight.

Eric had taken his vitamins and both his socks were drawn up to exactly the same height. A navy-blue peaked cap protected his barely discernible bald spot from blistering; his crisp white shirt, not a wrinkle visible, warded off the cancer-inducing sun. Bliss for any man. Or it should have been. This, the flotilla's first full day at sea, had not started well for Eric. True, he had rather over-indulged the night before but that first day had been pretty traumatic, what with the attempted ramming by *Moby Dick*, the crossing to Sivota under engine without the teeniest hint of a breeze, and the successful ramming by *Moby Dick* when they had all eventually anchored up for the night.

It would have helped, thought Eric bitterly, if Ted Banks had been there in advance to shepherd them all in. He was, after all, supposed to be the damn skipper of the flotilla. If Sally had not been so convincing about the need for Ted to check out the coast some five miles south of Sivota for the next day's sailing, the crews might have suspected he had got lost.

Still, Eric had to admit, it had been a great evening. Even the St Clairs seemed to have joined in the general spirit of bonhomie, Tara unexpectedly demanding a tango with the waiter. There was something about these upper-class women, hoity-toity one moment, the next teaching the wild tribes of Afghanistan how to knit one, purl two.

Gerhard Felgruber had been a bit of a show-off, throwing plates in the air and kissing the hands, and any other part available, of practically every woman. He had got his come-uppance when he had grabbed Clara Chippendale's paw and, finding it smothered in squid gravy, had skidded half-way up her ample arm before falling off his bench.

The evening had been only slightly marred by that unpleasant little yob – Eric twitched uncomfortably at the sudden thought that Darren was actually no smaller than himself – making up to Trudy. Thank goodness she had the sense to concentrate on her lemonade while the 'youf' made his moronic grunting noises at her. He would have stopped her from volunteering to teach Darren some Greek phrases if his attention hadn't been drawn to his own sons, both of whom seemed to be unnecessarily excited at helping Sharon to mop up the wine she had spilled in her lap. Those Armitage children – well, looking at the parents, he should not have been surprised.

Still, the coloured lights had been pretty, the food passable, the wine nearly drinkable and the stars romantic. And the stars, in a way, had highlighted, as it were, the problem. With the children in their bunks, the lights out, and a last-minute check to make sure that all ropes were neatly furled, he had only to take his Vitamin E pill, his garlic heart capsule and his cod-liver oil capsule before climbing into the welcoming arms of Penny. She, too, was warmed by the Ionian breezes and the sweet music and had sensed, from the way he had forgotten to check that all the life-jackets were handy in case of an unexpected storm, that Eric was as near to being abandoned as he ever would be.

And then. And – then. It was happening too often. True, he reasoned, it happened to every man at some time or other. Particularly when they are nearly fifty. No, it had nothing to do with age; it was – it had been – a case of, of *brewer's droop.*

Too much wine. That was certainly it. Those brewers

knew a thing or two, it must have often happened in brewing circles, particularly when such an unfortunate occurrence was named after a specific trade.

Eric scanned the horizon miserably. Liver spots floated before his eyes. He blinked rapidly but they remained obdurately in his line of vision, even appearing to grow larger. Too much alcohol – oh God, was he becoming an alcoholic? Let's see, say three glasses of wine, there'd been a beer, a large one in fact, and what was that white medicinal stuff Steven, looking unpleasantly amused and superior, had passed him? Ouzo. Like drinking Vick; an odour which had momentarily recalled a vision of childhood when, at the first sign of a sniffle, his mother had filled a bowl with hot water mixed with Vick and he was made to sit over it for hours with a towel over his head.

"Dad!"

Eric drew his head from the steam bowl.

"Dad! That's land over there. We're tacking too much to the east – we should be going west if we're going to Lakka."

Alan, busy scanning the chart, was pointing in the direction of Eric's liver spots which, to his profound relief, had formed themselves unquestionably into a rocky coast punctuated with tiny welcoming bays.

"Well, we'd better reef in and use the engine," Eric said, "There's not enough wind for us to keep tacking across."

"Hey, Dad, there are caves over there, look: a really big one and some smaller ones. I think they're joined up."

Mark was standing at the bow, binoculars focused on a point about a mile distant.

Alan scrambled up from the cockpit to join his brother.

"Dad, let's go over to them," he yelled. "They look great. We could anchor up and use the dinghy to row over. Come on, let's do it," he exhorted.

Penny's head poked out from the cabin.

"Go on, dear," she said, climbing out into the cockpit,"there's no rush. You take the children into the caves while I get lunch ready. I wouldn't mind a quiet half-hour with my book."

Eric was a stickler, a man who liked to keep to a schedule that had been set. A tinge of guilt, though, at last night's performance, or lack of it, quelled his objections. The sea was mirror-calm, clear as a pool and totally inviting.

"Good idea," he assented, "let's get the sail down and motor in."

Twenty minutes later, Alan let the bow anchor drop and *Nemesis* drifted lazily to a halt, some two hundred yards from the caves. The breeze had dropped entirely: even without the anchor, the yacht was unlikely to drift. From the deck, the sea floor could be clearly seen, small flurries of tiny fish darting through the weed.

The boys unhooked the stern ladder, untied the painter and lowered themselves into the rubber dinghy.

"Come on, Trudy, jump in, we'll fish you out," called Alan who, with his usual presence of mind, was carrying a torch.

Trudy threw down her towel and stood poised on the deck edge, her pretty figure poised for a dive. Despite her one–piece floral bathing suit, with its silly frill around the waist, she looked distinctly appetizing.

"Well, I'm not sure," hesitated Eric, "I think maybe the men ought to explore first in case – in case of problems."

"Oh Daddy," protested Trudy, "I'm a jolly sight better swimmer than you are. Don't be silly."

And before her deflated father could object any further, she sprang from the edge, cleaving the water gracefully, to be hauled into the dinghy by the manly brothers.

"For God's sake, be careful," warned Eric anxiously, "that dinghy can easily turn over."

The boys groaned in chorus. He was at it again.

"Humour him, Tru, before he has a fit," nudged Alan.

"Daddy, we could swim to the bottom and back in one breath," humoured Trudy. "Look, it's absolutely clear as glass, it's *fantastic!*"

"Well," said Eric, "well...all right."

To his eyes, it looked a little murky down there. Actually, a lot of things were looking murky to Eric these days. Truth was, he could do with his spectacles more and more, but they remained packed away for emergencies – such as needing to see where he was going.

He squinted at the horizon.

"There's a yacht over there. Where did she come from? There was no one around a moment ago."

Penny sighed patiently.

"Darling, we haven't yet bought the Ionian and I don't think it's Long John Silver. Now do get in and enjoy yourself. Just relax. That's what you need."

Eric felt there was some significance in that last remark but forbore to comment.

"Well, we're off then. Won't be more than an hour. I think you'd better radio Ted and let him know where we are, just in case. Can you do that?"

"Yes, Dear," answered Penny, almost shoving him headlong into the dinghy. "I think I can just about do that. I can also see the caves quite clearly so I won't be at all worried. In fact, I'm feeling like having a rest so I'd be quite glad if you'd *go*."

With an inward sigh at the tetchiness of women, Eric wobbled into the dinghy, took the oars with confidence, checked his socks for knee height, and commenced to row his children towards the caves.

Ever practical, Penny did not stand at the rail concealing a tear and waving a silk hanky. She stepped down the cabin steps, switched on the radio and called *Ulysses X* which, perhaps wisely considering Ted's vigour below deck, had no code-name.

"*Nemesis* to *Ulysses X*. Over."

No reply.

She repeated the call–signal.

The radio spat out a few crackles then Ted's voice, sounding just a touch winded, came over the airwaves.

"*Ulysses X* to Nem...Nem...Nemwhatsit, receiving you. Over," panted the athletic Antipodean.

Penny smiled knowingly – and a little wistfully.

"We're anchored about two miles south of Sivota just off

the coast. There are some caves here and the rest have gone
to explore them, so we'll probably be in to Lakka somewhere
about six. Do you want a compass bearing of our position?
Over."

Penny assumed that the silence was the result of Ted
working out the question. Not being suspicious by nature,
she knew that working out a compass bearing on his chart
would give him no problem.

"No probs. You go ahead and take it real blithe. Don't
go botherin' yer head over no compass readin'. We'll see yer
in the bay later. Olly, olly, Over an' Out."

And with that unusual farewell, Ted returned to whatever
required so much energy.

If Penny had looked out at that juncture, she might have
noticed that the yacht on their stern appeared to change
course which, considering its sails were reefed and it must
therefore be under engine, might have indicated that
someone, listening to her radio conversation, intended to join
them. But the midday heat, the early start and the prevailing
peace made Penny drowsy; climbing into their cabin, she
adjusted the breeze-chute through the deck skylight and
stretched out luxuriously to fall into a deep sleep with no
worries.

*   *   *

Luigi Giannovi smiled. It was not the smile of a nice man.
In truth, Luigi would not have been flattered to be called a
nice man. Having worked in a sardine canning factory in
Naples, he liked to think that seafaring was in his blood and
preferred to imagine his ancestors not as simple, God-fearing
sons of the sea but rather nearer to predators, the scourge of
the Mediterranean. This picaresque feat of imagination took
quite an effort of mind since his father had been a Fiat
mechanic and his grandfather had spent his entire working
life removing pits from olives for an olive-oil company, but
Luigi was a true romantic with hot blood – and a cold heart.
Quite piratical.

As his yacht, *Angela Mia*, neared the anchored *Nemesis*, he cut the engine and pressed his finger to his lips so that his exciting mate, Ariadne Xstanopoulis, should not give vent to her powerful lungs. Wearing only a G-string, her muscled Amazonian body a gleaming bronze, breasts thrust purposefully forward in the direction of the Warbelow's yacht, Ariadne was a fit companion for the lean Luigi, both darkly Mediterranean, both ear-ringed. Both planning something nasty for the unsuspecting Warbelows.

Angela Mia's bow gently nudged *Nemesis*'s stern rather like a well-mannered dog making an introduction. From the caves came muffled shouts of excitement as the dinghy edged into the tunnels. Otherwise, peace and quiet reigned.

The intrepid Luigi, pulling at his big black macho moustache, nodded to Ariadne who slid into the sea without a ripple disturbing the surface. He watched her lithe body appreciatively as she dived towards *Nemesis*'s anchor some ten feet below, a rope trailing behind her, the other end in her Latin lover's knowing hands. Deftly, she knotted the rope through the anchor chain and returned to the surface, scarcely needing to draw more breath into her lungs.

Luigi waited until her fine torso acrobatically swung on to deck before tentatively pulling on the rope. Nothing happened: the anchor remained fast.

Ariadne padded over to him, gestured that he should return to the cockpit, and proceeded to haul on the rope, her biceps gleaming proudly with the strain. The anchor gave with a barely perceptible nudge: hand over hand, Ariadne brought it to the surface, stooped over the rail and drew it on board. Pulling on its attached anchor chain, she steadily rattled it to the deck, followed by a length of rope secured to *Nemesis*. A testing tug and *Nemesis* drew perceptibly back towards the snout of Luigi's boat, like a well-mannered bitch acknowledging an interesting overture. With a grin of triumph, Ariadne signalled Luigi to start the engine.

The sudden rumble of the engine breaking the stillness seemed impossibly loud and the couple froze, scanning the caves for the sudden appearance of the crew.

Nothing. Not even the muffled shouts.

Pushing the throttle into reverse at low revs, *Angela Mia* strained with the added weight of *Nemesis*, shrugged, then began to edge backwards, gently pulling the Warbelow's yacht in her wake.

As *Nemesis* obediently followed her seducer, Penny dreamed sweet dreams in which her Eric more than made up for any shortcomings from the night before. Curiously, such is the stuff of dreams, he had developed an Australian twang.

* * *

"No, we'd better be getting back."

Eric was feeling anxious. None of them had a watch and he was sure that more than an hour had passed since they had entered the main cave.

"Dad, this is brilliant," said Alan, his torch breaking the blackness beyond.

"I'm cold," muttered Trudy, not wishing to be a soppy spoil–sport but covered in goose pimples.

"There, I told you this is men's work," said Eric tetchily, feeling chilled himself, "come on back to the yacht."

Using hands and oars to thread their way back to the entrance of the caves, they eventually emerged from the deep blackness after what, to Eric, seemed an age.

Momentarily blinded by the sun, their eyes blinked across the azure sea.

Nobody spoke.

They sat, gently bobbing, feeling faint. There was a reluctance to put it into words. Eric simply sat, transfixed. It was beyond his worst imaginings – and he was always ready to conjure up a few of those.

"Dad," whispered Mark, "the boat's..."

"Yerrrrrk," said the boggle-eyed father, rising to the emergency.

"I think," said Alan slowly, "I think we might have come out of a different entrance. Maybe we went up another tunnel..."

"Grooooh," answered Dad. He regarded his offspring with a wild stare.

"It's gone. IT'S GONE. THE BLOODY YACHT. IT'S GONE. YOUR MOTHER. SHE'S GONE."

It did seem somewhat indisputable and the children remained silent. They surveyed the empty sea.

Eric made a supreme effort. Panic would get them nowhere.

"We're in the middle of the Ionian," he panicked, "exposed to the sun, there's not a ship in sight, our yacht's gone, disappeared, there's no way of getting help, we'll be fried, get sunstroke, your mother could be drifting in front of a tanker..."

Trudy, who had inherited all of her mother's practicality and few of her father's neuroses, took over.

"Daddy, I'm sure it'll be alright. There's no current and no wind. Look, the dinghy hasn't moved while we've been sitting here. If our yacht moved, Mummy must have moved it. She – maybe she just wanted – to have a look along the coast – or something..." she ended weakly.

"So she just pulled up the anchor, started up the engine and headed off into the blue – do you really think your mother would do that?"

He paused. Would she do that? Was it – was it something to do with last night? Would she really...?

"I know," said Alan, "why don't we row up the coast back the way we came and find somewhere to land. Then we could get to a village or something, and get help."

Eric regarded his eldest with admiration. Even in such dire straits, it was comforting to know that his genes had been transmitted so effectively to his son. This suggestion succeeded in calming him. The more he thought about it, the more unlikely it was that Penny had upped and gone of her own accord. She didn't even know how to start the engine.

"That's right. That's good thinking. Perhaps – perhaps the anchor slipped, maybe there was a wash from something big and our yacht's drifted a bit. It's probably just beyond that bluff – just out of sight."

He took the oars, a man in charge of all their destinies. The dinghy, with its worried occupants, pulled away – in the wrong direction.

*   *   *

The atmosphere on board *Siren*, despite the prevailing calmness of the sea, was tempestuous. Bernie, with a beer in one hand, a blockbuster in the other, and a red knotted handkerchief on his head which made him look more than ever like Tommy Cooper wearing a flattened fez, should have been happy. The awning had been spread over the cockpit, cushions strategically placed under the parts tending to plumpness, and Julie had been busy below deck creating an hygienic environment worthy of an emergency ward.

That, indeed, had caused the squabble among the sirens. Liz, being short-sighted, had been taking a well-earned swim after sorting out Bernie's evening wear in consecutive order for the next twelve nights.

Not an adventurous swimmer, particularly when everything around her was as murky as an uncleaned goldfish bowl, she strayed no further than a few feet from the hull.

Everyone *knew* she was in the water, she had no doubt about that. So Julie must have *deliberately* chosen that moment to flush out the heads.

Whilst her sight may not have been perfect, there was nothing wrong with Liz's sense of smell. And it did not have to be keen to make her acutely aware that the Ionian had suddenly become a trifle niffy – not to say stupendously pongy, a rich, sewerish sort of pong that was all-pervasive... and all-enveloping.

As she reached for the stern ladder and rose out of the sea directly behind Bernie, he had leapt up as though struck by the sight – and smell – of a monster from the deep. Jaws could not have achieved a better effect. Hardly flattering and Bernie's behaviour lacked any evidence of tact or affection.

Lorraine, who had been sniffing the air disapprovingly from the sharp end, gazed at her fellow nurse with horror.

43

"Liz! Liz! Get back in the sea at once!" she ordered, "You can't – ugh! what a stench!" and she reached for one of her ever-handy packs of tissues.

"Good God Almighty!," exclaimed Bernie, reeling to the rail. "She's covered in shit!"

Liz glared in the general direction of Bernie's voice.

"Oh, don't state the obvious," she retorted, with heavy sarcasm, "don't tell the world, will you!"

Tears made funny little white streaks down her face. Bernie stared at the besmeared apparition until realization dawned, aided by the odorous clue. Then he began to laugh, a chesty sort of chortle, the kind that was insensitive and hurtful if you were the brunt of the joke.

"Liz, – hoot, hoot – your tan's coming off...it's dripping all over – snortle, snortle – the bloody deck!"

"IT'S NOT FUNNY!" she screamed. "You wouldn't think it was funny if someone emptied – emptied a dozen bedpans over you!"

Julie's head emerged from the cabin entrance.

"What's all the row – oooh, blimey, oh no, I can't..."

And she backed down the stairs clutching her nose, preferring the air below deck to the company of her crew mate.

"It's your damn fault," wailed Liz, addressing the mast, "you're not supposed to empty that toilet unless we're moving and we weren't and..." now sobbing, near hysterics, "..I was right in the middle of it and I'M COVERED IN IT!"

It is often said that nurses can be the least sympathetic in the face of extremity, practicality needing to replace emotion. In this case, though, it was laughter that overtook Lorraine and Julie, so much so that *Siren* herself bobbed with the combined wobble of Liz's three shipmates.

"I SAY, CAN YOU HEAR US?"

The voice came from a loud hailer, startlingly near. While Liz, dripping miserably on the edge of the cockpit, had been bewailing her fate, *Ulysses VII* – or *Annus Mirabilis* as she had been esoterically named – had almost come alongside, the Hon. Crispin St Clair, in neat white ducks, hanging on to the shrouds, loud hailer to his mouth.

"*Ulysses V* – CAN – YOU – HEAR – ME?"

Bernie, with his back to the St Clairs, couldn't: he would have found a loud-hailer useful in normal conversation. He had subsided to the deck, still clutching the rail as low gurgles of laughter doubled him up. On the whole, Bernie found amusement in simple things.

As Lorraine cupped her hands to answer Crispin, Liz decided that further accusations of deliberate sabotage would not solve her present predicament and, with a shriek of anguish at the inhumanity of women, belly-flopped back into the briny to execute a complicated series of porpoise rolls. The sight of Liz squirming as though she was trying to extract a jellyfish from her bathing suit only rendered Bernie even more helpless.

"COME ALONGSIDE," bellowed Lorraine.

"ER – NO, THERE'S A – ER, PECULIAR AROMA," returned Crispin, "PERHAPS YOUR GAS CYLINDER IS LEAKING. PUT YOUR RADIO ON."

Lorraine signalled assent and made towards the stern, pushing past the recumbent Bernie, still unaware of his neighbours.

"Julie," she yelled into the cabin, "put the radio on, there's someone trying to call us."

"You put it on," retorted Julie, "I'm not going anywhere near that stink, I'll be sick."

Made of sterner stuff, Lorraine descended the steps and switched on.

"*Siren* to – I've forgotten what your boat is – *Siren* to the St Clairs."

"We've been trying to call you up for some time," came the pointed tones of Tara. "What is that frightful reek coming from your boat? We're trying to stay upwind from you except there's no damn wind. The children have got their heads under their pillows and Arabella has already been sick."

Lorraine felt nettled.

"It's Liz, she's had – had a little accident. And you're

supposed to say 'Over'. Over," she added primly.

"Oh, Over, then. I'm sure that helps. She ought to take kaolin-and-morphine, a nurse should know that. Anyway, there's a problem with the Warbelows. Their yacht's gone aground, somewhere along the coast past Sivota. Penny Warbelow put out a 'mayday' and we are going to look for them. Apparently she's still on the yacht but that worried little man and his children are floating around somewhere off the Greek coast. We are the only boats in the area, can you join us?"

Lorraine remained tediously silent.

"Hallo, are you – oh, damn and blast it, OVER!"

Lorraine crackled into life.

"Of course, we'll help. We'll follow you. Just wait a minute while we get Liz back on board. She'll probably want a shower. There's nothing wrong with her stomach – it's her *outside* that's the problem. Are you going to radio Ted and tell him what we're doing? Over."

"We've tried radioing Ted a number of times but he doesn't respond. How someone is supposed to be in charge of a flotilla and not be in contact with his crews is beyond me. Perhaps you can try him while you sort out that poor girl – I don't think we can stay here any longer. We're going about: there's no wind so we'll just chug on up the coast and you can catch us up. Oh, and by the way, our call-sign is *Annus Mirabilis*; you can give that to Ted. Not that he'll remember."

And with a severe 'Over' the St Clairs went off the air, turned tail and took themselves out of the *Siren*'s smell-range.

Bernie, his explosive mirth now under control, saw the stern of the *Annus Mirabilis* turn away from them, heading north. As *Siren* bobbed energetically in the wake, Liz, who had been groping her way up the ladder like a short-sighted limpet, fell back into the sea with an unheeded splash.

"What are they up to?" Bernie demanded of Lorraine who was searching for a business-like piece of carbolic to apply to the besmirched body of Liz, "Why are they going north? I thought we were all supposed to be heading for Lakka?"

It took a good five minutes and a lot of bellowing from Lorraine for Bernie to grasp the situation. Bernie's deafness required tact; the nurses tried to make it look as though it was quite natural for normal conversation to make their faces red and their eyes pop out with effort.

"Alright," said Bernie, rather relishing the role of rescuer, "let's get after them. Lorraine, you help Liz scrub down while Julie takes the helm. I'll radio the skipper and tell him what we're doing."

"Oh, I'll do the radio," said Lorraine, dreading the complications, but Liz had finally made it on deck and Bernie plunged below, anxious to avoid proximity with that particular faithful slave. While it was not immediately obvious what the attraction of Bernie was for his three plump nurses, it was certainly clear that Liz held no attraction for Bernie at this specific moment.

Julie, with accomplished skill, started up the engine and turned *Siren* in pursuit of the St Clairs while Liz stood naked on the forward deck, Lorraine holding the sun-hot shower bag over her, directing the nozzle at those parts where carbolic soap was needed most. Had the Greek sailors of mythology witnessed the sight of the bare-bodied nurse, soap running from her long black hair, bouncing off those truly wondrous breasts that looked like a pair of genoas under full wind, bottom wobbling to the rhythm of the diesel, they would have believed themselves to be cherished by the gods and fought any number of boring old minotaurs with hardly a thought for danger.

"*Siren* to *Ulysses* X. Over," said Bernie into the handset.

"*Ulysses* X to *Siren*, receiving you. Over," came the surprisingly prompt response.

"*Siren* to *Ulysses* X. Over," repeated Bernie patiently.

"*Ulysses* X to *Siren*, receiving you loud and clear. Over," answered Ted, equally patiently.

"Never seem to be able to get that Aussie bugger," commented Bernie over his shoulder to Julie. He adjusted the squelch, the radio indignantly emitting high–pitched squeals in protest.

"*SIREN* TO *ULYSSES X*, ARE YOU RECEIVING ME? OVER."

Bernie's bellow could have been heard in Albania.

"Chrissake, I'm not only receiving yeh, you've brought down a load of tinnies on my caboodle," roared Ted, forgetting his role of imperturbable skipper of the fleet, "THIS IS TED. OVER!"

"Oh, I've got him," said Bernie, pleased at his success. "*Ulysses* X, YOU'RE A BIT FAINT, I HOPE YOU CAN HEAR ME. UNDERSTAND *NEMESIS* HAS GONE AGROUND OFF COAST NEAR SIVOTA. WE'RE GOING TO FIND THEM WITH – WITH – ," he turned to the cockpit to address Julie.

"What's their name, I mean, what's their boat called?"

"Lorraine," called Julie, "what's the name of the St Clair's yacht?"

Lorraine momentarily reflected then appeared to receive inspiration from projecting the shower hose at Liz's bottom.

"It's the *Annus Mirabilis*."

"The *Annus Mirabilis*," Julie yelled into the cabin.

"The what?" ejaculated Bernie. Sometimes, he thought, his hearing was not a hundred per cent.

"THE *ANNUS MIRABILIS*," screamed Julie, grotesquely clutching the long wooden tiller between her legs while she leaned forward to bawl into Bernie's ear.

"Good God," muttered Bernie and took up the transmitter.

"*SIREN* TO *Ulysses X*. WE'RE FOLLOWING THE – THE – 'ANUS MIRACULOUS' UP THE COAST. WE'LL CALL YOU WHEN WE'VE FOUND THE –er – *NEMESIS*."

At least 'Nemesis' was a word you didn't mind saying over the radio. Half the boats in the Ionian could be listening on the same wavelength. Arrogant bastards, those St Clairs, to call their yacht something you didn't like to mention in ordinary conversation.

Ted, who had prudently covered his radio with a dishcloth to muffle Bernie's stentorian tones, was equally aghast.

"Stone the bleedin' crows, *Siren*, I don't mind what ye're followin', it's your holiday and I reckon you do what you like on yer hols but keep it to yerself now, will ye mate? Over and Out."

And Ted shut down with relief. O.K., fair dinkum, if a feller can get three sheilas to shack up with him on a cruise, that was his good luck or whatever, but shouting about arseholes over the water when there could be kids tuned in was a bit ripe. Bit of a humdinger, this going aground of *Nemesis* but he was a good two hours' motoring away from their position so he might as well wait and see what developed before putting his nautical mind to the task.

Besides, Sally was waiting for him to oil her back and previous experience suggested this could lead to other things.

*   *   *

It was the bumping and grinding that shook the hull of *Nemesis* which had awakened Penny from that deep and satisfying sleep in which she had dreamt that Eric, face unlined with worry and curiously having developed Ted's muscular physique, had performed feats of amazing sexual prowess. True to his real life image, he had kept his flippers on throughout in case of emergencies, but dreams are rarely totally devoid of reality.

She had peered out through the deck window to find *Nemesis* facing a curving sandy beach backed by olive trees and scrub. Facing the shoreline, reclining under the shade of a tree and surrounded by goats of many colours was a goatherd. She squeezed her eyes tightly, then re-opened them but it was no dream. This pastoral view, musically accompanied by the clattering of bells suspended from the neck of each goat, had replaced the caves into which her family had disappeared.

With a gasp of dismay, she hauled herself through the

skylight and scrambled on deck. *Nemesis* herself had become part of this idyllic scene; her hull was wedged in the sand some three feet below.

Penny clawed her way to the cockpit and, bending over the stern, peered below at the rudder. By craning further, she could see that the screw was clear. She reasoned that it was a shelving beach and that it might be possible to back *Nemesis* off under engine. A coil of rope, leading back to the stern anchor hold, lay on the sea-bed near the screw; hauling it in, she stared dumbfounded at the rope end, neatly sliced across.

Even Dr Watson would have instantly perceived that the rope had been cut, without resorting to Sherlock for a quick burst on his fiddle and a suitable theory.

Penny was not one for theorizing nor for spending time on useless analysis. For whatever reason, *Nemesis* was no longer where she should be and was grounded to boot.

She started up the diesel. Under the tree, the elderly goatherd looked on with lazy interest, one hand holding a wine bottle, the other scratching at irritations buried beneath layers of ill-defined garments. If the tourists wanted a picture, then a few hundred drachmas would result in a sylvan pose. In a pocket somewhere in his shaggy outer layer was a wooden flute. The tourists liked that touch, available for a few extra drachmas. Otherwise, their doings were of no interest to him, apart from a spot of voyeurism when a suitable occasion presented itself. He pulled a battered hat over his eyes, scratched what he thought was himself but proved to be an inquisitive goat, and relaxed into slumber.

The burst of reverse revs from the engine made *Nemesis* rock a little, sand, gravel and flotsam churning around her stern. She shook herself, then buried her nose deeper into the shore.

Wiping away the sweat, Penny tried once more. It was against all the rule books but needs must. Needs didn't and Penny cut the engine. She knew full well what the panic of her disappearance would cause in Eric's breast but giving way to despair was not part of her character: she had Eric to thank for that. Peering over the bulkhead at the goatherd, she pondered over the possibility of his help but decided this was unlikely. Anyway, picturesque as he may be, the pungent smell of goat which assailed her nostrils was enough to decide against any close proximity.

With a resigned sigh, she descended to the radio. Ted was the answer: this situation was precisely what flotilla skippers were for.

She called up a 'mayday' and was eventually much relieved when the Honourable Crispin St Clair answered her call.

Anchored up in Sivota, Luigi smiled his evil smile as he listened to Penny's plea for help. How nice, he reflected, to cause so much trouble so soon.

*　　*　　*

"Mummy, I can see them! Mummy, it's them! Over there! That's them in a dinghy over there! Mummy, it's that little man with that worry all on his face that you said, he's in their dinghy and those boys and that girl....!"

Lucien waved the binoculars frantically at Tara, clad fetchingly in a multi-coloured silk sarong and white turban. She drew up an elegant leg and raised herself on her elbows, almost putting herself in danger of allowing the sun to touch her marble-white skin. The masses might crave a tan but Tara, with the breeding of generations of Indian Army wives in her blood, would not permit the sun to take such liberties with her colouring.

"Crispin, darling, Lucien has found the Warbelows. They're over there somewhere," she announced, waving her languid arm vaguely in the direction of Greece.

"Good Show!"

Crispin was pleased. Class would out: whatever the murmurings of discontent, the people were glad to turn to their natural leaders in times of crisis.

And Lucien was shaping up, despite his housemaster's end-of-term comment that he 'at times failed to live up to the ideals of his House'. There he was, vigilant as look-out at the bow, his junior safari kit protecting him from the worst of the sun's rays, actually spotting the poor blighters.

All in all, Crispin was rather enjoying himself. His early bad humour had departed: being with a flotilla could be, he decided, quite jolly. The previous night he had actually joined in a conga, not something you would want witnessed by a chap at home but not such a bad wheeze when your hands are gripping the lissom waist of the affable Sally.

Following the direction of Lucien's important and rigidly outstretched arm, Crispin steered towards the blot on the horizon. As Arabella prepared refreshing cups of Earl Grey below, *Annus Mirabilis* homed in on the Warbelow dinghy.

Eric gazed up at his saviours with profound relief and gratitude. There had been nowhere to land on the rocky coast during the last two hours of rowing and the insides of his thighs were a violent red from sunburn. Having gallantly given his cap to his daughter who had nestled down in the shade behind his back, he was feeling an uncomfortable sensation of burning somewhere on the top of his head, an area which he inspected daily with growing dismay.

Mark and Alan had spent most of the time in and out of the water, cooling off their bodies which fortunately had tanned quickly enough to avoid frazzling in the sun. They had never been particularly worried and had rather enjoyed the drama, though the need to boost father's flagging spirit, such as lying about how long they had been rowing futilely, had grown boring.

There had, in fact, been quite an interesting diversion. Alan, having sighted a shoal of fish beneath him, had dived to get a closer look and had glimpsed some unidentifiable shapes lying on the sea bed. Without a mask, and in water too deep for close examination, the excited brothers had swirled around much to Eric's consternation, trying to make out the blurred shapes below them. That they were man-made objects of some kind was obvious, huge grey angular shapes lying apparently tumbled on each other, but beyond that they could not guess. Alan, lungs near to ripping their seams, thought he had glimpsed the murky outline of a white rounded object caught between the jutting angles of the blocks but had to shoot to the surface, gasping for air, and feeling rather spooked.

As the dinghy wobbled at the yacht's stern, Eric reached out to secure the ladder.

"Yowwwwwwwwww!" squealed Eric as greeting to the St Clairs. His salt–caked sunburn made itself felt at the sudden change of movement. "Oh, oooooohh!"

Mark grabbed the ladder and, with helping hands from above, Eric was gingerly landed on board. The children followed, Tara solicitously examining them for exposure, then sending them below to relieve their thirst.

Eric sat in the cockpit, his hands pressed to his burnt thighs. With his legs necessarily bent while he was rowing, unkind sunrays had travelled down the inside of his thighs and right up his bathing shorts, slowly basting the parts where only Penny had recently reached. He peered up at Crispin through tear-filmed eyes.

"I say, old chap, buck up," said Crispin heartily. He regarded Eric with some disapproval. Not done for a chap to blub on a boat. Some spirit needed here. "Everything is quite alright. Keep your pecker up."

He was not to know how ill-chosen his words were. With his wife having vanished at sea, Eric's awareness of his own inadequacies had never been higher.

"There's – there's nothing wrong with my pecker," he gasped bitterly, momentarily forgetting how far his sunburn had reached. "My wife's gone, the boat's gone, all our belongings have gone and – aaaghh – I've been roasted alive!"

He slumped in a miserable fried heap on the bench.

"Oh, she's fine, your wife, all in fine fettle. She beamed up on the jolly old radio about an hour ;o and gave us her approximate position. That's how we picked you up. Lucien, there," Crispin proudly indicated his successor, "he spotted you, and Tara has told the nurses' yacht to go on ahead and find her – Penny.

"Radioed?" The relief Eric felt was tempered by the

thought that Penny must still be aboard the yacht. So she *must* have gone off by herself. His thighs' burns felt suddenly more acute.

"What the hell was she doing, traipsing about the Ionian by herself? She must have bloody sunstroke."

"Steady on, now, there's a good fellow," remonstrated Crispin, blissfully unaware of the level of irritation which he could arouse, "she got in a spot of bother. Seems some blighter must have cut the anchor rope while she was indulging in a bit of shut-eye. Yacht could hardly have drifted under these conditions – she thinks it must have been towed up the coast then – then cast adrift, as it were."

"*Siren* to *Annus Mirabilis*. Over."

Tara called up from the lower deck.

"Can you answer that, darling? I'm putting some camomile on these children. Send Eric down and I'll put some on him too."

Crispin eyed the stricken Eric.

"You stay there, old boy. I'll send Tara to you. Doubt if you could make it down the steps with your legs apart like that. Be rather difficult for a crab, what?"

With what looked suspiciously like a suppressed grin, Crispin descended to the radio.

"*Annus Mirabilis* to *Siren*. Over."

Lorraine's voice answered. "We can see *Nemesis*. She's aground in a bay on our charts. It's just below Mourtos – it's marked for shallow water. We might be able to pull her off ourselves but we'd rather wait for you. You're about fifteen minutes from us under full throttle. Will you follow, Over?"

"Right ho," said Crispin. "We've got Eric and his children on board. Can you tell – er – Penny, they are all tickity-boo? Over."

"Tickety? – oh, yes. Well, she's not on board. Julie can see her through the binoculars, she's sitting with some local or someone, surrounded by goats. Oh, wait – Julie said she's spotted us, she's waving. What? Ah, Julie said she's waving a bottle and – and she's doing some sort of dance. With the

– er – local. Umm. I mean, Over."

Crispin pursed his lips. There was a whole lot more to this episode than met the eye.

"Well, ah, good. She must be – fine. We're on our way."

While this description of colourful local activities filled the airwaves, Tara had climbed out into the cockpit bearing a bottle of camomile and a no-nonsense look. Upending Eric on his back, she applied the soothing lotion as far as decency would allow, which was pretty far. Eric, like a tortoise with his legs waving in the air, was caught between the unexpected delight of this impromptu massage and the dark suspicions of what sounded like some Bacchanalian revel taking place in full binocular view of *Siren*.

For Eric, things could never be simple.

CHAPTER FOUR

Supper at sundown. Amy reveals her parts. Ted agrees
to a treasure hunt while Gerhard hunts after Sally.
Morals are discussed while Sharon and Arnold discuss
their practical application.

Amy Clawrer leaned back luxuriously, the plastic strips of the chairback making interesting patterns on her deep-tanned flesh.

This was the life.

There was still heat left in the dying sun, though the yachts, moored only feet away from the taverna, were beginning to play shadow pictures over the glittering sea.

"*Efcharisto*," she murmured with authenticity to the stunning–looking waiter who had taken less than an hour to bring a glass of Retsina. Time didn't matter, at least in her present mood.

She sipped the turpentine liquid with appreciation. Amy was going native: not even a splutter as she swallowed, though this was not the first of the day and she had had plenty of practice.

From the kitchen, enticing smells of grilled meat and fish floated to the tables, aromatic herbs beckoned hungry stomachs. Cicadas chattered in rivalry with the inevitable strains of Zorba-type music played for the benefit of visiting flotilla crews on the taverna's somewhat creaky sound system. In the deep cool shade of the bar, two locals argued over cards, flicking their cigarette ash over the displays of raw squid and meatballs.

Behind the taverna, wild olive trees scrambled up the steeply sloping hill, giving way to untended vines struggling through bush heather and thyme, until the village was reached, an illogical pattern of white-walled houses and narrow lanes. Trailing bougainvillaea and geraniums splashed their colours from roofs and balconies, vying with the rose bushes stretching up to meet them. Trees in each walled garden proffered lemons, figs, limes, apricots, providing the much-needed shade for pots of herbs and straggling melons.

From the village, the white-dusted road edged towards the left horn of the bay, past a dome-shaped shrine to St Nicholas containing an empty beer bottle, to end abruptly at a sheer drop to the sea with only a bent rail as a warning to the unwary. An old woman, dressed in unremitting black from head to foot, leaned on the rail contemplating the bay below, as she would every sundown for the rest of her days. The bay was her doorstep, the motley of fishing boats, visiting yachts and routinely lumbering ferries her source of gossip. As she studiously excavated her left nostril, she studied the crews of the Ulysses Flotilla with a professional interest. Though well versed in the ways of tourists, she had a knack with hyperbole which provided a useful source of evening entertainment for the village.

Amy would have been mortified to know that the woman was possibly ten years younger than herself, many of the 'grannies' caught in the tourists' camera lens not having seen fifty years.

"I think we should go look for those marbles. I mean, hell, it would be so *exciting*, to make this big discovery, we'd be in all the papers, just terrific."

This opinion was expressed to all the Ulysses crews in general, gathered for their evening briefing. With the taverna more or less to themselves – apart from the owner's mangy and flea-ridden mongrel which occasionally made half-hearted attempts to mate with Clara Chippendale's plump and enticing leg – the mood was sublimely relaxed. Ted's prophecy that there would come a point when they would all 'pucker together and become a blithe team' was at the point of realization.

The subject under discussion was the 'discovery' by Mark and Alan Warbelow of the mysterious objects sighted during their enforced dinghy expedition three days before.

No explanation had been found for the abduction of *Nemesis* and the sleeping Penny. The evidence of the cut rope and the removal of the yacht pointed the finger at an unknown party, but no motive suggested itself other than a very warped sense of humour.

In the intervening days, the yachts had sailed down the west coast of Paxos without mishap. Well, not quite: the Armitage boat, *Moby Dick*, unfailingly provided a dramatic high point to the day as Jack made several attempts to berth her.

This, though, had developed into a workable routine. Rosie would radio Ted to announce their imminent arrival into harbour, infuriating Jack by lapsing into gossip during this crucial procedure, and still confusing her 'moby' with her 'dick'.

Cap'n Jack would bellow confusing and irrational orders from the helm to his increasingly reluctant mate, Darren, who was much more preoccupied with presenting just the right image for the onlookers at the quayside. Constant immersion in the sea had bleached the colour from his Mohican, the sun and exercise had taughtened his towny torso and Trudy's eyes sought him out as the Armitages prepared for their customary crash-landing.

Sharon, whose lithe and luscious body was tanned to such a golden perfection that even eunuchs would at least have raised an eyebrow, stood aloof from all the commotion, all long legs amidship, a delight of sensuality for the eyes of every male on shore. Old men in the tavernas, catching their first glimpse of this sea nymph imperiously sizing up the local talent as *Moby Dick* edged perilously closer, would chew on their moustaches and smile rheumy smiles at some distant recollection of long–ago summer nights.

Ted, like a lanky and muscular shepherd dog, would rush up and down the quayside, arms semaphoring, shouting for ropes to be thrown and being bowled over when several kilos of coiled lasso predictably hit him in the chest.

While the Ulysses crews knew better than to be on board their yachts as *Moby Dick* came in to berth, other unsuspecting tourists sat sipping their G-and-Ts on deck with superior amusement until the repercussions of *Moby Dick* hitting her first neighbour of the evening rippled through the assembled yachts, sending the G-and-Ts, and frequently their owners, abruptly into their respective holds.

Perhaps this was one reason why the delightful and secluded port of Spartahori was left entirely to the Ulysses Flotilla. The Ionian was not, after all, such a big sea and word soon spread.

Crispin St Clair had communicated the excitement of a

possible archaeological find to the group. With the cries of mingled anguish and delight from Eric echoing in his ears as Tara applied soothing balm to his sore points, Crispin had debriefed the boys regarding their expedition in the caves. It was only that same night, a sleepless night in Mongonisi harbour, that his restless mind had recalled their account of 'weird shapes, sort of oblongs and greyish'. And, as his imagination began to embellish their description with details of his own, a frisson of exhilaration seized his Classical soul. The possibility... the faintest possibility... a discovery... *The Crispin St Clair Marbles*!

By next morning, Crispin had made up his mind – to find the St Clair Marbles.

Now, as the crews sat at assorted tables, the younger members either sitting in bored silence or wandering in haphazard groups along the beach, the discussion turned on whether the flotilla, as a whole, should go treasure hunting, or follow the prescribed programme organized by their leader.

Ted had his doubts.

"I don't know," he said slowly. Ted always said things slowly when his mind had to cope with unwelcome decisions.

"I mean, I hear what Crisp is sayin', it really gets the old gonads goin', all that thought of findin' those old stones and bits of ancient Greeks, but we're supposed to be on an organized trip down the Ionian, not turnin' the whole thing into a – a –" he sought in his mind for an apt simile, "a Search for the Golden Geese" he ended, pleased with the Classical allusion.

Jack Armitage snorted.

"Make up yer mind, lad, I thought we was looking fer marbles, not bloody geese. 'Ow are we ter find geese under the perishin' sea?"

Before Crispin could clarify matters, Sidney Chippendale chimed in.

"I don't think Ted means we should *literally* look for the Golden Geese," he squeaked, "since, in any case, he was referring to *Fleece*. It was Jason, you see, who had the task of finding the Golden Fleece before..."

"Jason?" Jack was both puzzled and irritated. "None of us is called Jason. We 'aven't even decided if we want to go arfter these bleedin' golden marbles yet and ye're talkin' of bringin' someone else in on it!"

"Oh, shuddup, Jack, and stop interruptin'," chided Rosie, aware of the collective suppressed sigh. "He's talkin' about those Greeks in olden times when – when that Julius Caesar was alive an' they all wore skirts. Don't yer remember that film on the telly with whatsisname, Jeff – Jeff Chandler, that was it, he played that Jason, yer kept interruptin' then sayin' those Greeks couldn't 'ave 'ad American accents in those days..."

"Todd Armstrong," said Amy dreamily, "not Jeff Chandler. *Jason and the Argonauts*. I was a sacrificial maiden and he rescued me from a bull. I remember, we had this steer on the set and someone tried to spray gold paint on it and it got real mad and stuck its horns right up Todd's butt. We shot it, I mean the film, in El Paso, I guess 'cos all those Mexicans looked kinda foreign, but the whole crew went down with sour belly, I reckon it was all those chillis."

This non sequitur left the listeners nonplussed.

The waiter arrived during the ensuing silence with another round of beers and ouzo. The sun crept into the sea like the smile of a clown on the far horizon, throwing long shadows at the contented party. The breath–warm breeze, the rosemary scents, the tinkling from the shrouds, even the three millionth version of *Never On a Sunday* with its slightly distorted playback, all these created a repast of amicability and sereneness. The booze helped.

Darren was impressed. He leant forward with interest, and with the intention of brushing his arm against Trudy Warbelow's, conveniently sitting next to him.

"Eh, are you a fillum actress then," he asked, casually cupping his chin in his hand so that his head angled towards Trudy's. Like opposite poles of a magnet, Trudy's bent towards Darren's, a gentle manoeuvering rather than the more reckless headbanging on Darren's home ground.

Steven sniffed audibly, in a mean sort of way. Amy preened, glad that one of these dim-witted Englishers had finally shown an interest.

"Well, honey," she purred, "I guess I've played a few parts."

"You can say that again," added Steven, but somehow it came over unkindly, as though he himself had only found out about her latest part. Perhaps playing a character much younger than she actually was. He certainly seemed gritty about something.

"What's that, Stevie?" Amy blinked at him, an anxious loving blink.

Steven smiled a twisted sort of smile.

"Oh-ho, you'd better watch that, sugar, you could be gettin' kinda deaf in your *old* age. And *don't* call me 'Stevie'."

Amy gave him the glare that the producer used to ask for in close up when she was about to be raped by a thousand barbarians – and possibly a Minotaur as well.

"It's a sad but true fact, Steven, that *some* people are born old and simply get more boring and more crotchety from their first day in the cradle. You don't have no call to be making insinuations..."

Darren looked at Trudy. The sun's dying rays seemed to sparkle in her grey-green eyes. Trudy looked at Darren. The sun's dying rays seemed to make a gurgle erupt from his throat.

"Wharrerabartcuminferawalk?" he gurgled, noting what the sun's dying rays did to her eyes. Trudy decoded this invitation accurately and looked apprehensively across the tables to where her parents were indulging in Anglo-Germanic socializing. She nodded with the smile that gave the Leeds fan such restless nights and they stole off into the dusk leaving the Clawrers clawing away.

"But, er, ver eez Arnold," wondered Elke König uneasily, "I vos thinking ee vos for a drink cummin."

Jürgen, who understood his wife's English only marginally less than her German, resorted to the latter.

"For Heaven's sake, will you stop mothering that boy? How do you expect him to grow up like a man if you keep him tied to your *dirndl*?"

To be truthful about it, he didn't actually say '*dirndl*' because they lived on a modern housing estate where anyone wearing a *dirndl* would have been kept locked up in her incredibly clean and efficient kitchen. Translators have this tendency to overstate national characteristics.

Eric, though, had understood Elke easily enough and shared her anxious kind of mind, the sort of mind that rarely counted blessings but rather counted the nasty things that *could* have happened – and then envisaged those that might.

"Hmmnn, yes, well," he said unclearly. "Notice who else isn't here," he added, with significant sidelong glances down the tables.

Penny and the Königs peered through the dusk, not quite sure what they were looking for. Most of the adults seemed to be scattered around the taverna's tables: most of the children seemed to have disappeared.

"See?" demanded Eric.

"Nein," answered Jürgen, "I don't know what it is that I am looking for."

"Well," said Eric, explaining the obvious to the less observant, "who goes around giving everyone the eye?"

"Aaah," said Jürgen, doubtfully. "Ja. That is right."

He peered hopefully across the now candle-lit tables but failed to discern any eye sockets being plucked nor any formal presentation of eyeballs. Gerhard Felgruber did, indeed, seem to be gazing with a peculiar intensity into Sally Carson's deep-black eyes but, as far as the dusk would permit, it did not look as though lust had overtaken Gerhard to the point where he had deprived her of an eyeball.

"Darling, *nobody* knows what you are talking about, including me."

Jürgen was relieved at Penny's practicality.

"What are all these winks and nods and shufflings? One minute we're talking about finding sunken treasure, now you're doing a sort of Quasimodo act. Just say it, dear, whatever it is."

Eric, as so often, was sorely tried. How many years would it be before Penny understood him, before she actually came on to his wavelength?

"Elke asked 'ver eez' – I mean, where is Arnold and I was *merely* pointing out that a *certain person* is missing who should be given a spanked bottom and put to bed," he replied tartly.

Jürgen smiled appreciatively.

"There are one or two here for whom I would be liking that," he sniggered, giving Eric a conspiratorial wink. "Zo you have found one! Is Penny permitting...?"

Eric was horrified at this misunderstanding.

"Of course not! I wouldn't dream...and with a minor! I think that's quite *perverted*! I mean, she's with your Arnold, I saw them going off together and personally."

"Zo," said Elke. Had she been French, the translator would have probably written '*Zut alors*'; if Mexican, then '*Caramba*'.

"Zo," said Elke, "Arnold is alone mit himself and your Trudy."

"Trudy?" gasped Eric. "I'm not talking about *Trudy*! What on earth makes you think I'm talking about Trudy?"

"Because she is not here," said Jürgen simply.

"WHAT?"

The twitchy father stood up and caught his head on the straw canopy.

"Penny! Penny! Where's Trudy? She's not here!"

"Darling, she could be anywhere on the island. She could be in our boat. She could be with the boys. She *is* fifteen, Eric. I'm sure she's enjoying herself somewhere."

"Oh God," moaned Eric, sitting down and massaging the sore spot which was just about where his bald patch sat. Probably highlight his tonsure in the morning, he thought gloomily. And those awful Greek drains were at it again. The air, where he sat, was distinctly pungent.

Jürgen resumed.

"I think you mean the girl Sharon, no? This girl is – is

very, er, sexy and I am thinking also that Arnold is, er, thinking this. That. But, you know, Eric, I am liking this. Arnold has had – er – a bad time with loving for an – ah – Italian girl and needs a new wummins."

"*A new wummins*! Woman! Good Lord, you don't – I mean, how old is Arnold, for heaven's sake?"

"Vell, he has sixteen years now and this is a long time to be without a wummin when a young man has all the – ah – juices – er – making him crazy; and maybe with Sharon..."

Jürgen broke off leaving the possibilities hanging in the air.

Eric was discomforted.

"Well, you *are* progressive. *Very* Germanic. It's a bit different in England. Morals are – are a bit different. We don't do that sort of thing. Not at that age. Why, *Mark's* nearly seventeen, he could be..."

He broke off. Unwelcome thoughts were entering his head.

"Penny, where's Mark? Have you seen Alan? Are..."

Penny smiled at the Königs.

"Actually, we *do* do that sort of thing in England. Quite a bit, in fact. Eric is a weeny bit...*possessive*. A bit old-fashioned. Thinks nobody should do what *he* didn't do. Though *why* he didn't do it is another question."

The Königs nodded with affable lack of understanding. The waiter was passing around well-thumbed menus and food became the subject of interest.

"Tell you what, Nick," shouted Bernie to the uncomprehending waiter. "How about meatballs for a change? Or, say, meatballs. Or perhaps tonight I'll have meatballs. Then, as a change, I could have meatballs tomorrow night."

"*Kali spera*," responded the waiter, Dimitri, looking Bernie straight in the eye. It's more than likely that he understood quite a bit of English and what he really said amounted to an obscene suggestion as to whose balls were likely to be grilled next, but translators tend to be rather proper and avoid the earthier sort of dialogue.

"I don't see any bloody spare ribs," misheard Bernie, peering despondently at the admittedly short menu. *Hummus* was losing its attraction for Bernie; as far as he was concerned, they ought to stick their *taramasalata* in plastic bags and sell it as wallpaper paste. Bernie was an eggs and beans man, preferring his eggs to come out of hens, not fish.

Nonetheless, Dimitri sorted out the various orders with acquired ease, chairs shuffled, children were sought, toilets flushed, the coloured lights came on and *Never On a Sunday* followed on inevitably from Zorba's Dance. Though it was *kefthedhes* in various forms, whether balled, skewered or squidged into *moussakas*, it smelt good even where Eric sat next to Jürgen. The entire team of the Ulysses Flotilla proceeded to do it justice.

Not quite the entire team. Had Eric been a witness to certain events in a rubber dinghy, he would have done his 'told you so's' very loudly. He would also have been a peeping tom, a shocking accusation for a man of Eric's moral fibre, and highly unlikely – unless the coast was absolutely clear. And then only with a constantly accusing conscience.

As it was on this balmy, romantic evening. The coloured lights of the taverna chased the stars reflecting in the water, the boats rubbed gently against each other, emitting little moans and tinkles.

And so did Arnold, lying pressed against Sharon in the tethered dinghy of *Moby Dick*. Arnold was learning to forget his Italian love – rapidly. It was difficult to pine for an enamorata, who now existed only in his mind, when he was entangled with a body clad only in shorts and T-shirt, live in his arms.

"I think," she murmured, her brown eyes, enormous in the light reflected across the bay, staring steadily into Arnold's dilated pupils, "you could be my first Kraut. An' to think of all those things me Dad says about Germans."

Arnold mumbled a polite 'Ja', his English not as fluent as his father's. But his hands spoke internationalese, one caressing her tight soft-hard bottom inside her shorts, the other pulling up her T-shirt from behind until her breasts were bared to the stars and his Teutonic lips.

The boat rocked slightly less gently as Sharon stroked the somewhat square head whose tongue was raising her nipples to such heights and moved his enquiring hand to a more rewarding position between her legs. Little moans escaped from both of them, scarcely audible but just loud enough to cover the slight plop made as a snorkel surfaces for air just behind a dinghy.

The snorkel, and the moustache beneath it, belonged to Peeping Luigi.

*   *   *

"...still to be found in these seas. Lots of jolly old treasure. These two young chappies," Crispin continued, indicating Mark and Alan who had joined the tables for supper, having given up trying to locate Sharon, "saw *actual shapes*. Lying higgledy–piggledy, but with straight lines to them. *Straight lines*. Even covered in barnacles, if man had carved them with straight lines, they'd still look straight, following the outline. So, if they *are* man-made, they could only be lying on the sea bed by *accident*."

"Eet eez – a mystery."

There was a collective start from around the tables. Nobody among the flotilla crews had ever heard the enigmatic Monika utter a word. Indeed, they were only dimly aware of her presence, a female Banquo who might well be concealing gory locks beneath her ever-present floppy sunhat. Sitting next to her father, at the end of the long row of tables where they had all gathered to discuss the proposed treasure hunt, her jumbo-sized sunglasses trained on them from out of the dark night.

"Eet eez – an excitement. Vee need excitement for to live."

She relaxed back into her own darkness, only a white, beringed hand lying visible on the table.

"God aw-mighty," breathed Jack Armitage to Rosie, "the Mata-'ari spoke. Gave me the bloody creeps."

Sidney Chippendale removed his admiring gaze from Clara who was tucking into a fifth slice of melon, the juice running down her dimpled chins. The mangy mongrel was feeling pleased with itself: while its attempts to achieve sexual bliss with Clara's leg had been rebuffed, there were enough scraps falling from her plate to see him through the rest of the summer. Being native born, he would have preferred a little more garlic in the meatballs but the occasional rasping lick up Clara's comely shin added the necessary seasoning.

"It doesn't, you know, er – follow. I mean, even if the boys saw some sort of *carved* shapes, they could be anything. They were – what – a mile or so from the coast. Some kind of blocks – *grey* blocks – with sharp edges and a white thing stuck amongst them. Well, could have been a boat, in a collision or something, perhaps quite recently. And the Germans, you know, they were all over this place during the war, probably sank anything they didn't like the look of on sight..."

His high-pitched voice trailed off uncomfortably, aware of Gerhard Felgruber's icy eye.

"Strike me, Chippers," said Ted, unaware of any tension in the air, "I didn't know the Jerries were around these parts. Was there anywhere the buggers weren't pushin' their trolleys?"

The question hung in the air unanswered.

"It was war. All men are responsible for war. Only men make war."

Flora Gillicuddy made this solemn pronouncement, and glared at her meek Hamish, a glare which implied he had much to atone for – and would.

Bernie came to the rescue.

"That sounds like a cue for more of the old Domestos. Nick," he bawled for Dimitri, "bring on some more disinfectant. Mucho Domestico. And the dancing girls."

He smiled at Flora's disapproving face, his ears not registering her acid response.

Rosie, comfortably dressed in a parachute secured at the arms and legs, beamed at the candle–lit faces of her shipmates.

"I saw this fillum once, about some town under the sea, it was called – called – *The Lost City of – the Antlers*, all about some Greeks or Romans who lived under the sea and – and had lost themselves."

With Jack's sense of direction, Rosie had no difficulty in envisaging such a possibility.

Ted started, the way he always started when struck by an idea. Sally hoped, for a moment, he had noticed that Gerhard's hand seemed to have developed a twitch, possibly as a result of her slapping it each time it landed on her smooth bare thigh. But Ted's mind was becoming gripped by the idea of a treasure hunt. If they could find something bogglesome, he, as the flotilla leader, would be famous.

"Hey, Crisp, d'yer think that could be it? Sort of *ruins*, like all those old bricks in Athens an' all?"

Crispin smiled genially.

"Well, it *is* possible they are remnants of a settlement. Brain-box is a bit fuddled these days, what, but I seem to recall that it was quite customary to have monuments carved on the mainland and towed, on rafts, to the islands. That's what *Baedeker* says."

"Well, that's it," said Ted triumphantly. "Let's put a call in to this 'Baedeker' an' ask him who was towin' what to where in those days."

"Baedeker," squeaked Sidney, "wrote travel guide books and is long since dead. But Crispin is right: the Minerva Temple on Paxos was actually carved on the mainland then reconstructed on the island. Rather like a kit you could assemble anywhere."

"We do that."

Darren felt he had a part to play in this adult conversation, particularly with Trudy's hand firmly held in his.

"Me Dad gets all our stuff from MFI and puts them together in our 'ouse. 'Cept," he added, rather spoiling Jack's glow of pride, "they fall apart again."

There was a general hum of conversation as differing

views were given as to what the Warbelow boys might have discovered. Ted deemed it time to show what made a real leader, stood up, then climbed precariously on to the raffia seat of his chair.

"Oh, do be careful," said Sally anxiously, putting a supporting hand on his leg. Not to be outdone, Gerhard put a supporting hand on hers.

"Alright, cobbers," began Ted, "let's put it to the vote. I have to tell you, I shouldn't even *consider* this, it's not part of my job. But there comes a time – or is it a tide, Sally? – in the – er – time of man when you've gotta seize – er – the time and I reckon it is the time. Or tide. When d'ya get the chance to find some treasure normally, eh? Not in yer average lifetime, mates. Too right! So, fellas, whaddya say? Shall we spend a few days tryin' to get our hands on Crisp's marbles?"

Since those nearest to Ted were looking straight up his shorts, it came as a relief to know that it was Crisp's marbles which would be the basis of the search.

"I think it's a load of crap," drawled Steven Clawrer.

This was a bit of a dampener.

"Just because a couple of kids see a pile of rocks, we're supposed to spend the rest of this holiday chasing after daydreams? You gotta be joking!"

And folding his arms truculently, he treated the Ulysses Flotilla to one of his best Southern Scowls.

Flora nudged Hamish.

"Aye," spoke up the wee timorous beastie, "we think the same." A sweep of his hand embraced the collective Gillicuddys who nodded in concert. "We came here to sail the Ionian – with a flotilla. We havena finished the first week yet and we're talkin' about back-tracking – it's nae reet."

Ted swayed spectacularly on his chair, Sally's steadying hand saving him from an undignified exit. With Gerhard applying an equally steadying hand to the small of her bare back and regions beyond, Sally felt like the subject of the song who had 'one eye on the pot, the other up the chimney'. The leg of Ted's shorts made a suitable chimney: she did not like to speculate on the pot.

Gerhard interrupted his exploration of Sally's backbone to suggest a solution.

"So, it is not a problem. Ve are having three days free sailing in our two weeks, no? So, those that are vishing to look for treasure are doing so; the – ah – others are doing vot it is they are vishing and after, ve are meeting again, isn't it?"

Ted looked at Gerhard with new respect.

"Right on, cobber, you said it in one. That fits with the programme and everyone gets what they want. Fantastico!"

"Ted, *please* get down, you're going to fall."

Sally made a great play of helping Ted to get off the chair and abruptly changed seats with him before they sat down. She moved with such graceful speed that Gerhard, who had placed his hand palm upwards on Sally's seat in readiness for her return, found he was cupping Ted's brawny buttocks.

Ted's spring to the vertical would have made a grasshopper green – well, greener, with envy.

"Whoa!", he ejaculated wildly, "that's not my scene, Gerhard, matey. I mean, fair do's." Germans, he had hitherto thought, were more into goose-stepping than goosing. He hadn't figured on including a raving poofter among his crews. Either that, or he was one beer short of a six-pack.

Gerhard, his blushes spared by the dim light, stammered an apology.

"No probs." Ted edged his chair a little nearer to Sally's. "So what we'll do is this. Tomorrow, we'll sail around Skopios – that Onassis play-pad I filled you in on, then anchor up in Abeliki Bay for the barbie. We all have a great night – I've got my guitar – then the next morning at sparrowfart we head off for our three days. How about that? Beaut, eh?"

Despite the reference to the guitar, this seemed to be generally acceptable and no objections were raised. The party began to split up with a noisy scraping of chairs, and make for their bunks.

"Our Sharon didn't come to the meal," murmured Rosie

ruminatively as they headed for *Moby Dick.* "I think she's out gallivanting with that German boy."

She seized the bow rail and, with Jack's gallant and grunting assistance, heaved herself on board in an untidy heap.

"Leave 'em be," gasped Jack as he hauled his bulk onto deck in pursuit of his wife's large luminous rear, out-moonying the brilliantly clear moon above. "Even Sharon can't get up to much mischief 'ere. She's probably back, anyroads."

*   *   *

Jack, however, was unduly optimistic.

Had either Arnold or Sharon paused for breath and looked over the sides of the dinghy, they would have realized that Spartahori was no longer visible on the horizon. In the heat of passion, though, keeping a look-out was way down the list. And the dinghy, inexorably propelled by a snorkel, a large moustache, a pair of fins and a wicked Italian finger, bobbed steadily out to sea.

Sharon, whose shorts and T-shirt were crushed somewhere around her pretty feet, had not yet surrendered her exceedingly skimpy panties. It was only fair, after all, that Arnold should also remove his shorts although, in his present state of arousal, that might have been difficult.

"Hold on," she gasped after a particularly frantic bout, "don't pop your cork!"

"*Was ist passiert?*" mumbled the sweating Arnold, desperately hoping his cork wouldn't pop.

"Wait a minute."

Sharon scrambled into a sitting position and looked around her.

"Oh my Gawd!"

The moon and stars shone on a black expanse of sea. All around. Emptiness.

Arnold peered over the side.

"Shee-it!" he cried, internationally.

72

Sharon grabbed her T-shirt and pulled it on.

"Where – where the hell are we?"

Arnold twisted precariously onto his knees and peered at the empty horizon. Even at this moment of drama, Sharon couldn't help noticing the bulge in his shorts, pointing in the direction of his gaze like a personal sextant.

"Zer – zer is nozing," he wailed, summing up the situation in one. He began to wobble to his feet, setting the dinghy into a violent rocking motion.

"Stop it!" yelled Sharon, "don't panic!" But it was too late. He staggered, recovered, staggered again, then leaving only the word '*Mutter*' in the dinghy, disappeared over the side. Ever afterwards, Sharon would never be sure whether she had heard a hiss as his shorts hit the sea.

His head broke water and he flailed for the dinghy, almost tipping it over. She grasped his hair, wishing Germans didn't go in for such cropped hair-cuts, and with her pulling and his scrambling, Arnold flopped back in to safety.

After expelling a fair amount of the Ionian from his lungs, Arnold felt calmer, more stoical, if a little wet and chilly.

"Ve haf," he said, with Goethe-like finality, "not here a pad-dull." He gestured to the lack of paddles in the dinghy.

Sharon could only miserably agree. Yes, she thought as they bobbed to a melancholy rhythm, we're up the creek without a paddle. Unbeknown to both of them, though, the mean shit was still in the water.

CHAPTER FIVE

DARREN ATTEMPTS WINDSAILING AND TAKES THE WIND FROM HIS MOTHER'S SAILS. MAKING A CRISIS OUT OF A PALAVER. TED DEMONSTRATES A LEADER'S QUALITIES, BUT LUIGI IS TRIUMPHANT. ONE DEPRESSED ANTIPODEAN.

Darren swayed unsteadily, thighs strained, biceps stretched taught, more concentration in his furrowed brow than had ever lodged there before, even when peeing into an empty lager can to throw at a visiting team.

Then the board tipped and he fell backwards into the sneering sea for the fifth time.

Windsurfing was not what it was cracked up to be. Apart from requiring a certain skill in physical co-ordination – something totally lacking in Darren's make-up – there was another essential ingredient lacking.

Wind.

The sun was beginning to make its presence felt now, the ever-cloudless sky taking on its customary blue, but Darren was still the only sign of life in the sleeping bay.

The effort of crawling out of his bunk to practise on the windsurfer unobserved had so far proved unrewarding. Trudy was unlikely to be impressed. In his mind's eye, he saw his bronzed gleaming body gracefully guiding the windsurfer towards the admiring crowd in the taverna, the spectators nudging each other with appreciative comments on his natural athletic ease.

At his present rate, his bruised and battered body was more likely to be laid out on a slab for a local funeral.

He grasped the edge of the board, jerked his torso sharply out of the water and managed to get both his knees on the bobbing platform before it tipped him headfirst back into the water.

"Fuck it!" he roared as he surfaced, then added for greater emphasis, "shit!"

The deckhatch of the fore-cabin on board *Moby Dick* creaked open and the tousled head of Rosie periscoped in search of her offspring.

As the yachts were rafted together, bows to the taverna, Rosie had to twist her neck at such an angle that her kneeling body was forced to follow, thereby causing Jack much discomfort.

"Grooogh," spluttered upwards from the cabin, "gerroff me bleedin' 'ead!"

"I'm sorry, love," Rosie apologized, shifting one plump knee into Jack's solar plexus, "it's our Darren wakin' everyone up wiv 'is language. DARREN!" she bawled, completing the task of waking up the entire Ionian. "Wharrerya doin'?"

Darren glared his speciality of a baleful glare.

"Whatsit look like I'm doin'?" he choked, trying to scramble onto the board.

"Looks like you keep fallin' in the water and swearin'," replied his mother in that unflattering but realistic way that mothers often have. "I've told you time an' time again to watch yer language!"

"Will yer gerrof me stomach?" pleaded her loved one, no longer worried by the possibility of his wife being anorexically inclined.

Rosie's knee found firmer purchase on Jack's thigh.

"Is Sharon up yet?" she yelled at her precariously-balanced son, thereby precipitating him once more into the drink.

His sea-soaked head eyed her malevolently.

"No, she ain't up, she ain't been down. The only thing in her bunk is that bleedin' stupid panda."

And with that, he dived unconcernedly under the board to escape his mother's howl.

Jack's head replaced Rosie's, the rest of him having much the same effect on Rosie as vice versa.

"Darren," Jack roared, ignoring the dull thud that signified his wife's departure from their cabin – head first. "Leave that bloody wind–server alone. Where's yer sister? 'Ave yer seen 'er?"

Disgruntled as ever, Darren swam to *Moby Dick*, pulling the victorious assembly along with him, and clambered on to the yacht.

He stood over the deckhatch, pleasurably dripping over his father's upturned head.

"I've told yer, she ain't on board. She never came back. An' the dinghy's gone too."

"Oh my Gawd," breathed Jack and his head subsided into

the cabin. The absence of the dinghy was bad news. Not unused to his daughter's frequent unexplained disappearances, he would have assumed she was on shore, or perhaps another yacht, fraternizing with any male worth a fraternize. The missing dinghy, though, had nasty connotations.

"Rosie," he hissed through the open cabin doorway, "you'd better get Ted!"

But Rosie was already on her way, dropping from the bow pulpit to the deserted taverna front like an untidy bundle of yachts' fenders and making her way to *Ulysses X*, moored at the opposite end of the flotilla. It was always the same: *Moby Dick* was invariably the last yacht to tie up which had the advantage that the majority of the other yachts could escape in the morning without getting entangled with her. Except for her frustrated neighbour whose yacht would be embraced by the web of Jack's mooring lines, inextricably woven into a cat's cradle.

Rosie grasped the rails of *Ulysses X*'s bow and put her beef into rocking the yacht, a vigorous motion that was communicated to the other boats.

"Oh, not *again*, Ted," came Sally's sleepy voice through the open decklight, "give me half-an-hour, lovey."

"TED!" squealed Rosie, tension getting the better of discretion. She gave the bows another frantic rock.

"Strewth," murmured Ted happily, "that's what I call a really impatient sheila."

"It's *not* me."

Sally disentangled herself from the amorous Aussie, knelt up and, pushing back the decklight, peered across the now sunlit deck at the distraught Rosie.

"What's up, Rosie?"

"It's our Sharon, she's GONE. Gone missing. And the dinghy's gone too."

"Well, perhaps she's just gone for an early-morning paddle – around the bay or something," said Sally, her hand reaching down her back to push away the lips that were being pressed against her bare bottom.

"No, no, she ain't, she's been gone since last night. She didn't 'ave any dinner, you know, when we were all talkin' and we thought she'd gone off wiv..."

Memory dribbled back.

"She was wiv that German boy, whatsisname, Arnold, that's right. He wasn't there either. I mean, he was wiv our Sharon, not 'avin' dinner. God bless an' save us, they've – they've gone orf together, they've ee–loped!"

And Rosie plumped down stricken into a plastic chair, with fleeting visions of her innocent Sharon being seduced on the high seas by a member of the Hitler Youth.

"Wait a minute, Rosie," said Sally, delivering a sharp slap to the Antipodean nose edging up the inside of her thigh, "I'll be with you in a jiff."

By the time a dishevelled Sally emerged in her bikini on deck, Ted having reluctantly allowed her to tie on her top piece without a hand enclosing each breast, the other crews were showing signs of life.

From *De Profundis*, the Königs' yacht, came sounds of consternation. Elke had made a similar discovery to the Armitages: an undisturbed bunk. Jürgen's soothing tones, which annoyingly betrayed to his anxious Frau a certain admiration for his son, could be heard trying to restore calm.

"He is telling Elke," translated Gerhard to the crews now gathered around the taverna tables, "that Arnold is only doing that which all boys are vishing to be doing to Sharon. But," he added unnecessarily, "Elke does not seem pleased."

Eric gave Penny a told-you-so look. This sheer indulgence of youth always required paying the piper. He glanced darkly at Darren who always seemed to be standing unnecessarily close to Trudy.

"Pleased!" yapped Jack, "I'll please 'is arse when I get 'old of 'im. Point is, they ain't 'ere and they ain't been 'ere since last night. Where the 'ell are they? They could be 'alf way to flippin' Africa by now!"

Rosie's wail did not deter Sidney Chippendale from a brief geography lesson.

"Oh no, no, no. Quite impossible. Not *Africa*, my

friend. You see, even Ulysses could not have made the North African coast without more nautical knowledge than he had available to him, and *certainly* not in a rubber dinghy. There's even some doubt that he could have reached Turkey..."

Clara, though keeping a keen watch for an early waiter to bring her first breakfast, had the good sense to put her considerable weight on Sidney's foot and put an end to his squeak.

Jack gave Sidney the look he reserved for motorists who go for a tootle at thirty–five miles an hour on Bank Holidays: he liked to clip their wing mirrors as he overtook them on dangerous bends. Sidney's ears would make a good substitute.

"Jack, what are we goin' to do?" sobbed Rosie, pulling at a corner of his *California Surfin'* shirt to dab at her nose. "Can't we get a helicopter or sumthin' to make a search?"

She looked around the taverna with the vague hope of glimpsing a nearby helicopter pad.

"Oh, jest call up on the radio," drawled Steven Clawrer whose impatience signalled a marked lack of concern. "Send out a mayday. They won't have got far, even if they paddled all night. If *paddlin'* came into it..." he added wickedly.

"They ain't got no paddles."

Darren, standing next to Trudy, his biceps bulging unnaturally as he clenched his hands to make them stand out, wanted to emphasize his keen powers of observation.

"They're still in the locker. Seems to me, she an' that Arnold must 'ave got in ter the dinghy fer a bit of the other. *You know.* 'An it must 'ave come loose, what wiv all the bumpin' around."

Rosie was too worried to challenge this view of events, a view which seemed only too likely. Jack, though, felt his position as head of the family needed some reassertion and smacked Darren smartly on the back of his newly bleached head. His son's indignation was only soothed by the pressure of Trudy's hand on his. Maybe it was worth the smack.

"Don't you go makin' such remarks about yer sister. Our

Sharon's not that sort of girl," he added untruthfully. "More likely that young feller got 'er in ter that dinghy an' pushed it orf so she couldn't get back."

"Oh, ja," grunted Jürgen König, towering above them from the bows of *De Profundis*, his enormous belly wobbling with *angst*, "she is a little – ah – innocent, ja, with her body wearing no clothez every day and her eye–ss on any mens..."

"Well, really," said Flora Gillicuddy testily, shooing Angus and Angie back to *Thistle*. "I was of the opinion that this was supposed to be a *family* holiday, not some sort of orgy at sea. Hamish, I'm going to give the children their muesli."

Hamish, looking sheepish, stayed where the action was.

"Now, please, let's be calm," said Sally, sensing an international incident. "Ted, you'd better put out a general alert. It's not yet..." she pulled up Ted's sinewy wrist to glance at his glistening multi-function chronograph but gave up the attempt to read it, "er – seven o'clock, so most people won't be up yet. They've probably been picked up already and just don't want to disturb anyone yet."

Pretty unlikely, thought Sally, whose judgement of Sharon had a lot to do with a sense of rivalry. Sharon would wake the dead if it suited her.

Ted swung himself back on board *Ulysses X* with an athletic bound.

"No worries," he said, then thought better of it. "No *real* worries. They'll be back in a jiffy. Might even have just gone round the coast. They could paddle with their hands, dead easy."

"Yeh, well, they'll have had plenty of practice," sneered the unpleasant Steven and, gathering up his towel and kit, made off purposefully in the direction of the taverna's erratic shower. The onlookers were pleased that a trail of loo paper leaked from his towel, making his 'sod-you' gait less impressive.

Ted, reflecting that Steven Clawrer was an absolute piker, disappeared below to twiddle his dials. The group stood around uncomfortably, uncertain what to do.

"So, it is better to be doing somethings. Monika and me – and I – vill take my *Becker* and look outside of the bay."

Most of the crews had forgotten that Gerhard had christened his yacht 'Becker' and were momentarily non-plussed. There had been some obvious confusion every time Gerhard had radioed the position of his *Becker*.

"What's he say he's going to do?" asked a puzzled Bernie.

"He's going to search around with his – his boat," yelled Lorraine. "We ought to too."

"That's the ticket," said the Hon. Crispin St Clair, "If we all go in different directions, we stand a jolly good chance of coming across them. Perhaps if you stay here, Sally, we can all report to you – and you can let us know if they turn up in the meantime."

To Sally, it sounded like a perfect recipe for disaster but she couldn't think of an alternative.

"Well, alright," she agreed slowly. "But can everyone please make sure that your radio is tuned in on ten and stay in touch. If we all motor for, say, an hour out and an hour back, we should have sighted them by then."

Gerhard sought to apply good German planning.

"Ja, that is good but it would be better if ve are returning on another tack because then ve vill not be simply doing the same things out and in."

This inescapable logic worried Eric.

"If we all go out in different directions, and come back in different directions, how do we know *which* directions we are heading for?"

Bernie, after a bellowed translation, was up to this.

"It's easy. We just go out, one after the other, then each one veers away after a bit, to the left or right. If the boat in front of you," he explained, mainly for the benefit of Jack whom he regarded as a basic thicko, "goes to the left, you go to the right. Like a fighter squadron."

"They did that in *Jackboot on Europe*."

Amy Clawrer had appeared on the deck of *The Bounty*. In almost her last film, she had been a Tahitian maiden and had received quite inadequate compensation from the studio when an ember from Marlon Brando's cigar had set fire to her grass skirt. Though burns were avoided, the film crew had been over eager in ripping off her skirt and revealing, much to her humiliation, the corset which had made her slim enough to join the cast.

Steven had thought of several anti-British names to call their yacht but had conceded to *The Bounty* when Amy's reassurances confirmed his own personal opinion that he bore a marked resemblance to Brando at his peak.

Though aware of the kerfuffle on the quayside, it had taken Amy a little time to apply just the right touch of make-up before making an appearance.

"I was the sweetheart of one of the bomber crews going off to flatten..."

"Well done, Bernie!"

Sally was feeling a little desperate. She could hear Ted on the radio and just hoped that there was a boat out there that could understand him.

Gerhard, a man of action, most of it with women in mind, patted her bottom reassuringly, then once more for the hell of it, and marched off to *Becker*, there presumably to summon his invisible daughter to help him cast off.

The others followed with the usual orders, advice and arguments. Engines churned up the sea, moorings were cast off more or less without mishap, and *Becker* was the first out, reversing expectedly into the bay, a beheaded figure at the helm. With a degree of co-ordination that surprised Sally, the yachts edged into the harbour, only *Moby Dick* predictably slamming *Thistle* amidships causing Flora to upset skimmed milk over her still-pale children. No harmful ultra-violet rays would penetrate the protected bodies of the junior Gillicuddys, even if Hamish's freckles were beginning to join together in some sort of tan.

As the flotilla left Spartahori bay, the white yachts trailing their thin wakes across the sparkling green-blue sea back to the taverna, Sally joined Ted at the radio.

"Anything?"

"Not a bite," replied Ted to whom the disappearance of

Sharon and Arnold represented only a temporary problem. In Ted's experience, most problems were resolved, one way or other, without too much cerebral pondering. You could get very upset by problems.

Sally breathed deeply. Breathing deeply was an indispensable part of their relationship.

"Ted, someone might hear us if you turn the radio on."

Ted gave Sally an admiring look. Admiring looks were also an indispensable part of their relationship.

"Kosher," he said, bringing life to the radio. He held the microphone close to his wide mouth and pressed the transmitter.

"This is Ted Banks, skipper of the Ulysses Flotilla. Callin' all boats in range. Bands seven to twelve."

He paused for thought. This was heavy going.

"Last night, we were all havin' a bit of a knees up, yer know, a few drinks, bit of a laugh..."

"Tell them where we are and who's missing," hissed Sally.

"Right. Too right. Well, we're moored off Spartahori, yer know, Andreas' place. An' we've lost two crew, not from the same crew mind, from *different* yachts – alright, Sal – they've gone missin'. Seems they were in one of our dinghies, got 'Ulysses' on the side, okay, an', well, last night, they were sort of – canoodlin', that's a word for it, ha, ha – sorry, Sal – an' they must have maybe drifted out the bay, been out there for – for, er, good seven hours maybe, *some canoodlin'* session, hey – I'm sayin' it, Sal – an' if they haven't hit the shore they could be somewhere out there. Or maybe someone listenin' has picked them up, a right sexy little blond, some looker that one – oww! – and a young German feller, black hair, they're around eighteen or somethin' like that."

"Oh, and yeh, they're called Sharon an' – what? – Arnold. Anyone hearing me out there who maybe has seen them: be more than grateful for the old speel on the airwaves. We'll be standin' by, good an' proper. Over!"

He put the mike down with relief and satisfaction. Not everyone could get it together like that.

"Ted," asked a worried Sally, "what are we going to do if we don't find them soon?"

He stretched out a manly hand and caressed her long, curling black hair back from her face. Those eyelashes were truly *a–mazing*.

"There's not a lot we can do at the moment, Sal," he husked. When Ted husked, he had one thing on his mind. He husked most of the time.

Sally pushed past her lustful skipper and climbed up the cabin steps to deck.

"The Clawrers are still here," she warned down to his upturned face. "You might know that mean Yank won't put himself out for anyone. I'm going to join him and Amy for breakfast. She could do with a break from his miserable face. I think you'd better stay by the radio in case anything comes through."

Steven had emerged from the shower and was seated, looking disgruntled, at a table with Amy. As Sally joined them, he took the opportunity to complain about the slow trickle of water in the shower, the dirt on the floors and the lack of hygiene where food was concerned.

"That goddamned mongrel is sittin' on that woman's lap in there while she's cuttin' up meat. I reckon these Greeks have got no sense of – cleanliness; no standards."

"If you want a McDonalds, you should have stayed in America," said Sally tartly. "The whole point about these islands is that they're not geared to mass tourism. Water is rationed, most supplies come by boat – and, anyway, if it doesn't worry the Greeks, I don't see why it should worry you."

Steven bridled. "Lady, it'll sure worry you if the whole of this flotilla goes down with dysentery and you get an ocean full of crap. If that stoopid mutt..."

Amy interrupted him excitedly.

"Sally, Ted's waving to you. I guess he wants you to go over."

Ted was beckoning from the bows of *Ulysses X*. Sally, glad to escape, joined him on deck.

"That Eyetie Luigi's got them. The kids, Sharon and whatsisname. He's just called up and said he'll give us the gen and to tell all the others to tune in on twelve so he can give us the yarn."

They dropped below deck and Ted reached for the transmitter.

"Wait a minute, Ted. What's he up to? Why doesn't he just tell you what happened?"

"Dunno, Sal, he just came in on ten and said they were on board his boat, that they were all pucker and he'd give the gen as soon as I'd called the other yachts in the flotilla and told 'em to tune in on his band. Maybe he wants someone near to him to take them off his hands. With that Sharon there, it'd be just as well, him being Eyetalian an' all."

Sally forbore to comment on the hot blood of certain Australians she knew, and they busied themselves instructing the Ulysses crews to tune in on twelve and listen for news of the missing couple.

It took them a good fifteen minutes to get all eight boats to radio in and adjust their wave bands. There seemed to be confusion reigning off the coast of Meganisi, Sally's misgivings about the manner of their search proving true. From their at times acerbic radio responses, it was easy to gain an impression that they were playing dodgems just outside Spartahori bay.

Eric Warbelow was the last to call up.

"*Nemesis* to *Ulysses* X. Over."

"Gotya, *Nemesis*. Over."

"Yes, well, we heard you," came Eric's peevish tones. "We could have called you sooner if we hadn't been trying to avoid being sunk. I told you it wouldn't work, half the yachts just turned in circles – oh, my GOD, WHAT IS THAT IDIOT DOING – "

Eric's screech faded into the ether, leaving Ted and Sally glued to their radio like Forties fans of *Journey into Space* waiting for next week's episode.

It was Penny who came back on the air. Even Penny sounded a little ruffled.

"I really think," she said sternly, "that you should require *some* experience of sailing before handing over yachts to some people. I don't think that Jack Armitage has quite grasped the principle of steering. If he *has*, then I can only assume he likes making Eric vomit with shock." She took a deep breath. "We're tuning in to twelve."

And all the flotilla, including the Clawrers who wanted to be in on the excitement, tuned in to Luigi.

*　　*　　*

The moustachioed skipper of *Angela Mia* was in seventh heaven, an affirmation of his belief in that place and of the power of his Catholic deity – a glittering gold crucifix – lying among the darkly-sprouting hair on his chest. If the other six heavens were half as good, he'd have no complaints when he hit the real thing.

Angela Mia was a larger and more luxurious yacht than the rather spartan collection of Cobras that made up the Ulysses Flotilla. No plastic shower bag hung from *her* mast. A touch-button electric job had caressed the honeyed body of Sharon who had shown her appreciation by appearing on deck clad in an alluring assortment of face towels – the only things she could find, hum, hum. Since Ariadne wore even less as a matter of course, Sharon did not feel that the ninety per cent of beautiful curves which she displayed were more immodest than the ninety-nine per cent of Ariadne's. Besides, a crisis of conscience concerning immodesty was hardly Sharon's line. What Sharon was naturally endowed with came to very few women – and yachts in the Ionian were not the place to hide it.

It had been extraordinary, amazing and brilliant luck that *Angela Mia* had been in the vicinity of the helpless dinghy around 2 a.m., with all hope of being picked up overnight having been lost. When the initial feelings of despair had been overcome, Sharon and Arnold had reasoned that *someone, sometime* must surely find them before their bodies became dried out husks stuck to a rubber dinghy. The panic having subsided, and the night air becoming coolish, they had found, more or less by experiment, that the closer they got to each other, the warmer they became. Had they been more widely read, studied, perhaps, accounts of Polar expeditions, this fact would naturally have occurred to them and they would have applied the principle as a matter of scientific procedure, a steady and purposeful mutual transmission of heat like two sticks rubbed together.

As it was, they were so encouraged by the results of their experimentation that, when the bows of *Angela Mia* slid out of the night and hovered ghost–like over their dinghy, what they had rubbed together had reached an exceedingly high temperature and was about to result in a mutual transmission of bodily fluids. It was only Luigi's melodic "*Grazie per la serata. E stata splendida!*" that made them realize rescue, and an audience, was at hand. Once again, Sharon retrieved her shorts and pulled them on beneath the admiring gaze of Luigi and the pursed biceps of Ariadne.

Clutching warming cups of hot chocolate, the shipwrecked 'children' had nestled comfortably into chaste and single bunks. Luigi had sat between them and recounted numerous tales of mishaps that had made any Ulysses Flotilla, particularly those skippered by Ted Banks, famed throughout the Ionian for cock-ups.

"Issa true," Luigi had assured them, "on the honour of my mother" – (she had run off with a Fiat foreman, his father's boss, who henceforth had suffered many jokes of the "I bet he's revving her up and giving her a good servicing" variety) – "this Ulyssesa is one–a bigga tea party, a *fiasco*. You will tell the others, yes, to – ah – say to 'ave their monies back and screw thisa company."

By the time he had finished, Sharon and Arnold were convinced that they were the victims of a shiftless Aussie who left untethered dinghies uninspected, sending hapless children out to sea in the dead of night. The avuncular and big-hearted Italian, true to his nationally characteristic love of children, then tucked them securely into their blankets – perhaps more assiduously in Sharon's case – waggled his moustache over Arnold's cheek in the way of a true *paterfamilias*, and bestowed several kisses on Sharon's delicate neck in the way of a true lecherous o.b.; until a sharp rap from Ariadne with a wrench on the back of his sizeable head neatly provided a full-stop to his bedtime story.

Now, after Sharon had donned her T-shirt and shorts for the umpteenth time in the last eight hours, they all stood in readiness before the radio, waiting for Ted to call them up on the long-range frequency channel: twelve.

"*Angela Mia* to *Ulyssesa Flotilla*, you are receiving me loud and clear, no, Over?"

"This is Ted Banks, skipper of the Ulysses Flotilla."

Ted thought it best to assert his authority. He didn't care for the rather summary manner of his rival in the flotilla stakes, but felt at a decided disadvantage: what he had lost, the obnoxious Eyetalian had found.

"Ah, bene, 'allo again Ted my frienda, all your boats are a–tuning in, Over?"

"Yes," said Ted shortly, "they're all ears."

"So, they are all there–a. We 'ave youra two poor little *bambini* 'ere. I find them in the sea, so cold and so tired, all the night longa they are, ah, dreefting in their leetle rubber – ah – 'ow you say, dinghee –"

"Great," Ted interrupted. "Can you bring them into Spartahori or do you want me to come and pick them up? Over."

"...an' I say to my – ah – lady friend, I say 'Ariadne, look, this is terrible, 'ow can this 'appen that they let two poora children go by themselves all alone–a'. An' she say 'Ah, Luigi, you knowa this must be the Ulyssesa Flotilla, always somethings are 'appening like this with them..."

Ted writhed with unaccustomed impotency, his ears turning red at the thought of his listening crews. "The bastard," he hissed at Sally. "He's really creaming this one."

"That's why he wanted everyone listening in," said Sally dolefully. "He's just scoring points, trying to discredit us."

The censorious Mediterranean tones continued.

"...so that they are lucky that always *Angela Mia* is

keeping watch, even at nighta, for any boats chartered from Luigi, is all parta of the serveece when you are a–coming to Luigi, an' now the leetle ones are 'appy an' Sharon, she wanna talk to the mamma."

There was a pause, then Sharon came on the air.

"'Ello, Mum? Mum? Can you hear this?"

Another somewhat lengthier crackle, then *Moby Dick* burst into life. It was the *papa*, though, who breathed heavily across the airwaves.

"...pressin' it, Rosie, I know 'ow to do it. Ahem. This is *Moby Dick* 'ere, an' over. To – er – the Eyetalian boat – er – *Angelica* – an' our Sharon. Er, over to you, like."

"Dad, there's no need to shout, you nearly blasted me ear off. We're alright, Arnold an' me, we're on this swanky number, it's got a proper flush loo an' a brill shower, just press buttons, and decent beds..."

"Beds?" asked Jack suspiciously, "You ain't in bed on no Eyetalian boat, are ye?"

"We just got up. They're givin' us breakfast, all sausages an' things. Anyway, Luigi's bringin' us back, so tarra for now. Here comes the bronzed hunk."

The undutiful daughter signed off with a giggle, to be replaced by the hunk himself.

"So – ah – we are coming to you with – ah – the childrens. In maybe one–a hour, OK, we are at Spartahori. Maybe," he added maliciously, "we picka up any others you are losing on the way, eh? Over and–a Out."

And Luigi, with the pleasurable sense of having landed one idiot of an Aussie right in it, sniffed the expresso-scented air appreciatively and turned to the important matter of breakfast.

*   *   *

Ted stared dully out to sea: the beauty of the bay, the calm of the Ionian, not even the light breeze which made for such perfect sailing conditions afforded balm to his troubled thoughts.

Ted had lost face, and when a man loses face he – he loses face. It was not merely Luigi's cockiness that had put Ted down, nor the way *Angela Mia* had turned into the bay in full view of the reassembled Ulysses Flotilla, letting off distress flares in triumph and using a hand-held siren to announce the Italian's imminent arrival. Lucky for *him*, Ted thought, that it was highly unlikely anyone in the Ionian would take any notice of what were supposed to be emergency procedures. No, it was the way his crews smiled at him politely, avoided eye-contact, and talked about the weather

One by one, Ted's crews had returned, save for the Clawrers who had seemed to steer *The Bounty* right into the midst of the returning yachts. Watching one outgoing yacht dodging eight incoming yachts in the neck of a bay reminded Ted of his windsurfing days on Bolongi Beach. He always seemed to be heading in the wrong direction, plunging out into the surf just as every lifesaver in the New World came hurtling over the crest of the wave in his direction. *The Bounty*, though, made out to sea unscathed, unlike Ted who had generally found himself face down in a quivering wobble of jellyfish.

As the yachts moored up at the taverna edge, Ted offered his services to each one, ready to catch the mooring lines, steady the bows, or even to sling his hook. But not even the Armitages needed Ted. True to form, *Moby Dick* weaved in last, Jack bellowing incomprehensible orders from the helm, Darren poised in the bows ready to leap ashore in that athletic way so admired by Trudy.

It was not his fault, as he protested later, if his father steered *Moby Dick* a mile away from any convenient mooring point and, anyway, the taverna tables seemed quite solid and he had no idea that, if he tied a rope to the table leg where Clara Chippendale was enjoying a third breakfast, *Moby Dick* would edge backwards and drag both the table and the breakfast into the harbour. Nor, he added bitterly, could he have known that *anyone* could be that fond of food as to follow their breakfast right into the sea and have to be hauled out like a cargo of quivering tripe back on to dry land by means of an Anglo-Greek co-operative of male muscle power.

So *Angela Mia* had nosed her way towards the taverna and, all available mooring spaces being taken up by the Ulysses Flotilla, had anchored just offshore. Luigi, sporting a perfectly ridiculous peaked cap complete with gold braid, had lowered his dinghy – a much bigger and more elaborate affair than any Ulysses job – and, with the statuesque and almost-clothed Ariadne sitting proud in the front, had rowed his way to shore, towing the dinghy containing the happily waving duo, Sharon and Arnold.

Ted thought that their welcome by his crews was overdone, all that whooping and shrieking and clapping, Rosie clutching her embarrassed daughter to her foil–clad bosom as though Sharon was the sole survivor of *The Titanic*. Only Jack seemed to strike the appropriate note, declaring that his wayward child should "have her arse smacked for causing all this bloody trouble", a sentiment to which Gerhard agreed with much enthusiasm and offers of help.

It now being midday, it was the unanimous opinion that a celebratory lunch should be supplied by Andreas, with Luigi as chief guest. The taverna owner did not demur, such custom being his stock of trade, but Luigi was not unknown to him and he didn't much like what he knew. Besides, a handsome Greek woman like Ariadne should know better than to share a cabin with a disreputable Italian, particularly when she could be sharing a taverna room with a no less disreputable Greek.

Apart from Ted and his sympathetic Sally, who harboured suspicions as to the presence of *Angela Mia* so conveniently at night in the middle of the sea, and whose analytical brain was recalling the mysterious beaching of *Nemesis* with only Penny on board, everyone appeared to enjoy themselves immensely. Even Bernie faced another plate of meatballs with equanimity, chilled beers and carafes of Domestica encouraging much feeling of camaraderie among the crews.

As Tara St Clair remarked, it was amazing how people who would go to some length to avoid each other at home should find each other's company so enjoyable.

It was Sally, ably disguising her irritation at the fêting of the majestic Luigi, who brought the lunch to a close by reminding the party of the barbecue that evening, to be held in Abeliki Bay. The breeze having become a light wind, conditions were set fair for a brisk two-hour sail and the charts were brought out to plot the course. Since even Jack Armitage could hardly fail to find the bay if he simply kept in sight of the coast, navigation was hardly necessary but Sally had hoped Ted would resume his role of skipper and take command. Unnoticed, though, he had left the crews to enjoy themselves and found a solitary knoll further along the shore to settle in his own little cloud of gloom.

Reluctantly, but bowing to the general mood, Sally had invited Luigi and Ariadne – whose undoubted attractions had tempted Gerhard into an experiment which had resulted in a sudden howl and Gerhard's abrupt departure to the lavatory, there to check that everything was still in its allotted place – to the evening barbecue. Now, with the Ulysses Flotilla once more at sea, Sally walked to the edge of the shingle-crushed beach to look for her man. Seeing his silhouette humped, Rodin-like, on a knoll, she called him back to the taverna. He shambled forlornly towards her, his customary lope extinguished by his depression.

They sat together on the edge of the mooring quay, her arm around his shoulders, watching the yachts disappear into the heat haze.

"Cheer up, love," said Sally, nuzzling his neck, her long black tresses stroking his bare shoulder.

"Bloody piker," he muttered, "lording it over everyone like that. Wasn't my fault those two went off like that. You'd think he'd found David Livingstone."

"Stanley," corrected Sally.

"Yeh, him as well."

"Funny he should just be on the spot like that," mused Sally. "All that stuff about keeping an eye out for his boats at night. Just as if...I mean, everyone says he lets out his boats to anyone, no questions asked. I think there's something fishy about him."

"He's an Eyetie," agreed Ted.

"No, don't be silly. I mean I think he's after something. We're not the first Ulysses Flotilla to have something go wrong, there's been quite a few other things we were told and if the company lost its licence, I'd take a bet he'd be in there like a flash..."

Before Sally could warm to her theme, Andreas appeared carrying a large box of uncooked meat, accompanied by his ever-hopeful mongrel.

"Eh, you two loving-birds," growled Andreas, "you want the food on the boat now for tonight, yes?"

"Come on," encouraged Sally, pulling Ted to his feet. "We'd better get the stuff on board. Chin up, it's barbie night!"

Andreas rested the box on a table and stood between them, an arm around each pair of shoulders.

"What is it, you are a miserable bastard, Ted? Look, look at this beautiful woman of yours, a man should die for this girl, look at that face, is an angel," his hand reached round to stroke her dimpled cheek. "Why she go for a bum like you when there is a man like me, I don't know this. But I tell you," he pulled them closer to a fishy-smelling sweat-stained vest, "I no like that Luigi, he is one..." he searched in his memory for a word from his merchant navy days, "nasty bugger, you do not trust him. Now, there is much food to get on and the flies are fighting for it so, come, get your lazy bum to action."

And bestowing a wet smacky kiss to left and right, he picked up the box and marched off to *Ulysses X*.

Sally hugged her hulk.

"Let's get the stuff and get going. We'd better radio the Clawrers and make sure they know where Abeliki Bay is. Alright?"

And she pressed hard against those finely assembled muscles, noting a certain lifting of the gloom.

"Alright, Sal," Ted husked.
Sally sure knew how to make her man husk.

CHAPTER SIX

OLEG, THE CASTAWAY OF ABELIKI. MONIKA JOINS IN THE GAMES AND WINS SEVERAL HEARTS. TENSIONS AT THE BARBIE, UNRELIEVED BY TED'S SINGING. AMY FALLS UPON A SURPRISED SOURCE OF SOLACE.

Oleg Grameshic Dhoni stealthily watched the rafting together of the Ulysses Flotilla in Abeliki Bay with the calculation of a fox eyeing a fat goose. Or geese.

Oleg was not concerned with collective nouns: he had literally had enough of collectives to last him a lifetime. Collecting the goods was more on his mind. After four solitary years living in the dense scrub and abandoned olive groves surrounding the bay, he had learned the art of survival, the simple art of putting himself and his immediate needs at the centre of his philosophical outlook on life.

Life, so far, was not bad – at least compared to life in Sinanaj, the small town in Albania where support of the glorious regime had been tempered by unrewarding drudgery. Oleg had been lucky: no, truth was, he had made his luck.

A handsome, fiercely bearded man turning thirty, he had been considered quite a catch by anyone with the means to catch him – which, in Sinanaj, were not that many. Oh, there were pretty girls enough and Oleg had dextrously avoided the vengeance of outraged males whose ancient solution to the dishonour of one of their women would have been to cut his balls off with a blunt knife.

Katrina's family had been different. Her father, being the superintendent of the jam-making collective where Oleg worked, had no desire for scandal to jeopardize his job. Marriage was agreed – at night, with Oleg held upside down from the family bedroom window, on the twelfth floor of the block – and the date was fixed. But the superintendent made a strategic mistake: he wanted his future son-in-law to cut quite a dash on the day when the Police Commissar would bond the happy couple, and he advanced Oleg several hundred *leks* for the necessary requisites.

With more purchasing power in his pocket than he had ever previously experienced, Oleg weighed up the advantages of buying a suit that Stalin would have approved of against those of acquiring a wife whose resemblance to that legendary figure had made her the envy of the Young Admirers of Stalin League – and found them wanting.

Indeed, he was found wanting on the day itself, having fled under the tarpaulin of a lorry bearing its jammy produce to the coast. Trading his dowry for another trip under a tarpaulin – one of the few things Albania was not short of – he chugged out under cover of night in a tiny fishing boat whose owner proved to be no mechanic. They had barely headed for Corfu when the ancient outboard called it a day and the fisherman called it a son of a bitch.

While Oleg peered fearfully from under his shelter, his fisherman friend proceeded to belt the outboard with a spanner, curses echoing eerily across the dark sea – and attracting the ominous looming shape of an Albanian patrol boat. Unmindful of his passenger's comfort and future welfare, the owner dived overboard with a howl, activated into a crawl that would have won him an Olympic gold medal. The spotlight from the P.T. boat swept across the sea, a staccato command rasped from the megaphones, and Oleg thought how nice Katrina was in a certain light, and what might have been.

Albanian spotlight bulbs, fortunately, were little better than Albanian suits and just as likely to burst, plunging the participants into darkness. Curled into a protective ball, it was some time before Oleg realized that the pursuer had headed for home, leaving a relieved fisherman to struggle his sodden way ashore and a reluctant bridegroom adrift in a smelly boat.

With no oars provided – Oleg had booked the economy package with no frills – boat and occupant bobbed on the tideless sea until the first streaks of dawn allowed for a cautious raising of the tarpaulin. Even Oleg's scant knowledge of the sea enabled him to perceive that he was roughly in the same position as when the P.T.'s light had gone out. And that position presented immediate possibilities of being picked up and delivered into the arms of his loved one – together with a ten-year sentence.

Furiously, he applied the owner's technique to the outboard, a wallop here, a bang there; but this time there was instant reward. One strong tug and the engine fired – oh joy – and Oleg was on his way. Although the coast of Corfu was in sight, he accurately surmised that he was still in Albanian waters and that any boat aiming for that den of capitalists was likely to be apprehended.

Pushing his luck as well as his fuel, he headed south and was in sight of Levkas before his diesel ran out. Instinctively feeling that the bottle-necked canal would provide a permanent barrier between him and his mother country, he determined to find a way through and was rewarded when a large white yacht pulled alongside in response to his frantic waving.

The French couple who owned the yacht could make nothing of his guttural utterances and cared even less. Theirs was an idyllic honeymoon, his fifth, her third, with twenty years between them in her favour – and with little else between them since they were of the nudist persuasion, a conviction which Oleg had not experienced but which delighted him nonetheless.

He was particularly impressed by the skipper who stood proudly at the bow as they edged their way through the Levkas canal, flying a kite. With very little wind, the kite flew in the slipstream of the boat as it motored carefully between the numerous sandbanks, appearing to have a life of its own. Indeed, it seemed to have a tethering all of its own, since the Frenchman at no time used his hands to manoeuvre it. Oleg's admiration knew no bounds when he realized to what the kite was attached: if this was the corrupt 'face' of capitalism, this was for him.

And so they came to the emerald waters of Abeliki Bay, gliding bows-in onto the soft sand and shingle of its shallow water to drop anchor. The beauty of it, the peace of it, the thyme-scented smells of it, as well as the isolation of it told Oleg that this was the place to take stock and think out the next move.

Four years later, he was still unsure of the next move. The French couple, persuaded by his vigorous confidence, had left him in the bay waving them and his memories of her bare-breasted beauty out to sea. A limited supply of truffles, cheese and wine – the couple were not so enamoured of the Greek Islands as to omit to bring their own Gallic supplies – were his sole means of support.

It became apparent to the castaway that the immediate area around Abeliki Bay was uninhabited. He knew, from his brief sojourn on the French yacht when not otherwise distracted by the naked helmswoman, that there were other bays on this island which could be inhabited but Abeliki seemed deserted. Exploring inland, he came across once-cultivated olive groves, stone walls that peasant hands had tortuously built, twisting between the gnarled trees, only to be abandoned.

His mistaken assumption that this must be due to lack of water was simply ignorance of the attractions of tourism and the greater profits to be made running sea-edge tavernas. Following a clearly defined track, he came across a tumbled-down stone dwelling built next to – and this was the real find – a crumbling well. Hours of labour and the removal of assorted debris, including the skeleton of a goat and a wooden lavatory seat crudely attached to a World War II giant army tin of condensed milk, rewarded him with the gleam of brackish water, at first foul tasting, then refreshing, scooped out with a French plastic yoghurt container loosely attached to the end of his belt.

So Oleg became the Robinson Crusoe of Abeliki, surviving by his wits which principally meant through theft. To be fair, he tried living off nature, who proved most ungenerous, wild figs having a catastrophic effect on his constitution. Since the plumbing had rarely worked back in Sinanaj, the disposal of his natural waste caused few problems apart from the time he found himself crouching over a scorpion claiming territorial rights. But a need for some solid food that would remain in his stomach without immediate expulsion from his bowels drove him to explore further afield until the day he overlooked, from his cover of trees and bush, the taverna at Spartahori.

His raids were discrete and carried out at night. A few bottles of water here, a dried sausage there, even a cheese or two. Andreas, unaware of the island's new arrival, had not noticed at first. When he did begin to notice that items were missing, he merely booted his cross-eyed cur for apparently having developed some gourmet tastes. A mangy mongrel, however, was unlikely to account for the absence of tin openers, knives and beer glasses, let alone help itself to a bottle of Retsina as it bayed to the moon.

So Andreas kicked first his wife, then his assistant, with minimal effect since this was nothing out of the ordinary. Whereupon he decided, a certain Orthodoxy having permeated his childhood, that the island had developed a spirit that required offerings; he took to leaving regular supplies which, just as regularly, disappeared.

This amiable solution became a habit – and in any case was paid for by the yachting tourists – and Abeliki Bay retained its permanent, if unseen, inhabitant.

The Albanian castaway did have a second source of supplies, which provided him not only with an exotic and varied diet but an assortment of clothes and belongings; these increased to the stage when Oleg seriously considered opening a store of his own.

Yachting flotillas arrived virtually every other day during the summer months, providing supplies and entertainment, much needed during the long winter nights when even the cicadas packed in their monotonous rhythm and called it a life. The barbecues were lit, the music throbbed, the games he-hawed, the meat roasted and the lovers headed into the scrub. As Oleg crouched observing naked bodies hurriedly satisfying urgent appetites, the solitude of his monastic existence was impressed upon him and even Andreas' flea–ridden hound took on a certain attraction.

Acquiring carelessly-dropped Walkmen had its consolations. It had taken him some time to figure out what to do with personal cassette players: eventually, after unravelling several cassettes, and using the tape as the most unsuccessful fishing-line to have been scorned by a passing sardine, he had mastered the art and now knew the lyrics of the Beatles' *Rubber Soul* by heart. Depending on a supply of half-used batteries had its drawbacks, resulting as it did in a style of singing that mimicked the slowing down of the tape. It gave the Beatles a curious Eastern flavour. There was some consolation, too, in the purloining of clothes, cameras and suntan oil – which he used for frying, thereby developing strange tastes with a particular preference for Ambre Solaire – but, at heart, Oleg Crusoe was a lonely man. Not to say a randy man.

Now, as the Ulysses crews dinghied and swam ashore, he moaned and muttered to himself as he picked out the sparsely–clad females alighting on the shelved beach. Even Clara Chippendale held his fascinated gaze, an abundance of female flesh wibble-wobbling out of a nearly submerged dinghy. Four years of solitude was a long time for a man of Oleg's appetites and such temptation made ducking behind a rosemary bush an extremely difficult position to maintain. With wild, unkempt hair and a beard down to his waist, a torn Jimi Hendrix T-shirt tucked into cut-off tracksuit trousers bearing the legend 'Beneto-' down one leg, and an ill-matching pair of trainers keeping out the pine needles, only his recently acquired Rayban shades gave him the coveted look of a sophisticated tourist.

He could hardly, though, make a casual appearance at their party, with only the lyrics of *It Must Be Love* (slowing-down version) as a means of communication. Besides, he was unsure of his safety, agents from Albania having a way of retrieving their exiles from the remotest places. Despite having attempted to keep track of time by various time-honoured methods such as notching tree trunks, he invariably forgot when and where he had started. He had a vague idea that maybe he was a couple of years older than when he had started out.

So he remained where he was, eyeing the unloading of provisions from *Ulysses X* and rocking with lust at the pleasurable sight of Sally's lean and glistening body pulling the food-laden dinghy ashore.

*   *   *

Unaware of the effect she was having on the sex-starved Albanian, but well aware of the effect on Gerhard Felgruber, whose helping hands she wished were elsewhere, Sally busied herself with preparations for the barbecue. She listened with accustomed patience to Ted's howls of dismay echoing across the bay as he attempted to wade ashore from his dinghy with a tray of sardines on his head. Since he always stubbed the same toe on the same rock, the ritual of trawling for the dead fish from the crystal waters preceded every barbie they ever held.

The flotilla was complete, Steven and Amy Clawrer being the last to arrive in the late afternoon, another burnt-out quarrel hanging in the hot air above their flapping mainsail. Steven's temper was not improved by having to raft up in a line with the others: Ted's insistence that anchoring alone would lead to drifting was met with a scornful silence and a deliberate rocking of the flotilla. Taking the usual place of *Moby Dick* at the end of the row was tantamount to being sent into the corner, too much of a reminder of Steven's unpopularity at his Southern Baptist school to make his temper sweeter. Hitting Jack Armitage on the nose with his carelessly-thrown mooring line was hardly compensation.

The others, though, were caught by a sense of communicated happiness, fed by the beauty of Abeliki, its blue-green clear waters caressing the soft shingley sand, and the prospect of a feast laid on by their amiable skipper – when not upending sardines into the water – and his capably exquisite Sally.

The aromatic fragrance of charcoal, singed olive-wood and lighter-fuel stole across the bay, causing noses to rise inquisitively, low murmurs of satisfaction and anticipation following its path. Sally, on all fours, was getting up a glow well in advance of cooking time. Gerhard, likewise on all fours and getting up a glow of a different sort, was blowing hard too: his ineffectiveness was largely due to aiming his puffs of excited air down Sally's cleavage.

The St Clairs were proving adept at organizing games, something to do with the boarding-school background they all shared. Crispin and Tara prodded the adults into lethargic action: Lucien and Arabella took over the kids. Even the diehards were not tough enough to resist the St Clairs. Tara told Steven "not to be a silly old Southerner" and warned him that he would be regarded as "nothing but a perfect old fart if he didn't get his arse into gear", a statement which so confounded him coming, as it were, from the mouth of a British aristocrat, that he meekly submitted to the organized indignities.

Arabella, deciding that only a woman should mistreat a woman, adjusted the straps of her flat one–piece with determination, filled a plastic bucket from the sea, and flung it without warning over mysterious Monika, sunbathing under her huge floppy hat on the prow of *Becker*. The hat collapsed around its owner's head, but the figure remained deadly still, little streams of water running out of an elegant blue sundress. Then the long, beringed fingers of one hand began a slow drumming on the deck, an extraordinarily menacing sound, far more effective than those Zulu drums which Arabella's ancestors had taken with a pinch of snuff.

Almost unnerved but made of the sort of spunk that regarded the old hot-poker-up-the-jacksy treatment as a bit of a laugh, Arabella would not let herself be intimidated by some phoney female who was German to boot. Besides, every six-former at Roedean adopted similar postures in floppy hats as the hormones worked overtime and third-formers developed crushes on them.

"Come on, Monika," Arabella exhorted shrilly, "everybody's going to play games. Don't just sit there. Have a bit of fun, it's super in the water and Daddy's going to organize games."

The sodden hat slowly turned in Arabella's direction. The enormous dark glasses rested on her like huge insect eyes in a monster movie. One of those long-fingered hands slowly drifted upwards, hovered languidly over the shades, then removed them slowly. Arabella was surprised to note how large and how blue were the eyes that fixed hers with such intensity.

"So da-dee is organizing games, is he? How terribly, terribly exciting – and British. Shall it be, how is it you say, hop-scot or cric-ket? Zo we can all be shouting 'How is this?' and 'Jolly Dee'? Vell, I cannot resist. Ja, I am coming."

Monika raising herself from the deck, unwinding, standing tall against the sun – an unearthly silhouette, black against the blinding sky. And Arabella less sure than she was of her six-formers, the sides of her mouth turning down as they always do when something unexpected and perhaps not altogether nice is about to happen. And wishing she could just squeeze the water back into the bucket and go away.

The hat removed. And the waves of crushed-gold hair tumbling to Monika's shoulders. The sundress unbuttoned, shrugged off, dismissed. Breasts, white breasts, of perfect symmetry and generous size, as proud and as haughty as the high-cheekboned face above them, raised their nipples to the sun, in greeting, not in worship. Unblemished white skin flowed from narrow waist to rounded hips, a silk thong disappearing into the V of her legs, a hint of blond pubic hair to be discerned by a more closely-observing and less embarrassed eye than Arabella's.

And the legs...legs chiselled, marbled, sculpted, created to perfection, in length, in shape, in – well, simply, in any way you can think about legs.

"Go," commanded the Goddess, "I follow."

Arabella withdraws, awestruck, thunderstruck, struck in every way.

As a hush falls upon those in the water with the appearance of this embodiment of Woman, Arabella falls victim to her first crush. Roedean just couldn't compete. And the males, he-hawing, chaps together don't you know, suffer a collective collapse of their libidos. Because they know, they *know*, they just couldn't make it. Come up with it. Couldn't get it up. No way. Faced with this perfection. And their own imperfections, magnified to the nth degree.

Jürgen, a Bacchanalian figure, looks at his stomach with dismay and lets loose a flow of bubbles which explode in minute gaseous disarray. Bernie, his peeling sunburn floating in ethereal strands, automatically ducks his savagely–red body behind his screen of nurses. Hamish, suddenly acutely aware of his spare skeletal frame unadorned by even one masculine hair protruding from his bony chest, turns to his equally spare children to convince himself of fatherhood. The Honourable Crispin St Clair wishes he were in formal attire, impressive in bow tie and tails, less impressive in his English posture of hunched shoulders and apologetic nakedness. Jack Armitage, his bombastic confidence burst like a balloon, wonders if he would have cut a finer figure in his C & A green-and-red striped shirt instead of his string vest. Sidney Chippendale, thinking that hair on his domed head would have been preferable to the fuzz that covers his pendulous breasts. Steven Clawrer, the sardonic sneer wiped from his face, *knows* that Monika would tread softly past him as though he were merely some crushable invertebrate species on the sea bed.

And Eric Warbelow. Poor Eric. Schmitten. On the spot. Standing in three feet of water on tip-toe, trying to look at least six foot tall, wishing that the ominous bald patch on the crown of his head were covered by water–slicked hair, that the deep, white wrinkles around his eyes, that defied the sun, should not make him look like a raccoon in Monika's eyes: Eric Warbelow, pushing fifty, overwhelmingly swamped with adolescent passion and fervour, had found his Lourdes, was at his Fatima. He sucks his stomach in so tightly that it makes an audible 'thuck', like a sink being drained.

The men might stand around, gasping, open-mouthed like Magritte's stranded fish, but the women were not to be so intimidated: there were plenty of ways to deflate the opposition, an inherited range of instincts that acknowledged an innate truth: while girls grow up into women, boys remain locked in the bodies of men. A reasonable proposition, from their point of view, and one that serves them well.

"Monika, how nice," said Tara, eyeing the *Fräulein* judiciously, rather in the manner she felt each tomato in a greengrocer's before committing herself. "Just as we're getting organized."

"What we're going to do is collect all the dinghies and have a race. Except, we'll turn the dinghies upside down and divide into pairs. One of you lies flat on his – or her – stomach on the bottom of the dinghy and paddles with his – or her – hands, the other hangs on to the end and pushes from behind, but only with his – or her – feet. Everyone understood?" she questioned in a tone that implied imbecility on the part of anyone who didn't.

There was a general stirring as dinghies were collected, a course agreed and the pairs began to line up. Tara made a mental note to be kind to Sidney whose Clara was the first to spreadeagle herself on their upturned dinghy, thereby pushing it so deep into the water that, from the rear, she resembled a couple of 1950s Lambrettas, the ones with protruding sides, from an old Fellini film.

A shout from Gerhard, wreathed in smoke like a Valhalla offering, whose observation of the preparations has led him to sense an opportunity in a pairing with Sally.

"Hey, vait for us, ve vant to play this too, Sally and me, ve vill race. That is permitted from you, Ted?" he added judiciously, but the bronzed beast had gone down with another tray, scattering olives over the sea-bed, and Gerhard seized Sally's reluctant hand and bounded over to join in the frolics.

Crispin, whose classical education had perhaps missed out one or two clues for living in modern times, was standing on the prow of *Annus Mirabilis* clutching – clutching what he believed to be an inflated balloon. Its curious black shape, ribbed with consecutive circles and slippery texture, made Crispin nostalgic for the bright balloons of his childhood, but Bernie assured him that such balloons were all the rage nowadays and that the nurses carried several as a means of concentrating their minds on the needs of children.

Flora Gillicuddy stared at Crispin with horror, *her* education having included the naughtier things in life as a way of learning how to recognize and avoid them. As Crispin stood proudly embracing what looked like the dong of Michelin Man, Flora shooed her whey-faced Angus and Angie out of sight – and range – of whatever might happen when the pin was applied to the massive inflated protuberance.

Pairings having been established, some more enthusiastic than others, the dinghies lined up rather haphazardly on a level with the yachts, and Tara stood at the shore edge ready to pronounce the winning combination.

Crispin raised his pin.

"Jolly good," he beamed, "Fair play all round, what? No bumping or barging, ha! Get ready, get steady..." and the pin jabbed home.

With their backs to the yachts, the competitors heard only the massive bang and failed to see the gallant Crispin blown overboard with the force of the expelled air. Gamely, he struggled to the surface, one hand still clutching the shattered remnants of a decidedly useless French Tickler.

With shouts and yells of encouragement and direction, the sea frothed to the kicking of legs and the paddling of hands. Some dinghies seemed incapable of heading towards shore. Sally noted with consternation that, however much she tried to steer with first one hand, then the other, Gerhard appeared to be pushing them towards a sheltered cove. She also felt considerably hampered by a nagging necessity to keep reaching behind her in an effort to stretch her scanty bikini bottom a little further over her almost bare cheeks. The happy German, hanging on to the end of the upturned dinghy with Sally's tanned legs on either side of his head, had no desire to be the first to finish. The sight of Sally's brown and white bottom rising scarcely a few feet from his glazed silvery eyes was too ecstatic to arouse his competitive instincts. What *was* aroused was in danger of being scraped along the shallow bed and Gerhard aimed for deep waters.

Arnold, too, was experiencing similar problems although his partner, Sharon, had none of Sally's reluctance in encouraging her panting propeller to great lengths. It was hard to see how waggling her delectable buttocks with such an exaggerated motion actually contributed to their speed but it certainly accounted for the satisfied smile on Sharon's face and the croaking moans from her eye–popping team mate.

Darren, on the other hand, was overcome by a mixture of gallantry and shyness and could not bring himself to take advantage of Trudy's prone position. He was not helped by the ferocious splutterings of Eric, endeavouring to steer his craft and Penny alongside his daughter like an inflated sheepdog while trying to catch the occasional glimpse of Monika, languidly extending a graceful if useless hand into the water while the despicable Steven, having abandoned Amy to a more generous spirited Jürgen, pushed her with his teeth set in the savage grin of a predatory shark.

It was a close-run thing and Tara had to make a judicious decision on the winner. It *looked* as though the American-German Axis had won the day but Tara had a suspicion that the bubbles rising behind Jürgen might have aided propulsion and mentally disqualified the team for unfair tactics.

She would have liked to reward the Chippendales for effort but their dinghy grounded much earlier than the others and remained stationary, despite Clara's frantic paddling and Sidney sucking in his stomach to dislodge it from the sea bottom.

Jack Armitage, with his customary navigational skills, had only succeeded in pushing Rosie in circles, while Bernie, the only man who had chosen to lie on the dinghy while being propelled by a perspiring Lorraine, succumbed to his afternoon beers and fell asleep, giving his dispirited nurse no assistance at all.

The Gillicuddys, only represented by Angus and Angie since Flora had taken exception to the innocent Crispin and his inflated ego and had forbidden Hamish to propel the partnerless Elke, fared no better. Both wore spectacles, attached to their head with sensible but tweaking elastic bands, and both were blinded by spray from the front–runners: they collided with Lucien and Arabella, which brought out the worst in Anglo-Scottish antipathies, sad in ones so young.

The close finish between Julie and Liz, a wild thrashing of pink flesh, flying wet hair and some rather coarse medical allusions, and the efficient but boringly-professional partnership, a sort of Becker-Edberg combination, of Mark and Alan Warbelow, was cheered on by a sardine-smeared Ted and a smirking Luigi.

"C'mon, yer creampuffs, they're creamin yer," yelled Ted hysterically, forgetting himself and reverting to pure Aussie, automatically supporting the male contingent. "Wharraya? Couple of pongos? Stick it to them bods, they've got their norks out in front, that's a right shonky when yer win by a couple-a tits! Right down the gurgler!" and he collapsed in disgust at Tara's decision to elect the nurses as the winning team.

"Thees ees very much the English, yes, to let the ladies win?" remarked Luigi in an attempt to engage Ted in conversation. He was acutely aware of Ted's resentment at the Italian's presence at the barbie and sought some way to ingratiate himself. Undercover hostilities were much more subtle than downright antagonism – the sort of thing, believed Luigi, that his ancestors got up to when poisoning rivals for the papal throne. Machiavelli, he knew, or any member of the Borgia family would undoubtedly have felt at home on the *Angela Mia*.

"That is you Britisha, always the *'honourable chappies'*, eet is something that everya-body is always saying of you, no?"

Ted fixed him with a real mean look.

"I ain't no pongo fer a start," he snapped. "An' don't think ye're stitchin' me up fer a wooden duck. I don't know why ye're tryin' to queer my pitch but I'm not away with the pixies. As far as I'm concerned ye can piss off like a bride's nightie."

And he stomped off towards the fire leaving Luigi uncertain of his exact meaning, but certain that it did not constitute a friendly overture.

As the sun sizzled into the sea, the crews began to assemble on the beach, an assortment of rumpled shirts, dresses and shorts having been yanked out of lockers to adorn their owners for the feast.

Penny had noted Eric's edgy preoccupation with his appearance, more than usually intent on finding a pristine pair of white socks to raise to just the right height below the knee. Bent double in their cabin, he had spent an inordinate amount of time parting his hair just so, an effect which he calculated concealed any tendency for the scalp to show where it shouldn't. She put away the hair lacquer that he had sneaked out of her soap bag, feeling somewhat flattered that he should take so much trouble for her sake.

The dinghies had been dragged ashore to be used, again upside down, as seats and it was Eric who found the now fully-robed Monika a place where the wind did not carry the bonfire smoke across her sensitive nostrils. Though the dusk had turned to night, the enormous shades were back in place under the floppy hat, but the wide, not to say sensuous – Eric rarely said sensuous – mouth acknowledged his consideration and a slim but firmly-fleshed hip made room for him to sit beside her, knees carefully aligned. He threw a baleful glare at Steven who, eyeing the opposition, summed it up and dismissed it, sitting down on the other side of Monika, a queen on a rubber throne flanked by her courtiers.

Plastic cups of red and white plonk combined with a crate of Ted's tinnies to recreate the atmosphere of bonhomie and relaxation which the dinghy race had temporarily dampened. Sally had reappeared, almost at a sprint, from further up the coast, with a panting Gerhard in tow, their dinghy over his back so that he looked like an Edward Lear limerick character, a rubber leer on legs.

Grilled sardines and meatballs, baked potatoes in foil, coleslaw, rice and olives, and ribs spurting their hot grease into the fire of resinous wood, charcoal and rosemary, provided a feast worthy of the balmy night. Ted was disappointed not to have a prawn to throw on the barbie, but such delicacies were sold at great profit on the Greek mainland and returned to the islands at a price which the Ulysses' skipper could not afford.

The fire crackled and the conversation sparkled, the dinghies drawn in a circle around the flames. Luigi, now joined by his stunning paramour whose long dress of red silk might have been inappropriate on a lesser figure but gave her the semblance of a fire goddess, was being particularly friendly to Crispin St Clair. Everything Crispin said seemed to carry great weight with Luigi, remarks of great profundity requiring deep consideration.

"Sharon, the so pretty leetle girl I have on my boat," Luigi mused, "she say you are such a – a man of knowledge, of knowing much of the – ah – Ancient Greek."

"Oh, I wouldn't say that," replied the flattered Crispin. "Just the jolly old facts that they flogged into us at school. You know, a bit of Homer for prep and if you didn't know it off by heart in the morning, the old smackeroos on the b-o-t-tom."

This was as incomprehensible to Luigi as Ted's native Aussie, but he persevered.

"Ah, si, the – er – smackeroons. Ver–ee nice. But she say, she say that you have found an exciting – ah – trea–sure, si? Trea–sure, much gold and the jewels and many old things under the sea, and that you all here," he gestured around at the firelit crews, "you are going backa to take up thesea things, no?"

Crispin laughed a deprecatory laugh.

"Good Lord, did she tell you that? I say, don't these young things like to exaggerate. Sorry to disappoint you, old sport, but nothing like. Would it were!"

The darkness hid Luigi's scowl. This was the famed duplicity of the British. His hand bit into the flesh of Ariadne's thigh with frustration, but even a harpoon would not have made much impression on her superbly–muscled frame as she continued to stare undisturbed into the dancing flames.

"Ah, but the children, they say you have made thisa finding, discovering, in the waters near Sivota. They tella me this when I am bringing them back from my rescue, when your capitan could not find them. Isa not a joke, yes?"

"Oh, no, it's true we did spot what *might* be some artefacts lying at the bottom of the sea. Or rather, those boys did, Mark and Alan. You see, we think some blighter shifted their yacht and they were stuck in their dinghy with their father for hours and hours. Could have suffered terribly from exposure. Absolute bounder, deserves a thrashing, if you ask me. Probably some beastly foreigner – oh, I say, present company excepted, naturally. Plenty of such bounders in England, of course. And one or two in America, I'll be bound," Crispin added thoughtfully, eyeing Steven Clawrer who, immune to Eric's glares, was passing Monika a plate of delicacies.

"So," said Luigi, not asking for a definition of the word 'bounder', "you are going for searching these – ah – *antiquariati* and whadda you do if you find them? 'Ow do you lift them? 'Ow do you takea them 'ome?"

Crispin cast Luigi a disapproving look.

"We wouldn't dream of taking them home. Besides, it would be rather difficult to stuff a Corinthian pillar or two in our baggage. We don't know what is down there, yet. Ted, our skipper over there, has an aqualung. He'll probably bring up any small artefacts but the point is to establish what is down there. Then we'll inform, well, we'll inform the Greek authorities."

Luigi was astounded.

"But that ees stupeeda. They will take them all, for why do you do this then in thesea cases?"

"For the sake of it, my friend, thirst for knowledge and all that. For the excitement. And I expect Ted will be very pleased, too, if there's anything worthwhile there. Think of the publicity his company will get around the world – they'll make him a big white chief, a director or something. I – er – imagine he'd like to impress the Ulysses people: had the odd spot of bother with a few flotillas, I believe."

Luigi silently agreed that this might be the case. There were two reasons for frustrating any such discovery. One was to remove anything of value himself should he find some way of getting there first, the other was to prevent Ted Banks from gaining any spurious prestige and in such way denting the perfect picture of Ted Banks, the Aussie Idiot.

The Aussie Idiot had, in the meantime, rescued his guitar from the shallows where he had dropped it from the dinghy and was now damply strumming a mean *Waltzing Matilda*, determinedly sticking to the only three chords he knew and mumbling the words which he didn't know. Never, in Ted's vast experience of twanging out the same song around countless bonfires, had anyone known the words of that famous song, though everyone thought they did and mouthed incomprehensible hums about 'wallabangs' and 'billabongs'. It was a traditional part of a barbie and expected of an Aussie, to be followed by *Michael, Row the Boat Ashore, Alle–loooo–lia* in a faintly depressing off–key with *Hang Down Your Head, Tom Doo–ooley* as an encore for those who hadn't burst into tears.

Amy Clawrer stood alone in the shadows listening to Ted's mournful dirge and his game accompanists, observing 'Stevie' giving rapt attention to the few remarks which fell from Monika's mouth. It wasn't that Monika was any less reticent than usual: she simply didn't have much chance to stem Eric's flow of middle–aged *angst*.

"...and then you turn round and the kids have grown up and don't need you so much, and argue with everything you say, and you wonder 'what happened to it all, what happened to all those things you were going to do?'..."

Monika's floppy hat bobbed up and down in apparent sympathy though, in the intermittent light thrown up by the wood-fed flames, it was possible to detect a look of boredom even from where Amy stood. It was also possible to discern that, while one hand squeezed Eric's with understanding and empathy, her other elegant digits were clasped in Steven's all-enveloping paw which offered the occasional caress and finger-in-the-palm intimacy.

*   *   *

Amy breathed deeply, despondently. This was not the

honeymoon of her dreams, this was not cosy meals and slippers before the fire at Last Chance Ranch. This was the mean, irritable, spoilt whelp who had deserted her in the dinghy race, leaving her to the indignity of tending to Jürgen's wounds where his stomach had scraped a small rock on the sea-bed as he grounded in three feet of water... and wondering why the Greek drains should be so pungent when there weren't any Greek drains.

This was the ungracious moaner who was clutching Monika's hand, when he should have been holding her own and joining in the chorus of *There Was an Old Lady Who Swallowed a Fly*.

Disconsolate, she pushed her way uphill through the undergrowth, unconsciously following one of the old paths that led into the abandoned olive grove, picking her way further inland through the dim shadows cast by the moonlight. Nobody noticed, nobody cared. She pressed on, unheeding of the bushes that clutched at her mou-mou, a garment that could only be found in America, a sort of wrap-around skirt and halter top made popular by Betty Grable in the Forties.

The sudden furtive scuttling of animals and insects, the grazing from a sharp stone, the plop of some indeterminate object from a disturbed branch, all passed unnoticed. A tumble of collapsed wall barred her way: grasping an overhanging branch, she hauled herself to the top of the precariously balanced stones, swayed momentarily, used the branch as a lever and propelled herself into the dark space below.

It's quite difficult to reproduce, phonetically, the collective sounds made when a crouching Albanian, gaining harmless pleasure from the study of the bare limbs of women around a campfire some way below him on a beach, is the recipient of some 150 lbs of American womanhood landing on his back in the dead of night. Despite differing national characteristics, some reactions know no boundaries.

Anguish played a major part, though possibly no more than surprise. Fear figured largely, on both sides, since Amy

Clawrer hardly expected to land on something that was undeniably alive, squirming, large and noisome, in a gurgling sort of way. Nor, indeed, had Oleg Grameshic Dhonia's four years' virtual reclusion on the island prepared him in any way for well-endowed American females ambushing him by dropping out of a tree while he was engaged in lustful thoughts.

"Jumpin' Jehosophat!"

Amy's expletive was scarcely appropriate since whatever she had landed on was in no position to jump, but it was indicative of her inner strength. Another woman – Rosie, for instance – might have resorted to screaming hysterically. Amy, however, came from a tougher breed. As a starlet in *Son of Quo Vadis* – her agent had specialized in epics of a classical nature, though this film had never been released since some egg-head had proved conclusively that Quo Vadis had never had a son, particularly after what Nero had done to him – she had performed much the same feat when she had been required to roll down a staircase and land on a stuffed lion in the arena. Oleg, in truth, felt a definite kinship with a stuffed lion.

Gingerly, she put out a hand and poked tentative fingers into the now almost inert object beneath her. Oleg had, in his more hopeful dreams, conjured up the image of being slowly explored by an experienced nymphomaniac, but this was hardly a turn-on. He lay still in petrified fear, pinned face down on the stony earth, while the hand examined his side, his thigh, his neck, his ear.

It found his arm and travelled down until fingers touched fingers, shot sharply away, then crept back and re-established contact.

Michelangelo probably got his inspiration from such similar circumstances. A lot of this sort of thing happened in Italy at the time. A small spark of mutual understanding, a transference of reassurance, and words were not needed. It happens in the most unlikely circumstances – and these were pretty unlikely. But Amy's hand communicated *something* to Oleg's, his returned that same *something*, and their mutual fear went into decline...

Amy, with some uncertainty, supported herself on one arm, lifted her rump off Oleg's back, and shuffled to a sitting position next to his prone body.

"Groooof," greeted Oleg as his lungs reverted to normal. He blew hard and finally discouraged a stag beetle from trying to enter his mouth.

"A-huh," answered Amy, by way of neutral greeting.

Testing his limbs for compound fractures, he was relieved to find that he was more or less working and struggled painfully to turn over and drag himself up to sit beside his unexpected visitor.

They surveyed each other by the light of the silvery moon.

At first sight, Oleg had more reason to be pleased. Amy's face in the pale glow lost many of those unkind wrinkles which Steven had taken to counting. Her dishevelled hair hung in blonde wanton locks about her shoulders and no moonlight was going to pick out the odd black root to betray the cosmetic hand. Her mouth looked full-lipped and tempting, her eyes sent back the gleam of moonrays and her nose, which she had once heard Raoul Walsh describe as 'pert' though, oddly, she had been facing the other way at the time, looked like the sort of nose on which you might plant a kiss. Add bare shoulders of alabaster and a generous cleavage barely three feet from his devouring eyes and you can well understand the effect on the woman-deprived Albanian, a man in his prime.

Amy's perception of Oleg, though, was not without appreciation. Perhaps the lengthy beard and wild spiky hair were not quite in keeping with her image of a Greek god but from what she could make out in the among the slivers of light and shadow, his arms were finely muscled, the ragged track-suit bottoms revealed fine calves and he gazed at her with lustrous, heart-melting black eyes. She had *known* Greece would be an adventure, was ready to be impressed by any amount of myth and legend; and, here, seated right next to her, was a true native of the islands.

True to her upbringing, she held out her hand.

"Well, hi! Amy Clawrer. How y'er doin'?"

Oleg stared at the outstretched hand. Back in his village, it was customary to spit on one's palm and clasp the other's proffered hand to clinch a deal. But Oleg had not been the Lothario of Sinanaj for nothing.

He took her hand slowly in his, bent forward and brushed it with his lips.

"Oh my," flustered Amy, "that's real cute."

A warm glow suffused through her body. On such a romantic night – well, a night that was romantic *now* – to meet a wild man with the charms of a Southern gentleman, the manners that Steven so sadly lacked...

"What," she asked as their eyes locked with the birth pangs of passion, "WHAT IS YOUR NAME?"

She enunciated slowly, the way foreigners like to hear.

Oleg was up to this, in any language.

"Ah, girl," he answered, somewhat startlingly, since he almost sang the word, dragging it out into a hushed syllable.

That warm glow became a furnace. It was a long time since Amy had been called a girl.

"Oh, gee, that's nice, that sure is nice."

She tried again.

"Me, girl," she said with a girlish blush. "You..."

No, she thought, that line's been overworked.

"Me, Girl. Amy. That's me. WHAT–IS–YOUR–NAME? NAME?"

"Namey?" queried Oleg, his deep tones adding to the lustre of his eyes.

"No, you sweet thing," tinkled Amy, patting him roguishly on a steely-muscled thigh. "Amy! I – AM – AMY. Not Namey," she giggled coquettishly.

Oleg giggled back and patted her rather more exposed thigh. She patted his. He patted hers again. The situation was improving by the pat.

He decided to take the plunge and make use of his carefully learned English. Though she could have been speaking Numerian Syriac for all he knew, the cadences of her language and pronunciation of one or two words fitted into his concept of another language. He may as well try his luck.

"Ees– there any–body goin' t'listen to ma–story?" he intoned, putting a most peculiar musical intonation into the words.

Amy was transfixed. It was a kind of English alright, but with an odd guttural type of moaning accompaniment. And sort of familiar.

"Heavens! You speak English! But – well, I mean, what are you doin' here? You look kinda, kinda like a castaway, that beard and everything. You been here long? I mean, on this island?"

Whatever she was saying didn't ring any bells with Oleg but they were conversing, in a way.

He summoned up another line.

"Whena think–of all thu times I've tried so–hard t'leavea" he answered with the smile that had worked wonders in the old days.

It worked wonders now.

"You don't say!" gasped Amy, though the dawn of recognition was filtering through.

"Af–ter all this time I donno why," Oleg added by way of emphasis.

"So you live here, on the island, all by yourself?"

Amy hardly noticed that they were holding hands.

"Still yu–don't regret–a single day," breathed Oleg, his face moving towards hers, his mouth reaching for her returning pucker.

It began as a gentle kiss, slow, faltering, tentative, then trembled into a passionate crushing of lips, a twining of arms, a grasping of bodies.

For Amy, mixed emotions blended with mixed aromas, identifiable in more calm moments as male sweat tinged with just a little goat and perhaps just a touch of suntan oil in which Oleg had earlier cooked one of Andreas's stolen chickens.

But when you've spent a miserable honeymoon with a horned toad like Steven, and felt that everyone else was enjoying themselves, who can blame you if a stranger, a Greek native, who looks at you as though *you* were the Greek goddess, and then sings – yes, that was it, *sings* a Beatle number at you, she'd got it now – who can blame you if you seize the moment, if you give caution to the winds, if you give your mou-mou to the winds as, indeed, Oleg was helping her to do, and take love when it comes to you, in the whispery, balmy, starry night of dreams?

From down on the beach came the strains of *She'll be comin round the mountain, when she comes.*

On the whole, it was pretty accurate.

*   *   *

The barbie was beginning to break up, some dinghies having already ferried their owners back to their bunks.

Bernie has lost contact rather early, the sun being responsible, and nothing whatever to do with a dozen cups of punch and a pack of tinnies. Flat out on his back on their upturned dinghy, his three sirens tenderly lifted the lot without disturbing his even snore and swam with their burden, silently and in syncopation, to their yacht, a whale tended by his school of porpoises. Delacroix, had he been whooping it up at the barbie, would have been inspired to paint 'The Wreck of the Medusa – Part II'.

Flora Gillicuddy, having mistakenly thought the punch to be non-alcoholic, had performed a surprisingly athletic reel before unsurprisingly throwing up over her astonished offspring, much to the secret pleasure of Hamish who would be able to cast admonishing looks at his wife for weeks to come without fear of retribution.

Angus and Angie were in a state of saintly shock at the terrible spectacle of their mother who, demonstrating a particularly difficult twist in a sword dance, suddenly turned to them, pausing as in an action replay, then honked all over them from a not inconsiderable distance. They were led down the beach to the water by their holier than thou father to be bathed, both physically and spiritually. Removing

traces of salami, carroty coleslaw and something best not
identified from the – now that he thought of it and
particularly in moonlight – somewhat carroty hair of his
progeny, Hamish wished that Flora would regain her dignity
and stop thrashing about on the stand, screaming about her
'wee timorous beasties' and the denting of their future
prospects.

By the time Amy rejoined the beach party, there were few
left still draining the fly-floating remains of punch and Ted
had long since dropped his guitar in the sea again while
returning the barbie debris to *Ulysses X*. With some
reluctance, he had agreed that those who wanted to could
sleep ashore provided that no yacht was left totally
unattended. Previous experience accounted for the reticence:
too many naughties had happened in the night with past
flotillas and Ted had been forced, more than once, to
separate over-lubricated and over-sexed combatants who had
'mistakenly' investigated the contents of particularly alluring
sleeping bags.

Gerhard had stomped off to *Becker* in a huff, having
convinced himself that Sally would not be able to resist the
pleasure of hearing German folk tales by bonfire light and of
falling asleep beneath the stars and – he hoped – beneath
Gerhard. But resist him she had, rushing around with a
plastic bin liner to scoop up the paper dishes and plastic
cups, and bolting to the refuge of her yacht to be joined by a
tired and emotional Ted. Still irritated and annoyed by the
presence of Luigi, who had upstaged him by singing *O Sole
Mio* in a rather attractive and vibrant tenor, Ted's customary
'having a naughty before shut-eye' lacked the usual gusto,
and *Ulysses X* barely rocked in response.

Luigi and Ariadne had returned to *Angela Mia* with the St
Clairs and the Warbelows (with the exception of Eric),
offering nightcaps all round and assiduously but artfully
questioning Alan and Mark about their 'discovery'. The
group had finally dispersed with vows of eternal Anglo-
Italian friendship and Luigi, as proof of his deep-felt
affection, assured them that he would sail with them on the

morrow to help in the search for antiquities.

Amy was taken aback to see that both Steven and Eric had grown an additional leg whilst she had been engaged elsewhere. It became obvious, as she approached the dinghy, that the two extra legs belonged to Monika, not only because of their elegant shape and length, but because Monika's body was still attached to them. Eric's conversation had taken its toll and Monika had fallen asleep, lying back across the inflated support, her hat over her face. Steven, startled from his contemplation of the bare limb pressed against his, rose guiltily causing the dinghy to tilt in Eric's favour and roll Monika in a sleepy embrace around Eric's bottom.

The Americans headed for their boat, Amy walking with a particularly light and youthful gait and Steven plodding along in his usual morose fashion, leaving Monika to open her eyes sleepily and stare at Eric's moonie with incomprehension. With mutual embarrassment, they scrambled to their feet, awkwardly adjusting their clothing and scuffling their feet in the bonfire cinders. Then Monika, with the same amount of affection and indifference she would bestow on a favourite uncle, lightly kissed Eric on the cheek and strode off to hail her father for a lift in their dinghy back from the beach.

Eric, finding the only remaining dinghy was the one he had been sitting on, upturned it and dragged it to the water, propelling it to his yacht by pulling along the anchor line. He did all this like an automaton, his mind numbed by that fleeting kiss, the pressure of her lips still burning its indelible firebrand. Something so lightly given was something portentous to receive: Eric was full of portent.

From his observation post above the beach, Oleg Grameshic Dhoni regarded the break-up of the barbie with more than his usual predatory interest. For once, he was not about to go foraging for supplies.

He had made up his mind. He was leaving Mengalissi. Amy had awakened more than the most obvious desires and Oleg was buzzing with refreshed ambitions that would not be satisfied by the solitary life of a castaway.

Among the boats moored together was one which was bigger, more spanking than the rest, one on which it might be possible to conceal oneself for a short passage to a port on the Greek mainland or on Corfu – or anywhere other than Mengalissi. Somewhere *new*. With the natural caution of an illegal immigrant and his awareness that his sudden appearance in their midst may arouse suspicions, he reasoned that he stood more chance of leaving on one of those moored boats if the crew was unaware of his presence.

He had noted that the generous lines of *Angela Mia* appeared to be shared by only two people and had thus selected his quarry. When she put to sea in the morning, Oleg was determined that *Angela Mia* would be carrying one unauthorized Albanian, even if it meant squatting in the hold among all the paraphernalia of sailing.

He left his hiding spot and set off to the shack that had been his home for four years. Apart from his Raybans and his Walkman, there wouldn't be a lot to pack: there would probably be some rich pickings aboard *Angela Mia* which would help him get along for a few months.

Little did Luigi suspect, as he slept in the strong embrace of his flawless Ariadne, that he would be playing host to one who would make sure that the devious and piratical Italian would be more sinned against than sinning.

CHAPTER SEVEN

CRISPIN CONSIDERS THE CREWS. OPPOSITION TO THE TREASURE HUNT LEADS TO MULTI-NATIONAL FISTICUFFS. BERNIE THE PEACEMAKER. *THE BOUNTY* AND *THISTLE* OPT OUT. OLEG GETS A TOE IN THE HOLD.

The sun predictably peered over the horizon and decided to make a day of it, slowly, comfortably, stretching its warming fingers across the sea onto Abeliki beach.

It was not an early start. There was, after all, no great haste to get underway and most stomachs were still digesting the charcoaled edibles and inedibles of the barbie. Flotillas are not favoured by true yachtsmen, and the Ionian's beauty does not make up for the fact that it is regarded by the cognoscenti as the Hyde Park boating pond would be regarded by an Oxbridge rowing blue. It was rare for a brisk sailing wind to make its presence felt much before the afternoon, a civilized factor allowing a leisurely lunch, a refreshing swim, a glass or two of this and, for those so inclined, a touch or two of that.

A gentle swaying of the boat would then indicate that either the wind was getting up or that Jürgen was in the vicinity, or occasionally that both were combined. Either way, the wind rarely amounted to more than a stiff breeze, a *really* big blow maybe getting up to a Force 6 to 7, sending the more timid spirits scuttling for any port in the storm, while the true salt had his boat so far over that a passing literate dolphin could read its name below the keel.

On the whole, there was a general disinterest in splicing any mainbraces at an early hour among the Ionian sailors and the Ulysses Flotilla had a seemingly high percentage of lazy bums below decks. Crispin St Clair, though, was astir, standing at the bow of *Annus Mirabilis*, clad only in a neat pair of Hardy Amies shorts, gazing unseeingly at the barbie–littered beach.

Crispin had not thought he could be so happy. That first day of the holiday, the depression that had descended when he had – when the whole family had – realized that the choice was either going home or staying with a, well, with a lot of somewhat 'common' people, including some *very* common types – *that* had not been a happy start. Added to which, it had not taken long, about five seconds from when Ted opened his mouth, to scent that the skipper of the flotilla knew as much about navigation as Crispin knew about

'Grunge' rock. Crispin didn't want to learn anything about 'Grunge' rock and the first sighting of Darren, his eyes rolling and jaw lolling to the predictable thud–thud–thud of moron music skewered through his ears from one of those ghastly Walkman things had made Crispin's stomach churn with dismay.

Since the St Clairs had owned their own boats for several generations, the decision to charter something in the Ionian might have seemed, for a reasonably experienced sailor, an odd choice to those friends of the family who were not aware of the financial constraints they had been experiencing of late – not *disastrous*, but sufficient to make Crispin look at such cheaper options. As for giving Lucien and Arabella some experience with crewing abroad – absolutely essential for when they were to start running with their set.

Undeniably, though, the St Clairs were enjoying themselves. It was natural, of course, that they should feel, *actively* feel, fit and healthy. That was a predictable spin off, a debt to the sun, the swimming, the fruit, the vague sense of always being on the move, even if it was only sitting under the awning in the cockpit while the engine churned gently through the sea.

In truth it was more than that. It was the feeling on being in a team, and of liking your team-mates – well, most of them. It was the gossip, the small happenings, the 'goings on' within this microcosm of the world, coupled with the blissful relief that the plebs's music was not pouring out of ghetto-blasters (Darren's Walkman had fallen overboard – an act of revenge on Sharon's part for stringing up her pink and white Snubsy?). Not only did Crispin find most of the others bearable, he was actually beginning to *like* some of his companions.

The Warbelows, for instance, were a nice family. 'Nice' was the kind of word which Tara eschewed, but that was what they were. Eric was a bit of a bore with his constantly surfacing worries: he lacked the confidence which an education at a *good* public school would have bestowed, that was the real problem. Penny, though, was a good sort, a practical woman with a sense of humour, not unlike Tara but perhaps a little less formidable – perhaps 'homely' was the correct word. And their children, they exhibited good, solid, middle-class virtues, particularly the boys whose discovery of the 'St Clair Marbles' might well reinstate the family fortunes. After all, the Board would be unlikely to vote for his resignation if his name was associated in the papers with an important archaeological find. The Board had been a bit jittery of late: Crispin had a distict impression that having his name on the letterhead was rather less important in the nineties than it had been a decade before.

The Gillicuddys and the Chippendales – well, they were not the sort of people you would be desperate to have around for dinner, but here in the Greek Islands you could do worse for conversation in the evening over the meatballs and Retsina. Sidney had a tendency to pontificate – he reminded Crispin of a fat Pontiff – and Clara's appetite was an awesome sight, but they certainly were not objectionable.

Flora Gillicuddy had certainly got up his nose with her scathing remarks about the pollution spread by industrial conglomerates, particularly as her husband worked as a number crusher for a North Sea Oil company. He rather doubted if she would have been sailing in the Ionian if her husband had been staring up sheeps' backsides for a living as his crofter ancestors had done. The plane that had flown them to Corfu probably guzzled fuel from the North Sea. Still, she had made one or two telling points, points which he meant to raise with the Board on his return home.

Then there were the Armitages. That first day, during the briefing, the St Clairs collectively had eyed the Armitages with horror. Everything about that family had been off-putting, from the guttural grunts of father and son that passed for speech, to the dazzling shellsuit of the mother and the brazen flaunting of her sex by the daughter. And yet... And yet they actually weren't beyond the pale. Jack wasn't such a bad sort, willing to stand his round, attempting some pretty excruciating jokes. It was the Jacks of this world who had waited patiently on the beaches of Dunkirk for rescue, who had slogged through the desert to give Rommel his come-uppance. If Jack had been born ten years earlier, he would have been a 'desert rat', wearing silly British 'shorts' to his knees, carefully tailored to disguise the fact that males had – ahem – 'parts': now, though, he wore silly floppy British hats and T-shirts with moronic messages stencilled across his nipples, carefully designed to demonstrate the owner's lack of brain.

Which, naturally, made Crispin think of the Germans. What was he to think of the Germans? Like many Englishmen, he had a grudging respect for the Germans, mixed with a peculiar form of contempt that hid an underlying rivalry. Crispin, like his father and grandfather before him, had been expected to 'go into the army' which meant, of course, a career as an officer. But the aftermath of the Second World War and its consequent revelations had left an unpalatable taste in his father's mouth and the young Crispin was directed to be 'something in the city' – which included a few hand-me-down directorships.

Instead of regarding the Germans, therefore, as the natural military enemy, Crispin saw only the dedicated vigour of the German economy, an efficiency applied to commerce. And he had a sneaking feeling that the sort of contribution that he personally made to the British economy would be regarded with scorn in Germany.

So, unprejudiced in general outlook, he nonetheless regarded the Germans as a nationality with some suspicion, a feeling that he discerned among the rest of the British crews in the flotilla. Somehow, the general notion of being a team did not quite extend itself to the two German crews. Too many echoes from the past.

Jürgen and his family were probably not aware of this ambivalence: they joined in heartily with all activities, although Arnold's obvious passion for Sharon caused some restlessness among the natives. Sharon, though, was likely to cause chaos wherever she found herself.

It was Gerhard and his daughter who were difficult to classify. Gerhard's obvious sexual appetite and need to show off set him apart. It was noticeable that, when the crews gathered together around the tables in a taverna, an extra table had to be added to the gathering who appeared to have forgotten that the crew of *Becker* was to join them. The Americans were tolerated because of Amy's geniality, despite Steven's surliness, but, somehow, Gerhard and Monika remained left out.

Not that Monika helped. Her Garbo-like pose of wanting to be alone made her difficult to fit in, particularly as she rarely contributed to any conversation. And the stunning revelation of her beauty, with its obvious effect on the men, particularly on Eric who broke out in a sweat whenever she appeared, made for an undercurrent of disharmony.

Crispin sighed. There was so much to enjoy, so much visual loveliness, how odd that such unspoken antipathies should be present among them.

A tinkle from the shrouds of *Ulysses X* alerted him to the stirrings of their skipper. For someone who had dropped his guitar in the water so often, Ted had a remarkably happy demeanour. Perhaps it was related to the shroud tinkling.

"Good, eh, Crisp?" hollered the muscular skipper, before he executed a neat dive, cleaving through the crystal waters.

Crispin put aside his irritation with the diminutive and stretched out his hand to help the rippling phenomenom up the stern ladder.

"That's better," said Ted. "Needed that. Gotta mouth like an abo's armpit. Always the same after a barbie – yer think ye're goin' to be shoutin' down the great white telephone half the night, then yer take yer first dip and ye're fine an' ready."

He looked across the bobbing yachts with a pleased grin.

"Not too many up an' stirrin' yet, is there? Some night! We cracked a few tinnies, heh Crisp? I didn't think – well, you wouldn't, would yer, that old Flora, there, chuckin' up over her ankle-biters like that, yer just wouldn't..."

Ted faded into bemusement as they both gazed at *Thistle*, its lifeless deck concealing the turbulent conscience that held Flora Gillicuddy chained through shame to her bunk. The two men, one tall and pencil-shaped, the other slightly shorter and he-man shaped, stood together in a sort of unspoken comradeship, not a lot of common ground but sufficient unto the day.

"Hmmnn," assented Crispin, "I do admit to being somewhat surprised. Not that one shouldn't, on occasion, go..."

"...apeshit," put in Ted helpfully.

"...over the top," continued Crispin firmly, "but I hadn't thought that Mrs Gillicuddy – that she would, as it were..."

"...get rat-arsed," came from Ted, usefully filling the pause.

Crispin relapsed into silence, feeling that to continue this dialogue might lead to blows.

"Funny that," mused Ted.

There being no enquiry from Crispin as to what was funny, Ted had another muse, slightly louder. After all, Ted wasn't given *that* much to musing and felt that the effort required should be appreciated.

"*Funny that*," came the emphasized muse.

"Is it? What exactly?" said Crispin, squatting down on the deck and hurriedly jumping up again as he found himself gazing up Ted's shorts.

"Well, ye know, you call everyone, people, you call 'em 'mister' somethin' or 'missus' somethin' even when you've got their first handle. Like Flora, there, you've been in her company now near on a week and she's still 'Mrs Gillicuddy'.

Crispin found a seat on deck where the view of the sea was unrestricted. *Annus Mirabilis* rocked slightly as stirrings came from below.

Tara's head, its neat mushroom cut of fair-to-brown hair already carefully groomed, poked out through the stern gangway.

"So much for an early start, darling. I thought we were all leaving in a rush. We could just as well have had our own little exploration of each other after all. Doesn't seem to be... oh!"

She broke off as Ted's amiable visage smiled down at her.

"Always time for that," winked Ted, entirely unaware of Tara's discomfiture. "Not much point in rushin' off anywhere if yer ain't got time fer the good things in life. I mean, wha'ever yer do, its gotta have a point, stands to sense, eh? An' what better point is there than havin' the old mornin' glory before yer hit the road?"

Tara nearly understood everything he said.

"Quite," she answered frostily. She had not asked for an Australian homily before breakfast.

"I'm about to make some coffee. Would you like to stay for some?"

"No thanks, Tara. Sally's already brewin' up. I'd better get over."

As Tara withdrew to boil the kettle and meditate upon the exact nature of a 'morning glory', Ted padded aft along the deck to drop from the pulpit into the shallow water offshore. Otherwise, if he dived off the yacht, his newly-dried shorts would get wet again and he'd have to take them off. And Sally would...He padded back again to the stern in order to throw himself into the Ionian.

"OK, Crisp. Let's get everyone on shore for a briefing in half–an–hour."

He thought again.

"In three-quarters-of-an-hour. Finally decide who goes where, though I think we know what the score is."

"Fine," said Crispin, hardly heeding Ted's words. "You're quite right, you know. What you were saying about names. I *do* find it difficult to – to use a person's Christian name too promptly. Unless..."

He paused.

Ted looked at Crispin appraisingly and grinned.

"Unless they ain't in yer class? That it then, Crisp?"

This highly intuitive remark from such an unexpected source took Crispin aback.

"Well...no...yes...I suppose you're right. Yes, absolutely."

He looked resolutely at his skipper.

"If I'm honest with myself, I suppose that's why I can call

you 'Ted' so easily. Because..."

"Because I'm yer workin' class, that's it, ain't it?"

"Yes. I think that's probably right. And, of course, you've encouraged us to do so and everyone else calls you 'Ted'. That's the skipper thing, isn't it, the team-leader thing."

"At least," said Ted with conviction, "they don't call me 'Bruce'."

Crispin laughed.

"We're not *that* insensitive. Not anymore. There's too much Australian television, *Neighbours* and all of that sort of thing. And films."

Unintentionally, he made it sound as though he'd once caught a glimpse of *Picnic at Hanging Rock* through the window of someone's terraced house.

Ted scratched his nose ruminatively and eyed Crispin closely.

"Tell you what, though, Crisp," he confided. "*Ack*–tually, you'd 'ave been dead on. With 'Bruce'. It was the old cheese's choice: she was as daft as a two bob watch, though I 'ardly knew 'er. *Bruce Banks*. Gawd! She thought it sorta rhymed. We lived in Paddo, then – Paddington, in Sydney, got it? – an' she thought, well, I don't know what she thought 'cept maybe it was like a film-star name. So, anyway, soon as I got to Europe, I changed to 'Ted' 'cos a mate of mine was called that, seemed, ye know, familiar. Even Sally 'asn't a clue. So it's a secret, o.k. Crisp? 'Tween you and me?"

Crispin smiled. He felt rather touched at the confession.

"It's a secret," he affirmed. "It's a secret so long as you never call me 'Crisp' again. *Ever* again. If you do, I'll go right along to Sally and to everyone else and announce you as 'Bruce' to the whole world."

Ted's eyes widened.

"*I get ye!* I've been a right peanut then? I didn't think yer felt so strong! 'Strewth, you chooms are sensitive! I thought it was friendly, yer know? Crispin sounds – sounds –sorta posh, but...it sounds fine! I'd better push off."

And he did.

*   *   *

The sun's hat was well and truly wedged on his head before the crews of the Ulysses Flotilla were assembled on the shore. More accurately, all the crews had at least *one* representative sitting or sprawling on the soft–hot sand attending the briefing with varying degrees of enthusiasm.

Steven, sitting aloof on a tuft of sharp grass which did nothing for his normal irritated demeanour, was puzzled by Amy's drowsy state of contentment. She had been asleep, deeply and seraphically asleep, when he had climbed aboard *The Bounty*, leaving Eric in sole possession of a dinghy – and Monika. In her blissful repose she had looked, he had to admit to his hardened soul, encouragingly desirable and it was he, for a change, who had made overtures of a Clark Gable kind, even given to a tender stroking of the inert limbs. But there had been no response and he had quitted with an uncertain feeling of rejection which had carried through to the morning.

Eric was sitting with his sons, one on either side, casting occasional anxious glances at both them and his yacht, *Nemesis*, as if awaiting sentence from a tribunal of whom he was the most severe judge. Try as he might, Eric could not dismiss the memory of that long, elegant and decidedly enticing leg which Monika had stretched so casually in the direction of his fully-raised socks the night before: nor would the casual imprint of her lips on his cheek remove its presence from his tortured soul. Observing Trudy waving happily to Darren Armitage from the deck of *Nemesis* only served to increase his torment: how could a father lecture his daughter on the licentiousness of men in general, and a Leeds supporter in particular, when his own head housed images of forbidden fruits?

The Königs were assembled as a family, Jürgen comfortably easing the pressure of wind in his belly in the direction of the wild mimosa. Arnold cast longing glances in

132

the direction of *Moby Dick* which sheltered the invisible, but nonetheless exciting, body of Sharon, wrapped lasciviously around the unappreciative Snubsy. Elke had lectured him roundly on the soundness of Lutheran morality in modern times, with many needless references to the 'whores of Babylon', the latter only serving to conjure up images of the most outrageous kind.

The remaining Armitages were in a group which included Bernie and his entourage, the three nurses having thoughtfully brought ashore several beach mats on which lay the recumbent form of their kingly Solomon, his handmaids brusquely dealing with any curious fly intent on exploring this well-oiled land mass. Hamish Gillicuddy, looking surprisingly animated like someone whose conscience was clear yet was married to someone whose conscience was not, was actually engaging Lorraine in a spirited conversation on the subject of natural childbirth. Jack Armitage sat horrified, never having realized that there was such a subject, and with no desire to consider the possibility.

The Chippendales and St Clairs formed another group, Sidney comparing notes with Crispin on the likelihood of finding Greek antiquities, while Clara dispensed largesse in the form of melon slices the size of split wagon wheels, to Lucien and Arabella.

Ted and Sally, as befits the skipper and his mate, stood roughly in the centre of the crews' attention. Sally held up the chart in a way which caused Gerhard, seated with wrapt attention alone in front of them, to concentrate on the map, particularly where its edges bordered on Sally's body, with a rigidity that made his eyeballs ache.

"I think," began Ted, "that we've more or less come up with what we're goin' to do. Everyone except – er – *Thistle* and, what'sit – er, *The Bounty*, are goin' after those – uhmnn –Marbles."

Though Sally had explained to him that this term covered a multitude of shapes, Ted found it hard to erase the image of childhood bags of 'ollies' from his mental picture. It made the treasure hunt seem slightly ridiculous but he couldn't get his tongue around 'artefacts', Sally's suggested alternative, without smirking.

"This," said Ted, pointing at the chart with an old barbecued bone, "is the approximate position where Mark and Alan saw – whatever they saw."

"That sure is approximate," came the surly tones of Steven, "that covers about half of the Ionian."

Sally peered down at the chart to where the bone was describing a circle somewhere near her navel.

"No, it doesn't. The caves they were in are just here, a bit south of Sivota, and they were picked up here – Tara radioed in and they made a note in their log of their position."

Jack looked at Tara admiringly.

"That shows some gumption," he praised, then spoilt it by adding "yer wouldn't think a woman'ud think of that."

Only Tara's sunhat showed any signs of emotion.

"So," Sally continued, "if they partly rowed and partly drifted in this direction" – her finger swept down the chart in a neat line from her navel to a point where Gerhard groaned audibly – "we can narrow down the area within this sort of circle. With eight boats – nine with Luigi's – and *knowing* what we are looking for, there's a jolly good chance of finding the, er, treasure."

She beamed around the assembled crews.

"Let's call it *treasure*. It makes it sound so exciting – and worthwhile. Even if it isn't, even if it's not important, it still makes it an adventure."

"Like *Five on a Treasure Island*," suddenly chimed Darren, then froze in horror as he realized the awful admission of having read Enid Blyton. Fortunately, Trudy was too far away to hear the literary reference; just in case, he flexed a few biceps and relaxed into his Schwarzenegger pose.

"I think," said Hamish, less timidly than usual, "that you're all going on a wild goose chase." "And", he added boldly, looking around the assembly with the look of a man about to crack an unaccustomed joke, "it's not a *golden goose!*"

The assembly regarded him silently.

"Well, anyway," he pressed on, slightly deflated, "we're not going. We came here to have a holiday with a flotilla, part of a group, with – with a skipper to sort things out if anything went wrong. If Ted's not going to be with us..."

"...We stand a fair chance of getting to where we want to go."

Steven's acid tones churned up the relaxed atmosphere.

"I wanna'd a boat, I've gotta boat. I can sail a boat. I don't need no shepherd dog. If the rest of you wanna go after some old stones, you sure are welcome. I guess a refund'll be due back from the company 'cos we were abandoned – that's OK by me."

While Ted struggled to make sense of this implied threat, Sally let fly.

"For heaven's sake, Steven, what is the matter with you? Do you get some kick out of complaining all the time, looking miserable, ruining everyone else's enjoyment?"

Her dark eyes fixed angrily on his unperturbed face, the colour rising in her dimpled cheeks.

"We're *not* abandoning you. We planned at the start to have at least three days free sailing time and that's what we are doing. The *majority* want to go on the search, you don't, so no–one's forcing you. All we need to know is where you are going to be, then we'll all be joining up again. Why is that so awful?"

"Ja, vot is your problem?"

Gerhard had risen to face the American, a knight in shining trunks. The sinister eyes fixed on Steven's sardonic face.

"I am thinking that you are a pain in my neck, alvays with this complaining. And to a woman, a woman such as this."

Up to now, there hadn't been much of an atmosphere, but what there was perceptibly thickened.

Steven returned Gerhard's glare without flinching. He shifted his rump on the flattened spikes, the better to find a few sharp ones which would match his mood.

"Well, now," he drawled menacingly, "here's a gallant Kraut indeed. Gettin' in her good books, you reckon, makes it easier to get in her pants later maybe?"

Gerhard couldn't quite make out what 'good books' had to do with anything but he had no difficulty in understanding the rest of the sentence.

He strode purposefully to the American and planted himself firmly in front of Steven's seated figure, legs apart, his chest expanding with wrath.

"It vould be better if you are standing up for me to knock you down, you..." he searched for the appropriate word until inspiration struck, "...*palooka*!"

Steven laughed.

"Palooka, huh! Where d'yuh pick that one up? Some G.I. from the occupyin' forces?"

The enraged roar, though, that greeted this insult came not from a German but an Australian throat. Ted, always two sentences behind in any conversation, had grasped the meaning of Steven's allusion to Sally's pants.

He plunged forward to inflict some damage on the American, and collided with Gerhard who moved with a similar intention. As they sprawled in a confused heap at the feet of the mocking Steven, Bernie leapt from his bed of beach mats with surprising agility and imposed his considerable bulk between the warring factions.

"Hey, come on, pack it in," counselled Bernie as Ted and Gerhard scrambled to their feet. "You can't do it, you know, not on holiday – I said PACK IT IN!"

"That nong, that piker..." spluttered Ted, attempting to get around Bernie's restraining arms.

"Hold on, Ted, just hold on."

Bernie stood solid between Steven and four clenched fists. The rest of the crews were all on their feet, faces stretched with concern, except for the junior members who were rather enjoying the drama of adults getting into trouble.

"I think we're all getting too het up," said Bernie. "It's all this sitting exposed in the sun. And I *do* think," he turned to Steven with a level look, "that a bit of an apology is called for."

Steven sneered.

"You can..."

"I'll say it again – we'd like to hear an apology."

Steven eyed the masterful Bernie malevolently, knowing that Bernie had probably misheard what had been said anyway. But he didn't feel too confident about taking the big Englishman on: Ted might look more like Mr Atlas but Bernie had an air of authority that suggested a good deal of trouble if he was challenged. And the three nurses had grouped behind their leader, a formidable trio of flesh.

"I guess...I guess I – uhm – spoke out of turn, no offence meant – to the lady," he drawled, looking at Sally and carefully excluding Gerhard from the apology.

The tension was broken by a fortuitous and startling blast from a siren, causing the assembly on the beach to turn as one to the source of the sound.

Luigi stood at the prow of *Angela Mia*, his swarthy, hairy arms raised in supplication.

"My friends," he intoned, "for why are you making these troubles in this *paradiso* when you shoulda be so 'appy? I 'ave never seena such a thing with a flotilla, isa tra–ged–ee!"

Jack Armitage turned to Rosie.

"Come on," he said loudly, for the benefit of everyone else, "the Eyetie's right. Gettin' upset because some silly arse can't stop 'imself makin' cracks. Glad to see the back of the bugger."

"Pick that stuff up, Darren," he continued, indicating Rosie's extensive collection of beach necessities – large white-framed sunspecs, an enormous bottle of Superdrug's cheap version of someone else's tanning lotion, a Jilly Cooper paperback about posh people, Jack's current hat, one plastic shoe and, implausibly, Darren's set of earphones, now rendered useless due to water in his Walkman. These objects were all that were needed for moving less than ten yards from the boat: any further and Rosie had to spend an hour packing.

The St Clairs, too, had obviously decided that the meeting

was at an end.

"Yes, I think we're all ready to go, Ted," said Crispin, smiling around him with a view to spreading general bonhomie. "I take it the Warbelows are coming? Not much of a treasure hunt without you lot!"

The awkwardness of the confrontation fizzled out with the general movement to the yachts. Sally, not sparing the still-seated Steven a glance, took Ted's hand and propelled him to *Ulysses X*, flashing a brief smile of thanks to Gerhard and Bernie, who likewise saw that the row was at an end.

"Zo, eet ees time to go, eh, Ted?"

Luigi was tactfully acknowledging the skipper as leader of the expedition.

Ted felt that, somehow, he'd conducted the whole affair with the natural authority of a man born to command and, bucked by Luigi's apparent deference, resumed his natural cheerful spirits.

"Pucker," he announced, "let's get ship–shape and – er – shipped out."

Magnanimously, he turned back to Steven.

"That was – er – not in the schedule. Sorry. Got out of kilter, eh? Bit of a misunderstanding. Alright?"

He held out his hand and Steven, with a barely perceptible pause, shook it though his eyes did not meet the frank look of the Aussie.

"Yeh, well, I guess these things happen. Amy and me, we're heading for Cephalonia. Circle the whole place and back through the Levkas Canal. Join up on, uh, the Wednesday, yeh?"

Hamish Gillicuddy, flanked by Angus and Angie, formed an anxious little group around the former combatants.

"Aye, well, that's what Flora – that's what we want to do. It's – it's for the more experienced sailors. What about, d'you think, us being together? I don't mean *all the time*," he added warily, having had some experience of being turned down, "but keeping in contact and maybe anchoring up together; I've heard ken that Assos is a right neat place to be spending a night?"

Before Steven could reply – and his ear took some time to comprehend the broad Scots vowels – a happy yowl of greeting floated towards them from *The Bounty*.

Amy Clawrer had finally stirred from her deeply satisfying sleep to greet the day and her companions with a blithe and contented spirit. As she had lain naked beneath the cabin skylight, a tousled sheet pushed down to her feet allowing a faint breath of wind to caress her body, she had tried to piece together the events of the previous evening.

The pieces didn't quite make up a whole. Had she – or hadn't she? Was there – or wasn't there? There had been similar mornings in her younger days, not *that* many, but a few. That Cavalry movie, for instance, about Custer's Last Stand – well, the title said it all. And having had his last stand, he'd literally dumped her in an oasis.

Could she have been dreaming? A castaway who had only uttered words – lyrics – from a pop song. She didn't, as a rule, remember dreams so clearly yet the words from the Beatles' *Girl* floated into her consciousness.

Dream or not, she felt like a million dollars, a zillion dollars. All the old optimism had returned, the belief that good things could – *would* – still happen. There was the sun, edging over the glass window, peeking down at her and telling her she looked great. She stretched sensuously under its embracing rays then realized that it must have been up some time before her and maybe it was time to greet the day.

"Hi, you guys," she chirruped to those guys, "aincha feelin' just fan–tas–tic?"

Angus and Angie waved palely at the large American lady wrapped in a colourful sarong, yellow tresses streaming girlishly over nicely plump bare shoulders.

"Jest the day fer stubbies," answered Ted jovially, pulling out the legs of his baggy black shorts in a mock curtsey. "Ye've missed the meetin', Amy. We were all sayin' our fond goodbyes 'til we see ye in a few days."

Amy looked blank.

"So who's sayin' goodbye to who?"

"We are, honey. We're saying goodbye to the rest of

them while they go – treasure huntin'. 'Cept for the, er, Hamishes here who'll be sailin' in our direction."

"Gillicuddys," corrected Hamish while Amy absorbed the shock of being addressed as 'honey' by her man. The last time he'd sounded so affectionate was when she had paid the hotel bill for their honeymoon suite at the Slumber-Tite Motel. *Something* sure had happened last night.

"Well, that sounds just dandy," cooed Amy, giving her Steven a winsome smile, "I'll just slip into my mou-mou and be ready for the off."

And she turned to go below, drawing her wrap tightly around her to leave them with a happy memory of a cuddly bottom.

*   *   *

The nine yachts heading in search of possible fame and improbable fortune eventually left around midday, later than Ted had intended, but he had, of course, forgotten Jack's ability to snare his neighbours' anchors – which caused the usual hour's confusion and exasperation.

The situation was not helped by Sharon's determination to take a deck shower in the midst of the entanglement, causing a lack of concentration on helmsmanship by Arnold who caught the tantalizing glimpses of wet-satin skin whenever Rosie failed to keep the screening towel in position. Fortunately, the only damage caused by the collision of *De Profundis* with *Becker* was the banging of Gerhard's nose forcibly against the cabin window where he had been kneeling on a bunk, observing the same scenery. Possessing a large, swollen probiscus did nothing for Gerhard's ego and his hopes that, sooner or later, one of the many females he admired among the crews would fall victim to his charms.

With *Ulysses X* in the lead, and the graceful *Angela Mia* taking up rear position, the flotilla looked quite an impressive Armada as it left the gentle waters of Abeliki Bay.

In the hold of the Italian yacht, Oleg Grameshic Dhoni had made himself as comfortable as an assortment of ropes, anchor chains, diesel cans, flippers and other sailing accoutrements allowed. While Luigi and Ariadne had taken their morning dip, he had surreptitiously left his lair, made his way below to the galley, and expertly purloined enough foodstuffs from the well-stocked cupboards to keep him going for a day without it being missed by his unknowing hosts.

It was not the most comfortable of berths, but Oleg didn't mind. Comfort was not his immediate preoccupation. It was the wide world which beckoned Oleg, beckoned him with an urgency which had been awoken by the strange encounter the previous night with the amorous blond woman of uncertain years. Oleg wanted to live, live, live and his years as a castaway now seemed like a long tunnel of barren exile, without the warmth of human contact, of a woman. The throb of the diesel as *Angela Mia* cut through the sea was a hymn of freedom, a hymn Oleg hummed to himself as he accompanied the expedition in his dark, oil-smelling locker, in search of a treasure which the others on board the treasure-seeking yachts had long since found.

*   *   *

Back on the island, Amy and Steven Clawrer stood arm in arm. Admittedly, Amy had hauled Steven's arm into hers, but he hadn't drawn it away impatiently as he had been prone to do the last few weeks or so.

"Seems kinda odd," mused Amy as the flotilla grew smaller on the horizon, "like we're sort of abandoned. Apart from them," she indicated *Thistle* where Hamish and his offspring where engaged in restoring Flora's equilibrium, "it's like a desert island."

Her eyes swept the shoreline, narrowing as she surveyed the tangle of olive trees and brush that lead mysteriously into the interior.

"You lookin' for natives or somethin'?"

Steven eyed his wife keenly. There was still a faintly odd air about her, a sort of dreaminess, a contentment that had him foxed.

"Natives? Oh no, you must be kiddin'."

"But," she added, as her eyes picked out a shadowed path that seemed to disappear into the scrub, "you never know... you never know what you might find on these islands. You just never know."

CHAPTER EIGHT

The Chief of Police in Thessadikios ponders on promotion. Jack is all at sea and Rosie spills the beans on the air. Major Swit ponders on demotion – for General Hockhymer – and goads the General into thinking positive.

Georgiou Komoulides watched the fly and the fly watched Georgiou Komoulides.

They had a mutual respect for each other.

The Chief of Police in Thessadikios might be somewhat past his prime, might have put on a few kilos since the glorious days of the Colonels when he had so enjoyed arresting foreign girls for wearing indecently short miniskirts; he might wish that the thick black curls which had made so many of those girls willing to be arrested had not long since departed from his skull leaving a few carefully–combed strands spreadeagled across his sweating skull; but he still had an appetite for the hunt.

Sprawled before his desk in a wicker chair that creaked and groaned with the effort of supporting his weight and girth, he eyed the fly without malice. There were many such flies – most of them foreign. Foreign drunks, foreign punks, foreign *hippies*, the Chief regarded them all as so many flies to be swatted. They kept him in work, of a sort. They made him the Chief, and though Thessadikios was hardly the summit that he had once aimed for, he did have the respect of the community – and most of them, including the *Papa* from the local church, in his pocket.

Whaaam!

The shutters, partly drawn over the grubby windows to keep out the midday sun, stuttered in annoyance then settled back into their heat-soaked doze. Overhead, the unwieldy fan continued its leisurely whirl, scarcely disturbing the leaden air or, for that matter, the black hairs that lay in a perspiration–soaked mat on the Chief's ample chest.

The fly settled scornfully on Georgiou's desklamp, daring the swat to descend on the Chief's only up-to-date appliance. It was a skilled tactical manoeuvre which the Chief appreciated.

He pushed the crumpled piece of greaseproof which bore the remains of his honey–soaked *baklava* in front of the faded photograph of his wife. The more faded the photo became, the better he liked it.

Scratching his clammy crutch, Georgiou waited for brains

to outwit basic instinct and pondered on Luigi's radioed message to the Chief's brother-in-law, Stavros.

He often received messages from Luigi via Stavros, whose ancient coaster proved so useful for delivering unspecified cargo at night. There was no love lost between Luigi and the Chief; they were two of a pair and recognized each other as such, a mixture of mutual regard and distrust.

But the entrepreneurial skills and mobility of the Italian complemented the official status and useful influence of the Greek, a combination that allowed for the import of certain goods – generally classed as 'luxuries' and including antiques, spirits and interesting videos of an 'athletic' persuasion – without the necessity of paying restrictive taxes.

The message from Stavros had been garbled, which was not unusual as anyone stupid enough to marry the Chief's sister must be a natural garbler.

Muttered in over-dramatic conspiratorial tones down a phone line that just about had the energy to make the Chief's phone tinkle in a peculiarly dismal way, the gist of the message seemed to be that a bunch of foreigners in sailing boats had discovered a treasure of National Importance, in waters that could be regarded as being under the Chief's jurisdiction. Luigi, once the booty – the National artefacts – had been located and identified, wanted the Chief to home in and confiscate the lot.

Then, after judicial consideration of what should rightfully go to the nation, and what could wrongfully be divided between Georgiou and Luigi, Chief Komoulides could publicly announce the discovery and gain that elusive promotion. Having Ted arrested in an attempt to steal from the Greek government would undoubtedly spell the end of the Ulysses Flotilla and Luigi, funded by the sale of a few undeclared artefacts, would reign supreme in Mengalissi.

Zzwat!

The over-confident fly made the mistake of thinking the photo frame was sacrosanct and paid the ultimate penalty. So did the Chief's wife as the glass splintered on the desk and the photograph soaked up the remains of the Domestica which had spilt from Georgiou's glass. He peered without regret at his wife's dissolving face: there was something symbolic about her abrupt disappearance, but it was much too hot to work it out.

The guardian of the law in Thessadikios became aware of a dismal keening coming from the bowels of his domain. If the atmosphere had not been so stifling, he might have given a start at the memory of the British yobbo he had locked into a cell the previous night for disturbing the peace – *his* peace. Perhaps he ought to feed him. Perhaps not. One thing at a time. The yobbo could wait, maybe another day or so.

The chair swore helplessly as the Chief settled back into thought. There was more than one option: he could arrest the lot of them, Luigi included, and snaffle all the treasure for himself; or he could declare it all and become the saviour of his country's honour, a National Hero. There had been that Mercouri woman who had got enough publicity over some old bits and pieces that were now sitting in a museum somewhere or other.

He ran a hand over his beaded scalp, had a better idea, and reached for his greasy but imposing peaked cap. Polishing the badge to a shine with his sleeve, he clamped it on his head, heaved his bulk to his feet and went into the lavatory, ignoring the pitiful wails that increased in hopeful volume as their owner heard the steps in the corridor.

Not a man to waste undue energy, he had fitted a mirror over the urinal so that he could do two things at once.

Quite an impressive figure, he thought, as he sucked in some of his gut; his photo would make quite a splash in the papers. Sucking in your gut when peeing in a low urinal does not aid accuracy. The Chief eyed his wet boots with a fine sense of irony: he had already made quite a splash.

*   *   *

Jack Armitage gazed in perplexity at the deserted expanse of sun-rippled blue sea. Following a course of 45 degrees was so simple: all you had to do was look at the compass in the bulkhead and twitch the tiller thing so that '45' kept wobbling against the black line.

Yet all the other boats had got lost.

"Bloody ridiculous," he snorted at Rosie for the umpteenth time. "Ye'd think they know 'ow to do sumthin' like that by now."

"They'll turn up, dear," answered Rosie comfortably, wiping some peach juice off her Judith Krantz. "You just keep chuggin' away an' you'll see. Turn it a bit the other way, Jack, I'm all in the shade."

Stretched out on the seat in the cockpit next to her ancient mariner, Rosie was enjoying life at sea. It could be very relaxing. Getting a tan was a doddle since all you had to do was twiddle the lever thing 'til the boat gave you maximum sunshine exposure.

Jack bestowed a glare on his reclining wife. Women just didn't understand the responsibilities of a skipper. He was not 'chuggin' away' – he was setting course.

His daughter was no help, lying there half naked – *three-quarters naked* – while Snubsy bobbed up and down on her stomach to the rhythm of whatever cacophony boomed in her ears. Thank God the engine drowned out her row.

Mind you, his mate was no better, sprawled in the dinghy while the yacht towed him along. About all he was good for.

He scanned the horizon, an unrewarding scan which signalled only emptiness. Not a mast in sight.

"Rosie, yer'd better get on that radio."

Rosie put her finger on the line where Princess Daisy was at it again and cast him a reproving look.

"Why can't *you* do it, Jack? You've only got t'switch on the button thing and shout – shout '*Moby D– Dick*, callin' *Ulysses X*, an' Over', an' Ted'll be there. If 'e's not at what 'e's usually at," she added, as an afterthought.

The skipper sighed a sorely tried sigh.

"I'm drivin' this boat, ain't I? 'Ow can I do all this steerin' an' call that Aussie at the same time? Anyroads, that sort of talk's not right for a woman."

Moby Dick swerved abruptly as his eagle eye brought her

back on course after wandering a little owing to stress.

"Dad, what's the matter with the boat? I nearly rolled off!"

His topless tactless daughter sat up and retrieved Snubsy from near peril as he rolled towards the sea.

"There's nothin' the matter with the *boat*," snorted Jack wrathfully. "It's the bleedin' crew who are no use."

"Oh, alright," soothed Rosie, uncurling herself from her snug nest, "I'll do it."

She ducked down into the cabin, presenting the helmsman with a pair of crimson cheeks which had been in contact with the cockpit seat for the past hour. Jack restrained an impulse to follow his ample spouse down the ladder. It wasn't, after all, Saturday night. Right was right, even at sea – whatever Aussies got up to.

The radio did its best to annoy Rosie, but hers was a practised hand and a touch of 'squelch' put an end to its mischief.

"*Moby Dick, Moby Dick* to *Ulysses X*. Over," she announced to perfection.

After the third try, Sally's voice responded, a little breathlessly.

"*Ulysses X* to *Moby Dick*, receiving YOU – you. Over," came back Sally, with what sounded like a clunk against a hard object in the background.

"Sally, where are you? Jack says ye've all got lost an' 'e's gettin' a bit moody–like..."

"Rosie, we're all here, in sight of each other. Except for you. Where are – never mind...what course are you on?"

"Wait a bit," said Rosie. She poked her head out of the cabin.

"Sal says what are you on? Which course is it?"

"The bleedin' course she told us to be on – 45 degrees North," answered the irritated Jack.

"He says the bleedin' – the course wot you said, 45 degrees North," she told Sally.

"*54 degrees North*, we said, Rosie. You're heading toward Cor – STOP IT, TED – Corfu! You'll have to correct

a bit. Turn towards 40 degrees North, then – let me think –
then you should see the coast. The Greek coast."

Sally unwittingly made it sound that, with Jack at the
helm, it could be the coast of China.

"Then just keep following the coast and you'll see a
lighthouse. You can't miss it. There's a village behind it, it's
called Thessadikios, you'll see the houses. It's marked on
your chart, you know, the one we use for briefings."

"Oh, that one," assented Rosie, "that map thing. Our
Sharon's sunbathing on that. Says it makes 'er feel on top of
the world. She's a one!"

Sally silently agreed.

"We'll be waiting for you. That's where the St Clairs
think that the treasure is. Crispin thinks that whatever is on
the bottom was being brought to that village. It was
probably much bigger in those days."

"Well, alright, Sally, but you wait fer us. We wanna be
there when you start findin' all that stuff, all those marbles
an' that. Jack says it'll be in all the papers and our Sharon
wants 'er photo in *The Sun* wiv all that treasure an' – an'
urns, an' – an' gold!"

A light laugh from Sally.

"Okey dokey, Rosie, we'll make sure you get your share
of excitement – and the treasure. Over and Out."

And Sally returned to whatever had caused her moments
of distraction.

At the American School of Archaeology in Athens, a
young 'student' removed his headphones and spun back the
tape-recording of their conversation.

Ten minutes later, General Samuel B. Hockhymer's phone
danced on his desk.

*   *   *

"Phone's ringin', Swit."

General Hockhymer tucked his chin into his collar and
smiled secretly to himself.

He enjoyed irritating Swit, watching the predictable tide

149

of red sweep up around his ears. What Swit was, Swit was a fucking martinet, that's what Swit was. What Swit wanted was to smack heads, snap orders, grill spies. Particularly, grill spies.

Instead of which, he was having to stride from the filing cabinet over to the General's desk to pick up the receiver which sat two inches from the General's paw.

"Yep?" snapped Swit.

Abruptly, his figure took on an alert, martial look. Security clearance was being given to an outside line and anti-monitor locators sealed the call.

This was more like it. Major Gabriel Swit squared his square shoulders.

"Okay, shoot," he ordered the conspiratorial voice down the line.

"Yep..."

"Yep?"

"Yep!"

The cradle winced as the receiver cracked smartly into place.

Swit stood for a moment in thought. He looked like a soldier standing to attention, but thoughtwaves slithered under the crew-cut.

The general regarded his aide with a jaundiced eye.

"Well, Major? Sumthin' happen out there? You look like you've jest had a carrot rammed up yer ass. Weren't those security bleeps I could hear on thuh line?"

Major Swit metaphorically removed the carrot. His colourless eyes swivelled around the General's office, a nice sort of old-fashioned affair of leather and mahogany. NATO had allowed the General to bring his furnishings from the States since the Headquarters for Balkan Operations was situated in a particularly depressing modern block in downtown Athens.

There were, Major Swit observed, few evident spies in the room. As he swept the room almost hourly for bugs, and had received a severe blow in the crutch from the coffee lady who objected to being body-searched without a formal introduction, he knew the room was clean electronically-wise.

"Sir," he hissed, bending forward so that a crease nearly appeared in his crisp tunic, "It's the Brits. They're stirrin' up some shit."

The General did not seem as taught with excitement as the Major. Taught was not a word to apply to General Samuel B Hockhymer: he hadn't been that way for some thirty years. He was a peace-time General who hadn't even visited Vietnam. He'd never had the chance to waste anyone.

Now in the sunset of his military career, he wished he'd had just a little engagement to commemorate on his chest. He was sick of all those bastards who had seen Korea, Vietnam, Cambodia – wherever – casting their eyes along his gongs. He could see the flicker as they picked out his highest honour: a medal from the Belgian Government – *Belgians*, for Chrissake – for organizing traffic during a police strike. There was a silly picture etched in the gold medal of what looked like a clown with a baton in his hand doing some sort of dervish dance. What else would you expect from a nation which was only famous for chocolates? Or was that those Swiss?

So the portly General did not feel the frisson his aide evidently felt.

"Major Swit," drawled the General deflatingly, "The only Brits here couldn't stir their asses out of the top floor bar. Tell me more. And, by the way, next time hand over the phone to your superior when you reckon it's important."

Swit's eyes narrowed. He didn't think much of armchair generals, particularly those who were lapse in their appearance. Hockhymer wore the uniform but looked more as though the uniform supported him. Overall, when he strode down the corridors among so many other uniforms, he looked okay; but there was something slightly messy about him, he looked lived in, like an old armchair.

"I – er – figured you may not want to get involved, sir. It seems like something pretty odd is going on in the Ionian, sir."

"I'd hate to think, Major, that there wasn't *sumthin'* a bit odd goin' on in a sea that big. Or on it. Can you be more specific?"

Major Gabriel Swit was stung. Having to take sarcasm from this no-account high brass was a bitter pill, but one he had to swallow on the road to his next promotion. The trouble was, the General wouldn't get directly involved and there would be no action to participate in.

"Sir, that was a call from our plant at that archaeology place – you know, the one with all those subversives we were asked to keep an eye on. Leftovers, dickheads from the Sixties, welcoming every commie bastard..."

"I think I know the place, Major. I suppose Jimi Hendrix had already snuffed it by the time you were in diapers. Well?"

"Sir, there's a British flotilla heading for a location off the coast, between Sivota and Parga. We're running a check on the guy who seems to be in charge. A..." he consulted his pad, "a Crispin St Clair. Some sort of royalty. Undercover agent, General, as sure as hell. They're after, well, they call it 'treasure'. We're decoding but haven't come up with anything yet. Our agent there is not so hot but he's got a tape and we're going through it. Stuff about 'marbles' and 'gold' and photographs. They probably know we've got tabs and are trying to confuse us, sir. Our *allies*."

Major Swit did not like the British. 'Perfidious' was a kind adjective to use about the British. 'Cock-up artists' was nearer the mark in his opinion. Everything the British started, the USA had to finish. They were starting something now – but they would have Major Swit to deal with.

General Hockhymer stirred uneasily. This happened frequently nowadays, accompanied by gurglings in his stomach which left a nasty taste in his mouth. Along with Major Swit. Surreptitiously, he eased a button on his tight shirt and felt a gastric juice shoot free in his capacious system.

"Yeh, well, I don't see that this is any business of ours. I mean, these are Greek waters and the Brits are allowed to operate in them, even lookin' for their – marbles. Don't see the harm in that."

The martinet ground a granite jaw.

"Sir, these guys are up to something and we've got no operations going on under any NATO ordinance. So it's clandestine, they're not telling us, filling us in. We've got to at least look at what they're up to."

The General picked up the phone.

"That's easy done. I'll call Meddle Tweddle."

Major Swit put a restraining hand on the receiver.

"Sir, that feller won't tell you anything. He comes over like a smart alec but 'Sir Garth Tweddle'" Swit said this in a bad imitation of a British accent from a Thirties movie, "may be more of a sonofabitch than you realize. Remember that dinner he told you was a fancy dress party and you turned up as Buffalo Bill and everyone else was in black tie?"

The General paused. It had been when, yes, that was it, the first of April, a day when the British played stupid jokes. He remembered them standing around haw–hawing as his0 leather chaps made slapping sounds when he was announced at the British Embassy. They kept asking him if he kept his six–shooter oiled.

"Yeh, sonsofbitches," he murmured.

Swit seized the advantage.

"That's what they like – to put us down. It's 'Yanks Go Home', but smothered in smarm. But if they're up to some game and it's unauthorized, you could catch them with their pants down. Send a gunboat, officially, as Chief of Operations, investigating unauthorized manoeuvres in neutral waters. It would cause a helluva diplomatic stink – and you'd get the credit, sir, for putting them in their place."

And the flack if it goes wrong, thought Major Swit, seeing the possibility of swift promotion opening up.

A gleam almost stole into the tired yellow eyeballs of General Hockhymer. Here was a chance for action. Congress would give warm approval to a general who smacked the uppity British one in the kisser. And perhaps boost his pension.

"Major Swit," he said in the tone of a man of decision, "put a gunboat on standby. Get a 'copter up to survey this flotilla and their destination. I will personally supervise this operation – and you will accompany me."

"Sir," snapped his efficient aide, turning smartly on his heel.

The US of A was not about to be trifled with.

CHAPTER NINE

OLEG IS KNOCKED COLD IN THE HOLD. LUIGI PULLS A FAST ONE. *MOBY DICK* PULLS AN EVEN FASTER ONE. ERIC TAKES THE PLUNGE. OLEG TAKES THE COUNT. LUIGI MAKES HISTORY. THE CREWS MAKE WHOOPEE. OLEG MAKES AN APPEARANCE.

Oleg squirmed uncomfortably, dreading the return of cramp in his left leg. The locker of the *Angela Mia*, which had been virtually his home for the last two days, was roomy enough for the yacht's needs at sea – diesel fuel, fenders, spare rope and chain, a grappling hook, and other bits of seafaring paraphernalia. There was even sufficient space for the odd case of contraband, though Luigi only used such an obvious hidey-hole when greed overcame caution. The two large diesel cans, in fact, gave out an odour more reminiscent of whisky than fuel and Oleg had found that the stuffy warm air of the locker, pervaded by whisky vapours, had quite a soporific effect.

Nevertheless, he'd had enough. Creeping out at night, like Dracula climbing out of his coffin, had been his only chance to stretch his limbs and grab food from the galley – garlicky food which caused much upheaval in his stomach and turbulence in his bowels. The atmosphere in the locker had thickened perceptibly. Dracula would not have felt at home.

Oleg had hoped that the two occupants of the boat – and despite his years as a castaway he knew them to be a man and a woman – would drop anchor for a trip ashore, but there had been no stopping to idle the hours away. It was clear that *Angela Mia* was a boat with a purpose.

Only once had he been able to leave his locker in daylight, when the absence of footsteps and voices left the solitary sound of the engine drumming routinely as *Angela Mia* maintained her course on automatic pilot.

Raising the lid slightly, he had peered at the empty cockpit through dazzled bloodshot eyes and had calculated his chances. He would have glanced at his watch, but whoever had forgotten it on his island had had the best of the battery and Batman's arms remained forever poised at half-past-six, giving Batman a curiously furtive look with his hands stuck between his legs. Oleg did not have to be an expert mariner to judge from the heat and the sun that it must be mid-afternoon: it was but a short jump to the deduction that Luigi and his mate were probably taking a post-prandial nap.

Warily, he had eased himself onto the deck and crouched behind the wheel, his eyes straining forward, ready to bolt. It was his ears which had told him that the coast was clear.

From the master cabin, directly below him, came the sort of sounds which signified either mud wrestling or erotic pursuit. Deciding it was the latter, and at some mid-stage, Oleg had stolen down the steps and into the capacious dining area where the best part of a meal remained on the table. With his ears attentive to the rearward grunts and groans, he had gathered wine, fruit and cold meats in a collective sweep then turned to face the steps – and the master cabin.

The sight, through the open door of the cabin, of a naked Ariadne kneeling astride her hairy Italian lover had rooted him to the spot. Like many Albanians, he knew some very rudimentary Greek and Ariadne was uttering some very rudimentary commands. How Luigi retained his dashing skipper's cap while imitating a piston at full speed was a matter Oleg could ponder later: he had bolted for the steps with his booty and sought the sanctuary of his locker.

But all that seemed hours and hours ago. He couldn't stay any longer in his sweat-imbued pit. So *what* if he gave himself up? They were not likely to turn back to Abeliki and dump him back on his island. Nor would they just throw him overboard: he had seen the other yachts sailing in the same direction as *Angela Mia* during his brief sojourn and guessed that they were travelling in convoy. There would be too many witnesses to any unscheduled flights overboard – someone would pick him up.

Even as he reached up to push open the lid, he became aware of something different. The engine had stopped. And there was a lot of shouting on deck, tramping of feet, the running of the anchor chain.

Struggling to his knees, he balanced on two fenders and pushed the lid gently with his head. As the locker formed a seat in the cockpit, the possibility of someone sitting on it was not remote and a vigorous shove would send an unsuspecting body hurtling over the side – with consequent retribution. But the lid gave easily enough and he peered through the tiny gap, his eyes squinting painfully in the sunlight.

Oleg squeezed away the tears that sprang from his sorely-tried orbs as the glare of the sun from the white empty deck slapped into them. From below, he could hear Luigi on the radio.

"Issa this spot, no, you are right, yes?"

An unfamiliar voice responded.

"Yer not wrong. Too right. Leastaways, this is the spot that the kids think they saw the baubles an' beads."

"The bubbles...?"

"...an' beads. The treasure, sport. What we came tear–arsing all this way for. They reckon it's somewhere here, below us."

"Ah, si, I am getting you, Ted. Issa okey-dokey, we put outa the dinghies now."

"Hey, hang about, now, Luigi, the others haven't completed the circle. As soon as I've got them all anchored up, we can have a bite an' then get down to work."

"Ah, well, this issa not a problem. Ariadne and me, we are ready now to look a leetle bit."

"*Luigi*, there's no rush. With the flotilla in a circle – if that nong Jack Armitage knows what a bleedin' circle is – we won't get any boats on our patch. We're the first cab off the rank, there's no push now. An' I'm so hungry I could eat a baby's bum through a cane chair!"

And with that mystifying observation, the radio lapsed into silence. Oleg remained as still as a Rodin statue with a lid on its head. His knowledge of English being restricted to The Best of The Beatles played at slow speed, he could not fathom the meaning of what had passed for English between the Italian and the Australian.

"That Ted, 'e is one stupeed son-of-a-beach," was Luigi's succinct description of the flotilla skipper, uttered from the bowels of the boat. "Ariadne," he roared, "I theenk we get the dinghy and the scubas and take a look first, eh? You jumpa down and getta the stuff ready, si, and I getta the camera ready."

Unfortunately for Oleg, his view was restricted to the horizontal. Had he been able to examine the vertical and look up, he might have seen the approaching doom.

Luigi's roar had been necessary since the Greek Goddess was forward on the top deck, that gloriously gleaming, bronzed and muscular body clad ready for action – in a thong. She turned from watching the yachts manoeuvering into a circle, ran nimble-footed along the deck, and jumped from the top of the wheelhouse – onto the locker.

Ariadne was perfectly proportioned. Few men would have proposed any rearrangement. But she was not possessed of any elfin attributes. Built on a handsome scale, combining muscularity with grace, when Ariadne landed on anything solid from a six-foot leap, the gross weight per square inch was, well, awesome.

Since the locker lid was supported by Oleg's head, it was the latter whose square inches experienced the gross weight converted, as it were, to a downward thrust.

Oleg took no further interest in the proceedings. In Ted's vernacular, he had 'come a gutzer'. Oleg was out.

*　　*　　*

Sally had been pleased with the crews of the flotilla until she remembered that *Moby Dick* had yet to join them. The excitement generated by the possible presence of some sort of archaeological find had kept the crews in good spirits, despite the pace which had been set.

Once the Warbelow boys had identified the approximate location of their 'sighting' – after much argument with their father, whose idea of the location was somewhat hazy since he had been groaning with sunburn in the bottom of their dinghy when the 'discovery' had been made – the yachts, together with *Angela Mia*, had formed an almost perfect circle around the agreed search area.

It had been decided to pinpoint the believed sighting of the treasure as the centre of the circle and confine the first search of the area to a perimeter some two hundred metres from that point. For the mathematically minded, which rather excluded Ted, this meant that boats opposite each other on the circumference were four hundred metres apart. Only Bernie could be heard at that distance but everyone had their receivers tuned in and and were in sight of each other.

Then *Moby Dick* had been spotted on the horizon by the St Clairs and Sally was anxiously clutching the shrouds of *Ulysses X* as the Armitages approached the circle. Shrouds were, indeed, being universally clutched on all the yachts as each crew wondered which space was in the mind of Jack Armitage as his boat grew ever closer at what appeared to be full speed. There was a lot of space in Jack's mind.

There was also a lot of sea inside the flotilla's circle. Neither Mark nor Alan Warbelow was sure of the *exact* position of their discovery and they could only make their judgement in relation to the Greek coast, just visible about a mile away. Once the dinghies were lowered, however, they felt confident enough that whatever had aroused their curiosity lay somewhere within the limits of the boundary roughly outlined by the anchored yachts. And there was sufficient room between each yacht for an average-sized tanker to get through without mishap.

Average-sized tankers are generally in the hands of a competent crew under the guidance of an experienced captain. *Moby Dick* was lacking in both. Captain Jack's hand on the throttle of his diesel engine was capable of two speeds, 'dodgy' and 'dangerous'. His crew had only one level of competence – none.

If Luigi Giannovi had not been so intent on upstaging Ted's crews in being the first to find the mysterious deposits, either he or his voluptuous mate might have been more wary of the approaching yacht. Without the benefit of the flotilla's experience of the Armitages at sea, however, he lacked the others' shared premonition of disaster.

Ariadne, rootling in the locker for the two oxygen tanks and flippers, saw no sign of a comatose Albanian. When you are hit on the napper with a resounding force, you don't always fold yourself away in a tidy ship-shape fashion. Oleg's bits and pieces were sprawled haphazardly amidst the locker's contents and were not immediately identifiable to the cursory glance. He might have regained consciousness sooner if one of the heavy scuba tanks had not been clunked against his sorely-tried head as Ariadne lifted it out. The large lump on the top of his skull had grown to resemble one of the fenders surrounding him, it was not surprising that Ariadne did not recognize it as a head containing so many Beatle lyrics.

With little concern for any protest that might come from Ted or his crews, Luigi handed down the diving equipment to Ariadne, who stood perfectly balanced in the dinghy. He climbed down the stern ladder, untied the painter and, less agile than his partner, wobbled to a sitting position among the scuba gear. Ariadne gave the outboard cable an effortless tug, adjusted the throttle to just above idling, and the dinghy began chugging to the centre of the circle.

*   *   *

On board *Moby Dick*, tempers were becoming frayed.

"Slow down, Dad," yelled Darren from the pulpit, "we've got to get between two of those boats. You've got to go sideways so as to be in the circle they've made."

"What?" roared Jack above the boom of the diesel. "Wharrer you sayin'? You'd better get that anchor ready up there. Sharon, get back here. I can't do the steerin' and get this anchor out as well. We've got to throw one out at the back as well as the front. An' put yer top on – they're all standin' on their boats and watchin' us."

Sharon, with her back propped against the mast, was busy changing over her 'Take That' tape in her brother's Walkman – the one that hadn't been accidentally dropped in the sea. Sulkily, she rose to her feet, tied on her bikini top, and unhurriedly made her way to the cockpit, combing her fingers through her sun-bleached hair in case a movie director should be viewing her through binoculars.

161

The two nearest yachts, *Becker* and *Discovery*, bobbed a few hundred yards directly in front of them. Gerhard and Monika stood rigidly to attention on the former's deck, eyeing the speedy *Moby Dick* with a Teutonic sense of fate. On the *Discovery*, Sidney Chippendale was instructing Clara on how to survive a shipwreck. To someone with an academic turn of mind, the problem presented by the difference between the small circumference of the lifebelt and the large circumference of both Chippendales was somewhat challenging. There had to be a suitable theorem to explain how one fitted into the other. Clara, meanwhile, had already filled an inflatable bag with enough food to cover emergencies – she didn't mind which particular emergency as long as at least one demanded close attention being paid to the bag's contents.

Jack's hand on the helm began to betray some indecision in the brain of its owner. At times of great emotion Jack naturally became greatly emotional. Coaxing *Moby Dick* into the gap between *Becker* and *Discovery* now took on similar proportions to parking an articulated truck in a space big enough for a Mini.

"Right! Right! When I shout," Jack shouted to his petulant daughter, "throw that anchor out over the back there – an' make sure the chain follers it."

"Throw the... you must be jokin'!" was all he got by way of support, "I'm not bloomin' Wonderwoman... throw it yourself."

"Fer Gawd's Sake! Don't bloody argue – Rosie! Rosie! Gerrup 'ere!"

"Tea's not ready yet, love," came the placid reply from the galley. "Shan't be a jiff."

"Bugger the jiff, I need... Gawd Almighty!"

Zigzagging erratically, *Moby Dick* chose not the gap but the bows of *Becker* at an angle of ninety degrees. Gerhard's passivity was replaced in quick succession by stricken horror then galvanized terror. This prompted some active decision-taking, resulting in a few graphic German oaths and the abrupt departure of both Monika and Gerhard as they ran to the starboard railing and vaulted into the sea.

On board *Nemesis*, meanwhile, each member of the Warbelow family was reacting differently.

Penny, true to character, felt that a calm head was needed and tried unsuccessfully to interrupt Ted's frantic exhortations over the radio, beseeching the Armitages to steer clear of the other yachts and to wait until he dinghied out to *Moby Dick* and took over. All the crews had their transmitters turned on but it was only Penny who realized that the loud whistling noise which disturbed the air waves was not squelch: it was a boiling kettle. Rosie, she deduced, was making tea and was probably searching for tea bags.

Trudy's eyes were fixed on the gesticulating figure of Darren who seemed destined to be catapulted over *Becker* with the impending collision. Her mouth opened and closed with unuttered expressions of the sweet things she would like Darren to hear in his final moments.

Mark and Alan were oblivious to the drama unfolding around them. Ever since recounting their sighting of the dim shapes they had glimpsed to Crispin St Clair, they had been infected by his enthusiasm and excitement. Combing their combined memories, they had tried to give substance to what they could recall, had sketched an approximation of what their blurred sighting and fallible recollection could yield.

They had torn a page from their father's diary – being naturally honourable, they had tried not to read any of the entries but couldn't help noticing the last page was devoted to one word, 'MONIKA', which struck them as a little strange – and produced a pencil drawing which was then pored over by each of the crews participating in the search.

It definitely looked, Rosie had thought, like that Antlers place that had been lost. Crispin, having used Tara's water colours to give the sketch more substance, was more than ever convinced that the greyish oblongs were pillars and the whiteish object a marble bust. He wanted to be convinced, to silence any misgivings. It was he, after all, who had persuaded the others to undertake the expedition.

Now that they had reached their destination, the boys

were overawed by their responsibility, tight with apprehension, gripped with a feverish excitement. While the radio shrieked and spluttered, while Germans flew through the air, while Trudy erupted in odd squeaky noises, they alternatively pored over their sketch and checked their recollection of where 'X' marked the spot.

For Eric the moment had come. As *Moby Dick* bore down on *Becker*, he found himself yelling 'Monika, Monika', bounding frantically up and down the deck in his pristine whites, heedless of the effect on his blood pressure or the loosening of his socks.

It was at that point that the two Germans bounded across their deck, leapt athletically into the air – and disappeared into the sea. Clear as the water was, their momentum caused a shock of bubbles to rise above them as they plunged downwards, obscuring any sign of them to the myriad eyes scanning the surface from the surrounding yachts.

A large, floppy hat floated forlornly on the surface. Then, as a brown arm thrust up through the water, Eric reacted with a speed uncommon to someone coming up for the big five-oh: he tore the lifebelt from its support and flung it with an unusual degree of accuracy at the head which would appear to be related to the arm.

To say that Gerhard was not pleased is to indulge in typical English understatement. It lacks emotion. It lacks fire. It lacks rage. And Gerhard was pot-full of rage. When, without any choice in the matter, you have just explored the lower depths of the sea without air in your lungs, the last thing you need is some *Dummkopf* to smack your head forcefully with a lifebelt – particularly when you don't need one.

But Eric's adrenalin, backed by his regular intake of ginseng, was working overtime and he perceived his mistake even as the lifebelt left his hands. Gerhard was of no concern to him – but a floppy hat with no visible sign of its owner was.

Pausing only to pull up his socks, he stepped over the rail and launched himself into a dive which any self-respecting swallow would have disowned.

His arms cutting the water cleanly in a clockwork crawl, the man-machine in white shirt, shorts and sneakers that was Eric powered to the stationary hat – now slowly sinking into the sea. Gerhard awaited him, treading water and nursing a bruise on the temple, the lifebelt having been pushed disdainfully aside.

"Zo, you are going somevere?" asked Gerhard politely, if coldly.

"Wuurgh," spluttered Eric – an inelegant reply but understandable in the circumstances, "Monika! Where – gruuuh – she isn't – ooof – I saw her jump – where...?"

"Perhaps you are vishing this, yes?"

Eric allowed Gerhard to lift the lifebelt over his head, poked his arms through, and stared frantically around.

"Where is she? Where's Monika? Your daughter?" he added helpfully, by way of identification.

Gerhard pointed to Eric's yacht, *Nemesis*.

"She is there," he answered laconically, "standing on your boat. That is Monika vaving to you. Ja, she is also my daughter. She has been for many years."

The lifebelt swirled slowly round, its suspended occupant gaping in disbelief.

"But... but her hat's here."

The marked iciness of Gerhard's manner was not eased by the alliteration.

"Her hat is not here," he hissed. "Her hat is sunken. There is *not* a hat here. I have seen it sunked. I think, perhaps, it is a pity that you... SCHEISSE! *Schwimm*, swim, now, swim to your yacht, come..."

Suiting action to words, Gerhard grabbed the lifebelt and, pushing the bewildered Eric in front of him, kicked furiously in the water towards *Nemesis*. Far from being the courageous rescuer of the divine Monika who stood, her long soaked dress clinging alluringly to her divine body, alongside his gesturing family, Eric found himself propelled ignominiously like a decoy duck back to his own yacht.

And he was horribly aware that, positioned as she was

some six feet above him, she must have a clear view of that sensitive area of his head which he fought so hard to conceal.

Gerhard's sudden apprehension was justified. Jack had averted slamming into *Becker* head-on by throwing his engine into reverse, and throwing his family off their feet. *Moby Dick* shuddered, crept up to the bow of *Becker*, gave it a light kiss, then shot backwards.

Jack, as a rule, prided himself on not doing things by halves and he was not about to break a lifetime's habit. There was no easing of the throttle: the engine revved at full speed. Another quirk of his character, a distinct disadvantage for a skipper, was that he was incapable of doing two things at once. To attend to the throttle, he released the helm.

Moby Dick, stern first, described a generous arc and plunged through the gap between *Becker* and *Discovery*, entering the charmed circle of flotilla yachts. Grimly wrapped around the tiller, like a wrestler with an opponent in a half-Nelson, Jack yanked the rudder from side to side, causing the yacht to swerve erratically.

To each of the crews gazing spellbound and white-knuckled at the rogue cruiser in their midst, it seemed as if *Moby Dick* was seeking a mate at random, with the rapacious intention of instant intimacy and no foreplay whatsoever.

The piercing whistle no longer cutting through the airwaves, Ted's voice crackled into life on all the yachts simultaneously.

"Get yer anchors up! Everyone, skates on, get outta here! That dillbrain is gonna sink someone, get yer engines goin' an' move it, NOW!"

Without even giving a pinch of goat shit for the customary 'Over and Out', the Aussie intonations abruptly ceased as *Ulysses X*, anchors already hauled by the able Sally, pulled away from the circle with a roar from her engine and repeated blasts from her foghorn.

Darren Armitage, having been flung across the foredeck by his father's unpredictable steering, a plunge into the Ionian having been avoided by a shroud which caught him painfully if neatly between the legs, was beginning to show the true grit which lay in the soul of a Leeds fan.

Inching his way on his stomach along the deck towards the cockpit as the boat lurched from side to side, he reached the edge of the galley roof and bent down his head to peer into the cabin.

"Yeralright, Ma?" he yelled, tightening his grip as *Moby Dick* abruptly chose another direction.

Rosie was alright, just. If Sharon had not been flung headlong down the steps as Jack evaded collision with *Becker*, and if Rosie had not been standing by the stove with the boiling kettle in her hand, both might have been severely damaged. As it was, her mother made a reasonably soft landing-pad for Sharon, and the two had rolled between the screwed-down table and the bunk, a mass of familial arms and legs. The kettle had landed among the groceries, its contents emptying into a bag of rice which had now expanded, leaking over the edge of the draining board on to their heads.

Darren didn't wait to unscramble the torrent of disloyal abuse aimed at his father. Swinging his legs over the roof edge, he jumped into the cockpit, tripped over an untidy coil of rope, and landed sprawling at the feet of his skipper. Single-minded Jack let go of the tiller and solicitously bent down to aid his fallen mate, only to pitch on top of him as the rudder obeyed the untended tiller and threw *Moby Dick* in the opposite direction.

In what had roughly been the centre of the circle before the flotilla had fled for its collective life, Luigi was preparing to dive. Peering below the surface through his mask, while Ariadne chugged gently from one position to the other, had been unrewarding, if absorbing. Sufficiently absorbing not to notice the commotion taking place at the circumference of the circle, some two hundred metres away.

Now tanked, masked and flippered, the intrepid Luigi sat on the inflated side of the dinghy, his back to the sea, ready to descend to the depths. He rather liked the macho feel of the equipment, the knife sheath strapped on his leg – truly, an Italian Cousteau of The Ionian. Ariadne, aware that their early exploration was unauthorized by the Skipper from Oz, gave the horizon a guilty scan.

It was not the absence of the main constituents of the flotilla which petrified her: it was the presence of the stern of a yacht, proudly displaying the legend *Ulysses V*, bearing down on the dinghy at full speed.

With that inherited presence of mind that her Ancient Greek ancestors had shown when confronted by the endless monsters of mythology, she tugged the outboard into life and steered desperately out of the path of the oncoming yacht, an astounded and enraged Luigi clinging limpet-like to the empty oarlock.

Moby Dick followed.

To Ted, whose binoculars were trained on the dinghy fleeing a reversing yacht at full throttle in hot pursuit, the spectacle was not unpleasing. Though his mental abilities might not be a source of envy for a wallaby, even Ted could figure out what Luigi and Ariadne had been up to, and why *Angela Mia* remained anchored while the others had bolted.

It was almost as though *Moby Dick* sensed what he was thinking. With the entire wide-open sea to choose from, she abruptly gave up the chase for the dinghy just as an adroit swerve from Ariadne finally broke Luigi's grip on the oarlock and threw him, uttering muffled howls down his airhose, into the sea. Ariadne cut the outboard, bringing the dinghy to rest above the bubbles that were Luigi. For once, she had to breathe deeply: being chased around the Ionian by a pilotless boat at full power in reverse was enough to quicken even Ariadne's pulse.

Darren, extricating himself from the flailing limbs of his father, leaned forward from a kneeling position and grabbed the widly-swinging tiller with one hand, grasped the throttle with the other, and shoved it upwards into neutral. Henceforth, his family would take seriously his ambition to play in goal for Leeds.

As he regained his feet, what had once been his Mohican again stood on end as *Moby Dick* closed in on *Angela Mia*.

Yanking hard on the tiller, he pushed it 180 degrees in the vain hope of turning the boat from its destined path. Still carried backwards by its own momentum, the yacht's stern appeared to hesitate, then clunked into the immaculate hull of Luigi's second most proud possession, at wheelhouse level. *Angela Mia* rocked hard to starboard, then swiftly righted herself by violently heaving to port, giving *Moby Dick* a handsome wallop in return.

Below deck, the jigsaw of limbs that belonged to Rosie and Sharon was joined by the *pater familias* as he somersaulted down the cabin steps and joined his women in a complicated Armitage jumble on the floor.

Moby Dick had finally rejoined the flotilla.

*   *   *

Life, according to most philosophies, has its ups and downs but for Oleg Grameshic Dhoni, downs seemed to have taken over for the present. Perhaps it was a consequence of living life in a locker.

As consciousness returned for the second time, Oleg's lips moved first. "Pic–cher your–self in ah boat by the riv–er with tan–ge–rine trees an' marmalade skies" were the mangled lyrics that were keened into the muffled darkness of the locker. Though the meaning might escape the concussed Albanian, the imagery was strangely appropriate. A star or two would have helped to complete the wavering scenes that floated before his mind's eye.

Gingerly gathering together the bits that he sensed belonged to him, each one possessed of a dull ache, he struggled to a kneeling position and ever so cautiously pushed against the lid. Oleg knew the value of experience.

The sound of a diesel engine at full throttle decided him. Being a castaway on an island had been a solitary enough existence, but living your life in a locker definitely had no appeal left at all. Oleg wanted out. He would give himself up: even the prospect of an Albanian prison cell seemed a happier choice than solitary confinement with intermittent concussion in a box. With grim determination, Oleg heaved forcefully at the lid, throwing it back upon its hinges. The fading afternoon sky was kind upon his red-rimmed eyes, the tears squeezed away by a few thankful blinks.

As he clambered onto the cockpit floor, he sought in his mind for an appropriate lyric by way of an introduction to the foreigners. By chance, or perhaps by some musical sixth sense, he again struck an appropriate note.

"Help me if you can, I'm feelin' down–n–n" he intoned in that curious whine he had learned from fading batteries, "and I do a–ppreciate you bein' round–nd–nd."

He stood erect, his head turning in the direction of the roaring diesel.

As if in response, the engine suddenly cut out. The ingratiating smile on Oleg's face froze as the stern of *Moby Dick* filled his vision, only a hand visible on her tiller.

There was just about room for another lump on Oleg's head, and *Moby Dick* obliged. As *Angela Mia* healed to the impact of the closing yacht, Oleg's unsteady legs were swept from under him and he flew backwards, a human cannonball, to tip over the side of the locker and descend, yet again, into its familiar interior.

As he strove to disentangle himself from the loving embrace of his erstwhile companions, *Angela Mia* righted herself and the locker lid teetered, held a vertical position just long enough for Oleg to raise his head, then slammed shut.

Destiny is a strange thing.

*   *   *

Calm spread its gossamer presence from star to star, from yacht to yacht.

The flotilla had regrouped, no longer in a circle but alongside each other, Ted's boat at one end of the row, Luigi's at the other. *Moby Dick* was sandwiched in the centre, bow, midship and stern roped, knotted and tethered on each side to her neighbouring boats, the ignition key to her diesel safely in Ted's possession. Thus safely corralled, everyone felt warmly secure and the atmosphere among the crews was easy, light, jocular – and triumphant. Even forgiving.

The treasure had been found.

After all the vicissitudes, the day had proven to be a tremendous success, a vindication of their decision to undertake the hunt, an absolutely gold–plated one helluva fantastic cracker of an ending to the day.

And now, here they were, crowded together on the decks of *Angela Mia* and *De Profundis*, toasting Jack Armitage as the Hero of the flotilla! Jack Armitage, the purveyor of doom, the maniac of the waves, the idiot of the Ionian, here they were raising glasses of Domestica to his continued health, even if that included skippering *Moby Dick*!

The wine, liberally shared even among the children for the toast, spread a warm and gently bobbing feeling that was echoed by the yachts, their cabin lights reflecting back from the rippling surface of the benign sea – the tinkling shrouds an apt musical accompaniment to the chatter, laughter and general bonhomie that spoke of the euphoria felt by Ted's flotilla.

And it *was* 'Ted's Flotilla'. Though the Gillicuddys and the Clawrers were absent, there was a generally accepted feeling that the boats made up a team, that it was a versatile, skilful and triumphant team, and that, as teams went, it was tops.

Ted basked in the warm glow of well-being, a man who had suffered much but had survived. Scarred a little, true, a bit more cynical, certainly, but a man for all that. He looked upon his team and he saw that it was good. So were the dishes of food that were being passed round, harvested from half-melted fridges, pulled from bags that had lain forgotten since their first day on board. The squidgy tomatoes, pongy bits of goat cheese, dried-out slices of smoked ham, hard chunks of spiced sausage, two Toblerones firmly stuck together, all the battered ingredients that made up the feast this night tasted like manna from heaven.

While it has to be admitted that, without Jack, Luigi

would not have been thrown out of his dinghy directly over the sunken artefacts, in all fairness it was the Italian who had located these mysteries of the deep. It was typical of a bunch of English and Germans to deny an Italian the credit. It was probably due to not having experienced a Renaissance.

Fortunately for Luigi, his airhose and mask had been in place as he was jerked from the side of the dinghy so that his sudden immersion in the Ionian and rapid descent courtesy of his tank and lead-weighted belt were more of an inconvenience than a catastrophy. Cursing down his airhose, he eased out of his rapid descent and peered through the murky glass of his face mask, to get his bearings from the dinghy.

Five metres above him was Ariadne's bottom – to be more specific, the black flattened floor of the dinghy. He trod water, feeling that he might as well start the search from where he was. Ariadne's unmasked face broke the surface of the water, just where his bubbles erupted. Macho as Luigi was, he couldn't compete with Ariadne who never used a face mask and scarcely needed a tank of air. He raised a thumb to her disembodied visage, peering down at him through the water like a celestial being on a Vatican ceiling, with her hair floating outwards.

The face left the sea, and he looked down below his paddling flippers. The sun was in decline, promising only one more hour of daylight at most. There was sufficient life left in the refracting rays to see down to the sea bed, less than ten metres below him, where sudden flurries of sand indicated the presence of some fishy denizen of the deep.

Luigi's eyes followed a shoal of small fish speeding along the sea floor. He searched back for the predator that must be pursuing them: apart from some isolated clumps of white and green rock, there was very little shelter for the hunted in these clear waters.

Luigi started.

He screwed up his eyes, his hand involuntarily sweeping across his mask as though to clear his sight.

Kicking his feet behind him, and kicking himself mentally

for not having his camera with him, he swam down towards the dark and shadowy shapes that had attracted his attention. His heart beating faster, his flippers flipping more frantically, he closed in on what was evidently not the kind of natural phenomenon normally found on the sea-bed.

It was their shape – there were three pillars, or containers, or something – that made them seem so out of place. If it hadn't been for their long, straightish lines, they could have been dismissed as simply shell-encrusted rock. But rock doesn't normally have a regular outline: it tends towards the lumpish; and two of the 'objects' appeared almost uniform in size, their colour a mixture of sea-bed pinks, greens and whites, with streaks of grey and black running amongst the shells and weed. They were oblong, about three metres in length and one metre wide.

The third object differed in size and colour, being almost entirely white. Smaller than the other two, it was also more square-shaped. Whatever it was made of had attracted marine life that displayed itself with uniformly white shells: there was virtually no other colour represented, as though the shells had been bleached.

Luigi was in no doubt that he had found the Flotilla Treasure. The boys, without masks or air, had recorded quite a faithful, if filmy, impression of what he now saw before him. Words of self-congratulation and speculation sped down the airhose, to be pumped to the surface as bubbles of excited Italian.

As he turned to surface, Luigi faced a quandary. To tell or not to tell? That was the unscrupulous question. Whether it was better to say nothing, lead the flotilla away from the discovery and return perhaps weeks later when they all had returned to suburbia, or to lead them through the sea of bubbles which marked the spot.

After the welcoming arm of Ariadne had hauled him back into the dinghy, Luigi made up his mind while divesting himself of his tank and mask. There was nothing to lose by revealing his find since he had taken the precaution of alerting his 'friends' on the Greek mainland. The desire for glory was in his blood and blood would out. He clasped Ariadne to his wet breast, an extremely pleasant experience on both sides, and ordered the return to *Angela Mia*, having first taken a bearing on the spot in relation to his yacht. For the moment, the heady excitement of the discovery drove the significance of the boat next to his own from his mind.

It was just as well for the Armitages that Luigi was so buoyed up with his personal triumph. As the purring outboard on the dinghy propelled the happy couple towards *Angela Mia*, their memory of the furious pursuit of *Moby Dick* was refreshed by the sight of the yacht itself lying alongside the sleek Italian craft. There probably wasn't a boat in the whole Ionian that wanted the Armitages as a next door neighbour.

Jack, under radio instructions from Ted, had managed to drop anchors fore and aft without holing either boat, not an inconsiderable feat since it was Rosie who flung out the stern anchor, barely missing the hull of Luigi's yacht.

There was a long gash in the paintwork of *Angela Mia*'s hull, and the name proudly lettered beneath the stern rail had been reduced to '..gel. .ia', giving the misleading impression that Luigi was running a floating ice-cream parlour. Forgetting, in the heat of the moment, to remove his flippers, the enraged Italian had slipped and slithered up his stern ladder and stood in his cockpit like a furious frog cursing the incompetence of mad Englishmen who shouldn't be let loose with a paper boat in a paddling pool.

The arrival of the rest of the flotilla had restored sufficient peace and harmony – together with a muttered promise from Jack that he would see the Italian alright over the small matter of a cosmetic repair – to enable Luigi to make his dramatic announcement.

Waiting until all the boats had been anchored together in line, with a dramatic sunset as a backcloth for his epic performance, Luigi had taken up his loudhailer.

"Ladies and–a Gentlemen."

Heads appeared from galleys, ropes ceased to be coiled, shower bags stopped sprinkling.

"Ladies and–a Gentlemen."

Luigi stood on his foredeck, the gold crucifix nestled among the hairs on his chest sparkling in the reflected lights from the almost stationary yachts.

"I 'ave found it, the – ah – treasure."

He paused for dramatic effect, like any good tenor before hitting an aria.

He was rewarded by a momentary silence followed by an electrified jabbering. Waiting for the crackle of questions to die down, he proceeded.

"They are there, as the– the boys 'ave been telling, these–a treasures. They are, ah, somethings, I donna know. All, all 'ave on them many conchiglias, many sh– shellas, many – ah –feeshes 'ave made–a houses on them, but, sure, they are dropped on the bottom of the, ah, sea from men."

Again he waited as his words were interpreted and passed along the crowded decks, eventually spilling into Ted's indignant ears.

He worked his way from one boat to another, eventually reaching *De Profundis* with the help of a heave from Jürgen's beefy arm.

"Yer – yer've got a nerve," he panted, leaning against Jürgen's mighty paunch for support, "I told yer to wait for us, *we're* the flertilla, we didn't ask no blow-in to take over...

Luigi raised his hands in a conciliatory gesture.

"Ted, Ted, issa not my thinking to find one thing, I looka for fish for eating, you aska my Ariadne, eh?"

As no one apart from Luigi was capable of asking Ariadne anything, there was not likely to be any contradiction. She nodded vigorously to a voluble burst of Italian and made hand-gestures signifying the catching, cooking and consuming of a fish. It was not, perhaps, very convincing but it was prettily done and the audience appreciated the charade.

"It was 'im, the papa of the *bella ragazza*," Luigi was pointing out Jack who put a proprietary hand on the posing *ragazza*'s shoulder. "'E was the one issa finding it, 'e make–a me fall out and find it, eh? So maybe we should be makin' the–a thanks to 'im, to the papa. *Si?*"

It was an adroit move to share the glory with an accredited member of the flotilla, even if the most discredited among them. It brought a ripple of applause from the crews.

"I say, Ted, that's rather sporting, you know," said Crispin St Clair. "I mean, we've only got two days left and we might simply have gone home without ever knowing if we'd just wasted our time. Now, well, now it's quite splendid."

He peered across the shadowed heads in Jack's direction.

"Well done, Jack," he shouted generously. "A bit unorthodox, what, to lead a treasure hunt backwards and chuck your diver chappie into the old briney, but jolly effective just the same. I say three cheers for Jack Armitage – and for good old Luigi here. And for our skipper for leading us and – and entering into the spirit of the thing. Hip, hip!"

And like an assembly in the school hall, the flotilla members chorused a dutiful hurrah, more a tribute to Crispin's diplomacy than any heartfelt gratitude to Jack. Even Ted joined in, however uncertainly: though he had the suspicion he had just received the rough end of a pineapple and would have preferred to chuck a browneye, any objections on his part would now make him out to be an absolute piker.

*   *   *

And so tranquillity reigned once more among all the crews comfortably and companionably reclining on any available space on board *De Profundis* and *Angela Mia*. More bottles were emptied, genial jokes and anecdotes were exchanged, and even moans were stifled when Ted decided it was time to fetch his guitar.

Sudden flashes of white light followed Julie's ample figure as her camera shutter busily recorded photographs of this historic eve of the raising of the artefacts. She felt that Bernie hugged Liz and Lorraine unnecessarily close for their shot and that the one of Gerhard offering Sally a peeled banana in

176

a disgustingly suggestive way would not find its way into her album, but the family groupings, like the Warbelows, were nice – even if Monika did seem a little out of place with an arm draped around Eric.

Practicalities had been discussed, such as how to raise the 'objects' to the surface. If, as Crispin conjectured, they were stone or marble from a temple, they were going to need quite some lifting. *Angela Mia* was equipped with electric anchor winches, both fore and aft, but they would hardly be sufficient to lift such huge weights – and transport them.

Luigi appeared unruffled by the problem. He knew someone on the shore who could get the appropriate equipment and could be trusted, he had not the slightest doubt, not to make off with the booty. Besides, he declared, what he had seen on the sea-bed might be some form of containers: they had a box-like look. The first thing to do was to wrap a steel hawser around one of them, replace an anchor with a grappling hook, and give it a try.

This approach to the problem being deemed practicable, the company gave themselves up to the pleasures of the warm night and settled into soporific harmony, regaling each other with only slightly exaggerated accounts of their recent experiences.

Ted reappeared, stumbling onto *De Profundis*' deck with his guitar clutched to his 'Bondi Beach Bum' T-shirt.

"I've jest copped an earful from the others," he announced, turning with his guitar and slamming it against the back of Darren's head.

"Oops, sorry, young Darren. Well, it was Flora Gillicuddy, sayin' they're comin' to join us. Seems they tried sailin' with the Ya – with the Clawrers but they split up pretty well from the start. 'Parently that Steven an' Flora fell out over just about everythin' an' he offered Hamish a poke in the snoot so that was that."

Ted didn't seem unduly surprised.

"Anyway, both – er – *Thistle* and *The Bounty* are together now, they've holed up fer the night at Parga an' are comin' over first thing. Should have told Flora you can take a barge trip there, I mean at Parga, an' visit Hades, what those old Greeks thought was Hell. Mind you," he mused, flicking back his blond quiff, "she's probably already been there an' back, ha, ha!"

Nobody quite caught on to the joke but there was a ripple of polite laughter: any effort on the part of Ted's brain deserved encouragement.

Sidney Chippendale, whose thighs obligingly provided a pillow each for the sleeping Lucien and Arabella, chimed in.

"They weren't exactly encouraging, you know, or supportive, for that matter. They insisted on going their own way. Now they're coming back when we've done all the work..."

He left the thought to hover over those who were still listening.

Sally welcomed the opportunity to move away from Gerhard who was trying to pop polished grapes into her mouth. She knew where they were being polished.

"I don't think it really matters, do you?" she asked, picking her way over to the protection of Ted. "We're all part of the same flotilla – it'll be nice to share tomorrow with them, particularly if they haven't exactly enjoyed themselves, won't it?"

"Some buggers don't know how to enjoy themselves," opinioned Jack. He was wedged comfortably against Rosie's slithery shell-suit on the locker seat in Luigi's cockpit. "Still 'n' all, what's the odds, let 'em join in. Can't see as 'ow we could stop 'em, anyroads."

And another beaker of Domestica slid down his throat.

"That's settled, then," said a relieved Ted. "I gave them our position so we couldn't have done anything anyway."

There were some who thought that any position given by Ted was unlikely to be the right one, but mean thoughts on such an evening were not entertained for long.

Ted edged between Trudy and Darren, causing a momentary unclasping of hands, and pushed the sliding hatch over the companionway with his sandaled foot. Squating down, he dangled his bare legs over the edge into the cockpit, brought his guitar to the ready and beamed at the huddled occupants in the sterns of both yachts. Behind him, stealthy movements suggested that those lucky enough to be out of range of Ted's cheerful gaze were making sure their ears were out of range of his dulcet tones.

"Well, this is pucker, don'tcha think?" enquired the happy skipper, accepting a beaker of wine from Sally who crept up beside him. It was a measure of her support that, knowing the limitations of Ted's repertoire and appreciation of the finer points of singing, she was still prepared to sit within earshot, even if she did bury her head between her smoothly gleaming knees.

"What's it to be, then? Anyone care to suggest a ditty?"

Sharon, tucked between the cushioned softness of Elke König and the boniness of Arnold's over–heated body, looked up evilly at Ted from the shadows of the cockpit.

"How about *Get the Funk Outta Here?*" she suggested maliciously, then hurriedly averted her eyes as she realized she was looking right up Ted's shorts.

Sharon was bored, bored to death with sailing, bored to death with her family, and rapidly becoming bored to death with Arnold. Despite Crispin's well–intentioned attempts, at various calm intervals during the holiday, to interest her in the finer points of yachting, she'd had her fill of ropes and wires being called 'sheets' and 'shrouds', of 'heaving to' and 'huffing up'. Sharon was thoroughly huffed up.

She plucked the inoffensive Snubsy, who had shared Nelson's fate and lost an eye in the course of duty, from her lap and plonked him in Arnold's crutch. His remaining eye looked as shocked as plastic would permit at what it observed.

A 'tut-tut' from Rosie stole from the *Angela Mia* but Ted refused to be shaken by her request

"Not sure I know that one, Sharon. Doesn't sound like we could all hollah the chorus, though."

He strummed one of the three chords with which he was reasonably familiar.

"Anyone else?"

There was a pause as addled heads tried to come up with a mercifully short song.

Then hauntingly, eerily, and startlingly came a reply.

"It's been ah–hard day's night..."

A chill descended on the listeners. Ted's hand remained poised over the guitar strings.

The strange whining monotone, at once muffled and echoey, continued.

"...An' I've been wer–kin' like ah doh–oh–og..."

A solitary cloud stole softly across the face of the moon, dimming the reflected light from the gentle sea. No one spoke. Silence, save for a ghostly tinkling from the shrouds, a groaning from the hulls as they nudged each other for comfort.

Tap! Tap! Tap!

To those familiar with the movie *Moby Dick*, particularly the Armitages, the image of Cap'n Ahab stumping restlessly and relentlessly on a dark creaking deck came forcefully to mind. Gregory Peck's performance may have been as wooden as his leg, but critical analysis is inevitably in short supply when in the middle of the dark Ionian sea, at dead of night, with a disembodied voice hollowly exhorting a request.

Bernie, snugly pillowed by his three nurses on the coachroof of *Angela Mia*, became aware of a certain tension as his sirens sat bolt upright causing his head to contact the topping–lift with a sharp crack.

"What – what are – who...?"

He looked around, indignantly rubbing his head. His questions were echoed in the minds of everyone else, but Bernie had heard nothing other than the generally confused melée of sound, now conspicuously absent. The party was evidently petering out: it needed a bit of cheering up.

"Come on, Ted," he encouraged, "you're not *that* bad."

As the moon returned its benign beams to join those from the yachts' lights, Bernie was taken aback by Ted's horror-struck face, eyebrows raised and mouth open like a conjurer about to produce a stream of ribbon.

Thump! Thump! Thump!

"How about," said Bernie, determined to get things going, "how about *Roll me over, lay me down and do it again?*"

It was, he admitted to himself, a bit naughty but the kids seemed pretty well asleep and the rest of them, well, they all looked a bit gob–smacked.

Nobody seemed inclined to roll themselves over, let alone lay themselves down and do it again. Their preference was, apparently, to sit petrified with stricken countenances and rigid limbs.

Bang! Bang! BANG!

It was Rosie who broke the silence.

"JACK!" she shrieked, "Jack, it's comin' from you!"

"Wharrer..." spluttered the shaken Jack, just as he and Rosie were raised a couple of inches into the air, to plump heavily down with a snap of the locker lid.

"Yaaargh!" screamed Rosie, "It's a poltergeist!"

Luigi jumped up from the opposite locker seat, crossed himself, and began mumbling an Act of Contrition. However piratical by instinct, it just didn't do to take chances with the supernatural.

The rest of the crews had risen with one accord, as though summoned by a voice from the deep – children grasping adults, adults grasping each other. Gerhard grasped Sally.

But Bernie was immune to ghostly visitations.

"That locker – that one, Jack, what you're both on – the lid just moved. I saw it – the seat was just pushed up. There's someone in it. Someone just pushed up the lid."

Jack and Rosie rarely moved with the speed of light; it was not one of their natural attributes. But Daley Thompson could not have improved upon their performance as, in the blink of a Bernie eye, they leapt from a seated position to a rigid standing embrace like a pair of overweight figure skaters.

Slowly, tentatively, the locker lid raised inch by inch; so did the hair on the backs of the collective heads of the onlookers, their eyes riveted to the widening gap. Sidney Chippendale's bald pate was incapable of raising any hair:

instead, beaded drops of sweated fear gathered on his glistening dome, like dribbles of candle wax falling on an egg.

A spectral hand materialized, caught in the yellowish light which shone up the companionway, to be followed by a brown and hairy arm. With a final thrust, the arm propelled the lid back against the handrail, and the hand groped forward to grip the front of the locker.

A second hand, similar to the other save for the reverse order of digits, stole over to join its mate.

Only a little mew of horror from Rosie gave evidence of life among the flotilla crews, their eyes glued to the shadowed interior of the locker from which came sound of shuffling, clanking, and low moans of effort.

And then... the head. *The* head. A head from which long snakes grew, like tendrils, twisting and struggling, around a face whose features were smeared with dark stains, whose mouth lolloped open in an insane grin.

"I don't know why– you say goodbye–" intoned the head, "I say 'el–lo."

Oleg Grameshic Dhoni shook away the coils of rope clinging round his head and gave Rosie an ingratiating smile. But it was too late for Rosie to be won over: Rosie had hit the deck.

CHAPTER TEN

Eric faces the unknown. Ted faces his conscience. Penny leads an on-shore expedition. *The Bounty* and *Thistle* rejoin the flotilla. A sense of strained relations. The mood lifts as the treasure is raised. Georgiou Komoulides invites himself to the celebration.

The Warbelows, as a family, were no less transfixed by the apparition ascending from Luigi's locker than any other member of the flotilla. Grouped in front of the mast of *De Profundis*, they had a grandstand view of the unfolding events lit by the strange combination of an ethereal moonlight and the yellow glow from the cabins, with shadows thrown by the shrouds leaving curious striped lines across the frozen faces of the spectators.

Penny's arms had automatically encompassed her brood, drawing the three children together in front of her as though in a defensive scrum. There was no objection: nothing in their previous experience, not even the occasional horror video smuggled into the house by Mark when parents were safely out for the evening, could have prepared them for ghostly imbeciles rising out of black holes, gurgling incomprehensible laments.

For Eric, it was a different proposition: still smarting from his attempted 'rescue' of Monika from drowning, despite the sympathetic but condescending kiss she had plonked on his cheek by way of gratitude, any possibility of showing that he was the man who could be depended upon to rise to the occasion just *had* to be embraced.

Monika, the dried–out hat back in place, stood in the bow of *Angela Mia*, looking not unlike a spectre herself, draped in a long robe of some flimsy material which lightly swayed to the rare gentle breeze, outlining the sinuous figure that had taken them all by surprise. Her arm was extended dramatically, the graceful hand with index finger extended, pointing over Bernie's shoulder at the astounding Albanian.

It was enough. Though Eric's bowels gave a hint of reacting to shock, this was a man who had something to prove. When you're heading for the half-century, you want to show you've still got it, particularly if you're not sure that you ever did have it.

With a half-strangled cry that was meant to express defiance, aggression and, more to the point, self-encouragement, Eric leapt to the side deck, bounded over both guard rails, and threw himself into *Angela Mia*'s cockpit with such force that Jack collided with Luigi and tumbled into the astounded lap of Ariadne, the only person still seated in the entire flotilla. As her view of Oleg had been obstructed by the ample rears of Rosie and Jack, Ariadne was relatively unphased by the unexpected vision of a spook: besides, Luigi's sudden appeals for forgiveness to his particular deity were a common occurrence in times of stress.

Eric confronted Oleg. Oleg confronted Eric. Each was gripped with a deep sense of dismay. For Oleg, this white-socked, wild-eyed being which appeared to have dropped from outer space uttering mangled whoops did not signify the warm welcome he had been hoping for.

"*Koreshki gruniria selspr*," greeted Oleg tentatively, the Albanian equivalent in dialect of 'have a happy day'. More literally, it meant 'may your productivity in the factory today reach new heights' but the sentiments were roughly the same since a low productivity rate meant a *decidedly* unhappy one.

Eric was nonplussed. Without the wig–like adornment of the mooring ropes, Oleg looked distinctly unthreatening, rather like, in fact, an unkempt and bearded stowaway.

Eric remained rooted to the spot, his guard up in the traditional boxing defence he had assumed in the playground whenever, as a child, he had felt obliged to stand 'toe to toe'. Invariably, his opponent had simply socked him one in the gut or, equally despicably, had kicked him hard on the knee. But rules were rules, and the Marquis of Queensbury was not to be scorned.

"*Doblineska virinneski pretr*," added Oleg hopefully. Eric had never been involved in the manufacture of bicycles so this pleasing allusion to the bonus of an inner tyre for exceeding the month's quota somewhat escaped him, but he recognized the friendly and optimistic tone of the overture.

His doubled fists unclenched and he found himself, hand outstretched, replying "Good evening, I don't think we've actually been introduced."

Their hands touching uncertainly; the spell which had held Eric's companions in thrall was broken. The tension gripping the entire flotilla fled as Oleg, now manifestly a human being albeit a weird and unexpected one, climbed out of the locker and stood over the recumbent form of Rosie Armitage.

As blood flowed back into the members of the flotilla who began to crowd onto *Angela Mia* in force, Eric experienced the wamth of acclaim, Crispin's "Jolly good, Eric, old chap, right man at the right time" ringing in his ears.

Rosie, surrounded by a forest of legs, regained what passed for consciousness.

"Jack," she whispered plaintively. "'Ee looks just like your mother when you told 'er I was in the family way."

And Jack, cradling his Rosie in his arms, could only agree.

*   *   *

After such a late night, it was hardly surprising that the sun had been up a few hours before life stirred aboard the line of anchored yachts.

Even Ted, so prompt to face the rising dawn with the stirrings of an instinctive appetite, lay with his mouth nuzzled into the back of Sally's neck, an arm stretched protectively over her bare sun-glazed shoulder.

Ulysses X rocked as Penny Warbelow came on board, the gentle motion sending echoing ripples through the neighbouring hulls. Ted, his subconscious prodded by the delicate rhythm of the sway, began to feel those old familiar promptings as the warmth of Sally's bottom pressing firmly into his groin beckoned him to a new day.

"Ted," called Penny, down the open companionway, "Ted!"

"Hmmnnn," responded Ted with a wide range of responses.

"Ted," persisted Penny, "are you awake?"

A poke in the groin from a sharp elbow produces an amazing clarity and freshness of mind, as Ted now became aware. Turning onto his stomach, he slid back the cabin door and smiled that engaging Antipodean smile at the face peering down the steps.

"About right, Penny, I am too. How about you, you feelin' pucker after last night? Why don'tcha come down those stairs, save yerself some hollerin'."

"Fine. I didn't want to drag you to the radio or wake anyone who didn't need to get up."

Penny came down into the main saloon. She looked fresh and crisp in a blue button–up denim dress and sandals, rather more than was customarily needed for a day's sailing.

"Strewth, Penny, ye're all dressed up like a pox doctor's clerk. Hang around a second while I get the strides in place."

Penny laughed.

"I never believed Aussies really said things like 'strewth' and 'strides', Ted. I thought all that was for *Neighbours*, thrown in for the Brits."

Ted scrambled out of the fore cabin, both strided and strewthed.

"Well, yer know, if I didn't just be a *bit* Aussie, yer know...?

"Oh, I know."

Penny was irritated to find herself blushing, like a girl on her first date, as Ted cast around the saloon for a garment to cover his well–proportioned pectorals. A fleeting memory of that erotic dream, where Eric had assumed the body of Ted and vigorously made love to her wearing only his white socks, jabbed into her mind.

Brusquely, she came to the point.

"Some of us have decided to go ashore for a few hours. We want to, well, just go to a bar and have a fresh shower and a walk, and just be on dry land."

"And we'll pick up some food. Fresh bread. Mmmm. Fruit. Some ham, something yummy. I've made a list. We'll only be a few hours."

"Yeh, well, fine, no problems. So who's goin'? And how?"

Sally, peering through the doorway, called out over Ted's shoulder.

"Penny, Penny, I'd like to join you. Is that OK? We all need some things and I know where we can get them. Have you thought of how to get over to the mainland?”

“Hi, Sally. Yes, Luigi’s lending us his dinghy, the one with the outboard. We’ll be there in two ticks. There’s Tara and her two, and Trudy – the boys won’t come in case they miss anything – Elke and, oh yes, of course, Arnold, Rosie and whatsisname, Darren, and – and I think that’s it.”

Sally climbed out of the cabin, a tumble of shiny-brown legs, wild black locks and soft inviting breasts nearly concealed by a flowered kimono.

“We’ll need more than one dinghy. We can take ours as well, can’t we, Ted? We don’t need to have the outboard here.”

Ted thought, fortunately not a lengthy process.

“Can’t see as how that would give us any hardship. Maybe – no, maybe not.”

“Maybe what?” queried Sally, plonking a kiss on his cheek as she pushed past him to the galley. “Coffee, Penny?”

Penny accepted while Ted continued, pulling on his quiff to aid the brain patterns that lay behind his complex thought processes.

“It doesn’t matter. I was thinkin’ of that bloke, the one with a face like a stunned mullet we found in Luigi’s locker, I was thinkin’ maybe we should drop him on the coast over there. He’d be sort of in Greece an’ in Albania, he could take his pick. Go right or left. Leastways, he wouldn’t be *our* problem.”

As Sally splashed boiling water over the instant coffee, she glanced at Penny and was reassured that they were both thinking along the same lines

“We can’t do that. We *know* he’s Albanian, even if he only talks – sort of talks – in Beatle songs. I mean, he must have got on board Luigi’s yacht somehow, maybe he *swam* all the way from the coast, and you don’t do that unless it’s pretty awful where you come from.”

They sat on the bunks, Sally and Penny opposite Ted, eyeing him over the steaming coffee mugs.

Ted looked worried. His brow developed a furrow. The furrow developed a frown. It was a slow process.

"Sal, we've got ter think of the Flertilla. If we should be found with an illegal immigrant by the Greeks – or, worse still, one of their own by the Albanians, it would be worse than – worse than – worse than a banger goin' off up a frog's arse!"

Penny looked thoughtfully into her coffee mug. She received no immediate impression of the possible result of a banger going off as suggested, but the expression did carry a certain graphic force.

"Is there much chance of either of those things happening, Ted? I don't mean the frog, I mean the Greeks or Albanians discovering that poor man. I thought, anyway, we all agreed last night that we'd drop him off in Corfu on the way home. That's less than forty-eight hours."

Ted leaned on the screwed-down table and endeavoured to screw down his concerns.

"I *know* we said that last night, Penny, but I've been thinkin'."

He paused to let this sink in.

"We're goin' ter lift this stuff hopefully terday. We don't know what it is. That Luigi, he's as crooked as a dog's hind leg, we've gotta watch out fer him. We're goin' ter get it back to Corfu and announce it, declare it or whatever yer do that makes it all official, all in two days, right? An' now we've got this – this refugee, I suppose, an' who needs more problems? Besides, we're as near as a pee up a drainpipe to Albania an' we *don't* want to get involved with that little bunch of cowboys."

Sally gave him a hard look.

"Are you really saying that we should dump him, Ted?"

"Not *dump* him, Sal, I'm not sayin' that. Sort of *release* him."

Sally's mug banged down on the table, splashing coffee dregs on Ted's salt-white strides.

"I never thought – Ted, he's got nothing. Nothing. And he trusts us. You were among the first to start slapping him on the back, when we got over the shock. You stood up to Luigi – *he* wanted to throw him overboard there and then.

Oh no, give the poor bugger a chance, you said. You even got Jürgen to put him in their spare bunk. He's probably there now, having frankfurters for breakfast, thinking he's among friends."

Ted raised his hands in surrender.

"OK, OK, ye're right, Sally, we'll keep him with us."

He reached over the table to grasp her hand.

"It's the flertilla, ye know, the licence an' all. The company couldn't operate if they lost their licence and we'd – well, we'd be out of a job. I *like* this job. I've never sort of been good at anything much before and this, well..."

Penny gave him the reassurance he was seeking.

"And you're good at this one, Ted. We couldn't ask for a nicer skipper."

Ted beamed happily.

"Penny, ye're a pearler, a real beaut!"

He got to his feet with a manly slap of his thighs.

"I had a bit too much of that snake's piss last night. That Domestica. Makes yer feel jumpy. Course we'll keep him, what did Crisp call'm, Oh Leg. What a label! Oh Leg. We'll drop 'im off in Mengalissi – an' if Luigi says a word, he can choof off."

"Fair dinkum, Ted," smiled Penny. "Sally, the others should be ready. We thought we'd probably only take a couple of hours so we won't miss any of the excitement. Alright?"

Sally, giving her robust hero a swift hug, agreed and climbed back into the fore cabin to search for something suitable to wear in a Greek grocery store.

*   *   *

With Sally at the tiller of one outboard, and Darren at the other, the two well-filled dinghies headed for the coast, a chug of about twenty minutes. Sally had only been to Thessadikios once before, and had not been overly impressed, but there was a store of a kind and it would only take a further fifteen minutes walk from the coast to reach it.

At the last minute, Clara Chippendale had decided to join them, necessitating a judicious distribution of weight between the two boats. Darren's dinghy had drawn the short straw and it was noticeable that their craft was both lower in the water and slower than Sally's. Nonetheless, high spirits prevailed and even Darren forebore from surly remarks as he peered over Clara's plump shoulders and pursued Sally's wake.

They just missed the arrival of *The Bounty* and *Thistle*.

The two yachts tied alongside *Ulysses X* and the flotilla was complete for the first time since they had left Abeliki. That relations were strained between the late arrivals was soon evident although Flora and Amy appeared to have struck up a semblance of friendship – or solidarity.

It was Steven who remained below deck while the others fraternized on Ted's yacht. Angus and Angie were disappointed that the St Clair's children had headed for the mainland; they had had their full quota of adult company in confined quarters for some time. They sat despondently and palely in the bow of *Ulysses X*, wearing miserable expressions and equally miserable sun-evading hats, dropping bits of Ted's only jigsaw into the sea in the hope of attracting a vicious-minded shark.

"Some of it," said Amy brightly, determined to put a cheerful face on things, "was okay, huh?"

She turned to Flora for assent, but the latter looked meaningfully at Hamish's nose which outshone the rest of his off-white countenance. Having nearly acquired a tan, Hamish had reverted to his fish-like pallor. When you receive a poke in the snoot from a short-tempered American, you tend to sulk in your bunk.

"So did yer like Parga?" asked Ted, diplomatically breaking into the silence.

"Where?" enquired Flora coldly.

"Parga," replied Ted, the fount of amiability.

"Oh, *Parga*! I thought you said 'Paaguh'."

"Yeh, Parga. Lively little number, eh?"

Ted was used to misinterpretation of his impeccable

Greek accent.

Flora made a grimace.

"No, not really. It was full of English yobbos swilling beer and stupid pop music blaring out of discos."

"Yeh," said Ted, recalling happy memories, "that's the place.

"Oh, sure, I thought it kinda quaint," recalled Amy, drawing her chequered mou-mou tightly around her considerable hips.

"All those little houses, an' those Greeks breakin' dishes, 'cept when our waiter broke Steven's by mistake; he was liftin' up the table to balance it, hey, that was crazy, on his chin and Steven's plate slipped off and all that *moussaka* fell on Steven's new trousers; he'd just bought them in this real local place, tiny it was, yeh, it was called 'Beneton' though I said to Steven I guess that ain't no native joint..."

She faltered as she recalled the waiter's brothers closing in on her husband and the Clawrers and Gillicuddys racing for the ferry to take them safely back to their yachts.

"Did'ya ever see *Marco and His Brothers?*" she questioned ruminatively. "I was their only sister and was – was *despoiled* by this foreigner and they get ahold of him, and..."

Again she broke off abruptly. Amy's tan had already been in evidence before she joined the flotilla and had now acquired a leathery map-like patina, but it seemed to fade visibly as her jaw hung loose and her eyes pushed forward beneath their contact lenses. Her yellow-blond tresses might have stood on end if they had not been braided, Hollywood-Greek style, around her head.

"Sweet Jesus," she gasped. But it wasn't. It was Oleg.

Oleg regarded her without recognition. Even beneath the stars, a man who had been as hungry for a woman as Oleg had been could be forgiven if the other half of a brief encounter had been the sum of her parts rather than individual entities. A starving man will eat his fill, regardless of whether the meat is lamb or beef [Ancient Greek proverb.]

"Zo," said Jürgen who had accompanied Oleg onto Ted's yacht, "vee haf made him some Frü–, some breakfast. He has eated everything, like a vale."

If Oleg bore resemblance to a whale, it was a skeletal whale with an ragged beard and red–rimmed eyes but the 'vale' grinned cheerily, clad in a pair of Arnold's shorts: even those needed a safety pin to hold them up.

"Zer is no – understanding – as vith us," reported Jürgen expansively, "but I am liking him. I am thinking he is okay."

And he placed a meaty arm around Oleg's shoulders.

Amy rose dramatically, arm extended from a capacious sleeve.

"That guy, that guy was on Abeliki," she said in a voice cracking with emotion.

This observation was greeted with silence.

"Can't be," answered Ted, shaking his head. "We found him last night, in Luigi's – the Eyetie – locker. He doesn't speak the lingo 'cept fer some songs but we reckoned he must have got onto the *Angela Mia* when we were searchin' for the sunken stuff."

"Which you've found. I haven't congratulated you. Congratulations."

Steven had arrived on deck unnoticed. Though the sun was spreading its predictable heat in the cloudless sky, a chill seemed to settle over *Ulysses X*. Hamish's hand unconsciously cupped his swollen beak, as if to protect it from further assault.

"So," continued the unsettling American, "we have a stowaway. And you've met him before, Amy? Did you say on Abeliki?"

Amy gulped.

"He just looked sorta familiar."

Steven looked around, a malicious smile lighting the fuse of trouble.

"Sorta familiar. You seemed so definite. Anyone else see this guy on Abeliki? Must have been around, say, barbecue time as we were all together before that."

No answer.

Oleg, sensing some degree of mystification and feeling that he ought to contribute something other than his fixed grin, remarked "It's seesy – all yuh need is love."

By now he was used to the effect of his store of Beatle lyrics on his audience. Whatever their meaning, the reaction was immediate – puzzlement, vague recollection and, most importantly, amusement. Oleg liked to be the life and soul of the party.

Amy's reaction was gratifyingly vehement.

"Oh My Ga–a–d, it *is* him!"

Steven unceremoniously thrust Oleg aside and confronted Amy.

"Him who?" he asked, ungrammatically but belligerently.

Before the stunned star of many a filmed dramatic showdown could answer, there was a stentorian hail from below the hull.

Luigi, surrounded by hawsers, ropes and diving equipment, was in a dinghy borrowed from *De Profundis*, with Arnold at the oars.

"Eh, Ted, let's go, eh? You no longa wanna find the treasure, no? We are all a–ready, Ariadne issa bringing *Angela Mia*. You look, all of them are in the dinghies, come on–n!"

And sure enough, Eric and his two sons, Jack and an almost excited Sharon, Bernie and his three nurses, and Crispin St Clair who had gallantly allowed Sidney Chippendale to take his oars, were all following in the wake of Ariadne.

"Too right," yelled back Ted, then turned to the others on his deck. "This is it. If we're goin' to hump the bluey, it's now or never. Let's cut the crap and get over there."

Even Steven had to cut the crap as there was a general move to join the rest of the intrepid explorers. The dark look he directed at both Amy and Oleg suggested a resumption of his interrogation, but he would have to wait.

There were more important matters at hand.

"Jürgen, Sally's got my outboard. Can yer give me a lift over there with my kit?"

Jürgen looked at the departing Luigi, shouting incomprehensible orders to his son.

"*Nein*, Luigi has mine. I think vee get anuzzer, ja, I call Gerhard, he is with only himself."

As Gerhard pulled away from *Becker*, he responded to the call from his fellow countryman and rowed over obligingly. After Ted had dropped his scuba gear into the dinghy, he and Jürgen climbed in.

Ted looked up at the others still on board his yacht.

"Come on, you lot," he encouraged. "Get yer dinghy, Hamish, pile in. Let's get the game by the throat, eh? Steven, you an' Amy, why don'tcha stick old Oh Leg inta yours, alright? Right, Gerhard, let's get motorin'!"

And as Gerhard got motoring, the ever–tactful Ted left a curious silence behind him.

*　　*　　*

The operation to raise the curious oblongs from the sea bed proceeded with more ease than anyone dared hope.

Ted, Luigi and Gerhard were the divers, decided after Eric had made his first attempt to cope with an aqualung, resulting in a too-speedy descent and a mild attack of the bends. It had taken the combined attention of Flora and Jürgen to unbend him and it was agreed to use those most experienced in scuba diving. Though the depth was not great, and the wavering shapes of the divers could be observed and encouraged by those on the surface, there seemed little point in presenting Penny, still on the Greek mainland, with the corpse of Eric on return.

Mark and Alan rowed their father to *Becker* where Monika assisted in hauling him aboard, taking care not to snag his Marks & Spencer swimming trunks. The boys returned to the hunt, satisfied that the massage which Monika was applying to Eric's contorted limbs as he lay in Gerhard's bunk would do the trick.

To their surprise, the international under-sea expedition found that the oblongs shifted more easily than their

195

appearance warranted. While Gerhard and Ted lifted the first from one end, Luigi slipped a metal hawser underneath the shell-encrusted block and returned to the surface.

Ariadne attached the looped ends of the hawser to the electric winch of the bow anchor and repeated the manoeuvre at the stern when Luigi had secured the second hawser.

This was the most delicate part of the whole affair. If the block should prove too heavy, if the winches pulled too fast, if the hawsers should give way, disaster would be the result.

As Luigi signalled to his partners to swim clear, the rowers moved the dinghies away to a safe distance from *Angela Mia*. The rubber boats bobbed with anticipation, their occupants staring fixedly and anxiously at the electric winches.

Bernie stood at the bow winch, Ariadne at the stern. Liz, Julie and Lorraine each held an emergency first–aid kit, poised to apply surgical tape to any part of Bernie's anatomy that should suffer a scratch.

At a nod from Ariadne to Bernie, the winches were set in motion. The hawsers tightened, gripped, then wound slowly around the fly-wheels with a metallic whine.

Under water, Gerhard placed a restraining hand on Ted's shoulder, waving a warning finger in front of his mask to prevent Ted swimming forward to the visibly-moving oblong.

From the dinghies, all eyes switched to the frothing bubbles which indicated the position of the divers.

"There, there, look!"

The concerted cries from Mark and Alan were not necessary: every head was turned towards the streaming shape, its carapace of shell and coral reflecting pinks, blue and greens in the sunlight, rising to the surface, bedecked with weed and trailing flotsam.

The squealing winches continued to haul effortlessly and, though *Angela Mia* leaned slightly, there seemed to be no danger of her being pulled over by the added weight.

Another nod from Ariadne, and the winches fell silent.

Slung between the hawsers, hanging amidship at the side

of *Angela Mia*, was what could have passed for Neptune's coffin. That it was some sort of container was now obvious; if it had been a solid pillar, as Crispin had conjectured, it would not have arisen with such facility to the surface.

Water poured not only from the outside but more evidently from the inside, flooding from the angular lines of its base. The underneath, which had been embedded in sand on the sea floor, was a dull grey streaked with red: in the centre were sporadic slashes of white.

The three divers surfaced almost simultaneously, and made for the nearest dinghy, Crispin's.

Sidney was the first to squeak.

"It's a container, a box of some sort. A *metal* box. That's metal, you can see it underneath, you can see the rivets."

"*Si*," gasped Luigi, hanging with one arm onto the side of the dinghy, "we can see it with all our eyes."

He felt that Sidney's bald statement lacked excitement.

Crispin fought to hide his disappointment. All his hopes of discovering classical antiquities had faded. Whatever the thing was, it certainly belonged to a more recent past.

He looked down at Luigi's glistening head.

"The others – under the sea – they're the same?"

"They are the same–a, maybe one a leetle beet smaller but, *si*, I theenk are as this one–a."

Ted's head bobbed up between Crispin and Sidney from the other side of the dinghy.

"Whaddya reckon, Crisp, have we fished out one of them marbles?"

The other dinghies were cautiously edging towards the enigmatic oblong for a closer look.

Crispin heaved Ted's air tank aboard as the three swimmers hauled themselves into the dinghy, almost pushing it below the surface.

"I don't honestly believe that we have found anything of *archaeological* interest, Ted. I've no idea what it is – or what it might contain. From what we can see, it may not be that old – if it really is metal and hasn't rusted apart. Although the metal could, of course, be quite strong.”

Sidney began to puff at the oars, heading to where all the others had clustered around the hull of *Angela Mia*.

“But,” speculated Gerhard, “you do not make this very strong box for nothing. It is for keeping somethings very safe in – or out, keeping others out.”

“Can’t be *that* much inside it,” said Ted, rather dashing Crispin’s rising optimism, “ or else you and me couldn’t have lifted it up like we did. Or hang it up there. Maybe it’s just an old boiler or somethin’ like that.”

Mark and Alan had positioned their dinghy directly beneath the swaying container, oblivious of the dribbles of brown water leaking down on them from above.

“I don’t think those boys should be right under that thing,” said Lorraine. The nurses were somewhat disappointed not to have been called upon to practise their talents. “It could suddenly fall apart and drop on them,” she added in hope.

“There’s been writing on the underneath.”

Mark was pointing at the intermittent white squiggles, now clearly visible amid the patches of rust and grey metal.

“Look, Mr Saint – er, Crispin, you can see bits of paint, like old white lettering that’s come off.”

Although it was pleasing to be regarded as the authority, Crispin felt that such reliance was now rather misplaced.

He stared at the marks, faintly hoping that he would recognize some Greek proverb from his schooldays although, in truth, he could only have construed ‘the horse in the market place has damaged my slave’, a phrase unlikely to have been painted on a riveted metal box.

“No, I can’t make anything out. I believe there *are* ways of deciphering inscriptions with the aid of special equipment. That’s something that will have to wait until we hand them over.”

“Oh, come on,” drawled Steven, sneering at the group of upturned faces. He had made Oleg row their dinghy, gaining not only cheap labour but also the opportunity to glare at both Oleg and Amy at the same time. “Don’t tell me you’re goin' on with this caper. Haulin' up this stuff, for what, to hand it over to some junkyard? If it's really that interestin', just tell 'em where it is and let them haul it back."

If Jack had been experiencing any doubts, he put them aside now. That this cheeky Yank, who had poured scorned on their quest from the beginning, should return merely to scoff at them was too much.

"Bloody typical. There's always some bleedin' Jeremiah, always one ready to moan. Listen – " Sharon nudged his knee and whatever epithet he was about to apply to Steven was dissolved by the warning, "listen, Stevie Baby, we said we'd find the blinkin' treasure and we've done it. Uuuurhh!"

A trickle of rusty water from the blinking treasure baptized Jack's head as his dinghy floated within range.

"Give us me cap, Sharon. Right. That there – box – could 'ave anythin' in it. Plans an'– an' documents, old ones, worth money. May even *'ave* money in it, maybe that's why it ain't 'eavy, could be stuffed wiv notes fer all we know. An' the others, all stuffed with money. So we're not bloody giving it up now. That there box," he extended a pointing finger, "that there thing up there means money. So I says we carry on. Yer do nowt, yer get nowt."

There was a general chorus of agreement with that piece of profound philosophy and Jack looked suitably gratified. The past twenty-four hours had done much for his self-esteem.

Ted looked at Luigi.

"Whaddya reckon then, mate?" Their undersea alliance had dispelled Ted's distrust of the Italian.

"Carry on? Get the other two up? Or leave it at this one? It's your boat that will be doin' the carryin'."

"I donna understand. What issa the problem?"

Luigi addressed his audience with amazement.

"This ees a miracolo, no? We 'ave–a done this and you Ingleesh," he waved his hands helplessly, including all the nationalities present under the one flag, "you Ingleesh wanna no more, you 'avea no – *eccitazione*, issa crazy! *Si, of course* we do it, Jack issa true, this ees MONEY."

He stood up precariously, and banged the metal casing.

"Money, money, money! Issa *meraviglioso!*"

Gerhard grabbed him before he toppled out of the dinghy.

Bernie leaned over from his vantage point on *Angela Mia*'s deck, not having heard any of the debate below.

"What's next, Ted, winch this one in on deck? Luigi reckoned on piling them up 'cross the bows up here. Need a few up here to give a hand."

Hamish, who had been eyeing the container with an accountant's appraisal of weights and dimensions, came to life.

"There's nae need to do that. It could be dangerous, you couldna see where you were going. Besides, whatever is in them may not be safe, either."

That thought had not yet crossed the others' minds.

"I would suggest," continued Hamish boldly, much to the surprise of Flora who was not used to Hamish suggesting anything, "that we could tow the – the things. On the dinghies. Raft, say, three together and lay them across. The weight, as yon' man said, is not so great that the dinghies couldna' take them."

'Yon' man' was deeply impressed.

"Hamish, ye're a bloody marvel! A real credit to the Scotch!"

"Scots," corrected Flora primly, but with some pride and Hamish's face coloured to match the hue of his nose at the murmurs of approval from the other boats.

"That's it, then, cobbers, we get the other two up. If some of you want ter swim back to yer yachts or pile into each other's dinghies so's we can make three empty, we'll get it all done in two shakes. Right, Luigi?"

Luigi was already pulling on his flippers.

"*Si*, Ted, *splendente*! Everyone, everyone, all to work! I 'ave–a the 'Spumante in the ice, inna maybe two hour we make–a the celebration!"

And the mood of optimism and excitement restored, the crews set to work.

Exactly as Luigi had predicted, the bottles of Astispumante were being decorked two hours later.

Angela Mia had rejoined the row of yachts, having towed the dinghies without mishap supporting the three mysterious containers the few metres back to the flotilla.

One container, slightly smaller than the others, also proved to be more intriguing. Bits of metal had rusted from one end: at intervals among the sea-crust which had grown over the gaps, a smooth white surface could be glimpsed, untarnished by time. It was not, thought Crispin, marble: it was too uniformly white. Tentative knocks with the heel of Amy's shoe resulted in a hollow ringing sound, reminding her of the kind of sound she made when she got into the bathtub at home having forgotten to take her jewellery off. That comparison made the object more mysterious than ever and it was decided to abandon any further analysis in favour of liquid refreshment.

Eric appeared to have completely recovered under Monika's ministrations. More than that, he seemed almost uninterested in what had been achieved, listening with a faraway expression in his shining eyes, his replies to his sons' excited comments monosyllabic. Only Penny might have noticed that even his socks were at half-mast, a telling sign for some preoccupation. His gaze rarely strayed from Monika whose cryptic smile betrayed nothing as she joined in the celebrations.

Ted was puzzled at the continued absence of the party ashore, since Sally had seemed determined to be back in time for operation to raise the containers. While joining in with the endless speculation on the nature of their discovery, he kept a weather-eye out over the crystal waters for a sign of their return.

It was Jack, equally worried about the continued absence of his Rosie and the doubts in his mind over the wisdom of Darren taking charge of one of the outboards, who first spotted the coaster heading in their direction.

"Oi, Ted," he called, "you got any bine-oculars? There's

some sort of boat over there comin' this way. Can't quite make it out, but I think there's a lot of people on it."

Ted reached down Luigi's companionway and hooked a pair of binoculars free from over the radio.

He joined Jack at the handrail and raised them to his eyes.

The rust-streaked coaster, smoke billowing from its stack, was definitely aiming for the flotilla. And among the people on its crowded deck, he could make out Sally and Penny at the front, both of them waving in his direction. Between them a short fat man in uniform, a cigar clamped in his mouth, gazed directly into the binoculars, the sun striking a reflective ray from the gold badge on his peaked cap.

Chief of Police Georgiou Komoulides was, metaphorically speaking, riding into town.

CHAPTER ELEVEN

SIDNEY COMES A CROPPER WITH CLARA. THE CHIEF OF POLICE EXERTS HIS AUTHORITY. GENERAL HOCKHYMER EXERTS *HIS* AUTHORITY. THE ALBANIANS EXERT *THEIR* AUTHORITY – AND WIN. AMY DISCOVERS AN OLD EXTRA AND A NEW SCENE.

The Chief would have preferred a more imposing craft to make his dramatic intervention in the flotilla's activities than a beaten-up coaster whose last cargo had left an obnoxious smell

that crept up from the hold and enveloped those on deck with its clinging pungency. The mixed pong of hot engine oil and something that reminded Rosie of how she habitually held her breath when putting Jack's longjohns in the wash at the end of winter had already sent her to the rail several times – an unhappy, heaving shell-suit longing to return to the certainties and predictability of 83 Stanley Street.

The Greek government having overlooked the need to place a fleet of destroyers under the command of the Chief of Police of Thessadikios, Georgiou had to make do with a call to his brother-in-law, resulting in a hurried agreement to drop a charge relating to unnatural behaviour with a donkey in exchange for the use of Stavros's rust-arsed ship.

The shore party from the flotilla had conveniently arrived in Thessadikios just as the Chief was preparing to play his part in the recovery of national treasure. Having enrolled Eleutherios, the shop-keeper, and Nikkos, the moped mechanic, as his somewhat unwilling deputies, Sally's party were politely but emphatically escorted aboard the smelly crate in a state of confusion and indignation.

Sally's understanding of the Chief's broken English, which he had acquired during those happy days under the Colonels' régime – when British hippies could be arrested, given short haircuts at the government's expense, and then deported – was just sufficient to realize that the fat policeman had more than an inkling of the flotilla's purpose in the area. Wary of exacerbating a situation which might land the flotilla, and especially Ted, in deep trouble, she calmed her party with the assurance that it was being taken back to their yachts.

This was not the easiest task since Darren, with some experience of confronting officers of the law during the occasional fracas on the terraces, was all for confrontation. Though his dyed Mohican had long since given way to a bleached thatch, the Chief eyed Darren grimly, entertaining pleasurable thoughts of treating Darren to a shearing.

Sally's tact, and her dimpled smile, defused the situation and the Chief restrained any demonstration of his authority until they closed in on the flotilla.

It was Ariadne who came forward to stand by Ted as the towering coaster dropped anchor across the sterns of the row of yachts, its wash sending strenuous ripples through the flotilla. The rumbling engine cut, water gushed through the overflows and, without the ship's movement to allay it, the fetid stench settled over everyone in the vicinity.

"Stone the bleedin' crows," spluttered Jack, his hand covering his offended nose, "what a niff!"

Stavros, high in the control room, seemed as impervious to the reek as was his mate who joined him from the engine room. When you start your day with goat's cheese, a little garlic and a mouthful of *ouzo*, you don't have any softy city sensitivities.

It was not merely the uniform of Georgiou Komoulides that Ariadne recognized: it was his type. Short, fat men with a modicum of authority and lots of gold braid needed careful handling to stop them from proving troublesome, a lesson she had learned from adolescence. Although she had not met this particular example of the species before, she was well aware of his previous collusions with her Italian *appassionato* and Luigi had briefed her thoroughly on her role as innocent go-between.

"Leave–a the talking to Ariadne," whispered Luigi to Ted, as Sally and the shore party were allowed to laboriously clamber down the coaster's gangway and make the considerable drop onto the deck of *Angela Mia*. Sally joined the group around Ted.

"I couldn't really make out what he was saying, he just mumbled what he thought was English and kept saying 'hey, man' to me. But he knows what we've been looking for. He said 'treasure' quite distinctly as though he'd looked it up. How could he possibly know? Do you think someone at the taverna...? Was Andreas listening? Who...?"

She broke off as Luigi put his finger warningly to his lips.

"Issa better not speaking, eh? Thees man, if we make–a the trouble, maybe we are all not going home, *comprende?*"

"Oh, great," breathed Ted, his face registering abject dismay, "another flotilla banged up in a foreign gaol is just dandy."

If his eyes had not been glued to the martial figure of the law, Ted might have noticed a flicker of joy register fleetingly on Luigi's swarthy countenance. The latter turned to Ariadne and, in a rapid burst of Italian, warned her of Sally's suspicions.

All the crews were now safely scattered about the various decks of the flotilla, save for one Clara Chippendale who rolled to the end of the gangway and contemplated the drop with unabashed trepidation.

Sidney gallantly stood beneath the gangway with arms outspread to catch his alarmed Clara: gallantry has its place, but catching the equivalent of a baby elephant in mid-air is a trick better left to circuses.

With a happy gurgle, the airborne Clara plunged into her spouse's cushioned embrace with sufficient impact to rock the deck anew as Sidney crumpled beneath the mounds of flying flesh.

"Dear God," breathed Bernie, "the poor bastard's flattened. Lorraine, Liz, Julie, action stations! It's first aid or last rites for Chippers!"

While Bernie and the three nurses scraped up the comatose Sidney and, with heroic effort, heaved his poundage from *Angela Mia* to *Discovery* with the aid of several helping hands grasping handles of available flesh, the Chief of Police surveyed the scene coolly from the end of the gangway. He relit the stub of his acrid cigar and blew a perfect smoke-ring over the assembled heads.

His assessing gaze lingered thoughtfully as it fell speculatively on the indifferent Sharon who cocked her head on one side, met his eyes with calm disdain, then dismissed him with a flourish of her golden mane as she picked her way back to *Moby Dick*.

He smiled as he plucked the butt from his mouth and

continued his silent survey, pausing only fleetingly on Monika whose father stood with arms crossed beside her, the grim set of Gerhard's jaw suggesting a readiness for trouble.

With an inward shrug, he dismissed the thought of any salacious opportunities from his mind. Life in Thessadikios had its quiet side, but there were many opportunities for comfortable liaisons for a man of power and Georgiou had no wish to provoke any international incident which might require detailed investigation.

He gestured to his deputies to lower him to the yacht's deck. A Chief of Police does not risk his dignity by sprawling in front of his intended victims. His deputies, though, risked multiple hernias as they grasped his arms and lowered him until his tiny feet took the strain of his appreciable bulk.

There was no pay for deputies and business could fall flat when conducted with a protruding hernia.

As he straightened his crumpled tunic and aligned his cap to its most imposing angle, Ariadne stepped in front of him, for once wearing a dress, a summery red cotton frock that, while it did not hide her sensational charms, more or less kept them covered.

She addressed him in Greek.

"Luigi says we are to speak only Greek. He doesn't want them to know that he can understand. Not that he does all that much, anyway. I will translate into Italian and he'll tell them what is happening."

The Chief pursed his lips. Ariadne spoke without warmth, as though he was there just to do a job. A woman like this, she needed a strong, virile, Greek male rather like Georgiou Komoulides, not a crooked Italian.

"That one there," he nodded towards Sally, "that pretty one standing next to the big idiot flexing his muscles, she knows I speak English."

Ariadne shrugged.

"She says she couldn't understand you – except you kept mentioning 'treasure' in English. That was a pretty stupid thing to say. They'll know somebody tipped you off. And the 'big idiot' is the skipper of the flotilla. It's best not to make too much of this. Let's try and do it quickly. Your boat stinks."

This was even less pleasant for the Chief. He sensed scorn – and Chiefs do not like sensing scorn. But Ariadne had just written Luigi out of the scenario.

He rocked on his diminutive heels, his hands clenched behind his back, his paunch just touching Ariadne's firm belly, a reasonably pleasant sensation, if only for one of them.

"Tell them," he said with icy authority, "tell them that I have reason to believe that they are trying to smuggle examples of Greek art, and of Greek heritage, from Greek waters. And that this is a crime which carries heavy penalties."

Ariadne put a suitable look of alarm on her face and turned to Luigi. With Sally and Ted looking and listening attentively, she made a great show of unease and consternation as she rattled Italian into his ear.

"I don't trust the great fat pig. Tell them they're in trouble but watch it yourself – he's not going to do you any favours. Tell them he knows they've been hiking Greek stuff."

Luigi gave the Chief a swift hard look then, climbing on to the foredeck, faced a sea of concerned faces.

"What's old Dixon want, then?" asked Jack, grimacing as Rosie rubbed his sunburnt back with poncy-smelling oil. Rosie's stomach was feeling more at ease but the smell of suntan oil was at least helping to keep the coaster's odour at bay. "Goin' ter give us a parkin' ticket?"

"I, a-hem, wouldn't do anything to upset him, Jack."

The Hon. Crispin St Clair held a more realistic view of their situation than Jack who dismissed the policeman in his mind as a jumped-up insignificant foreigner, probably distantly related to Hitler.

"We have got those..." Crispin made darting movements with his eyes towards the tethered dinghies and their cargo, "...and he could, perhaps, feel that we shouldn't."

As Luigi was about to speak, there was a roar from *Discovery*. Though pretty well everyone was in earshot,

Bernie worked on the principle that if he could hear, all the others could hear. And he could just about hear his own mild tones.

"Sidney's knackered," he bellowed succinctly. "He's sweating away down there in that oven but we can't move him. He's done his back. Someone'll have to sail his boat back to Corfu – maybe me and Clara."

The name 'Clara' rolled tantalizingly round his tongue. Bernie liked big women: he had no prejudices against other types but, simply, his admiration was for females on a generous scale. And Clara made the three nurses look as though they'd joined the Lady Di Anorexic Club.

"Crikey, that's terrific, that is, that's about as useful as a dead dingo's dong."

Ted looked at Sally in despair. It was all going horribly wrong although perhaps not *quite* as wrong as it had presumably gone for the dead dingo.

Sally gave his bulging bicep a comforting squeeze and looked up at Luigi.

"Luigi, do get on with it. What did he say?"

"I'm–a wantin' this, to tell you. 'Ee says we 'ave the Greek things, are not ours, we are in deep–a sheet."

There was an immediate buzz of speculation and all eyes turned on the unperturbed Chief flanked by his smiling deputies. Being sworn in to help your Chief does not even entitle you to a uniform: neither Nikkos's green 'Castrol' cap, nor Eleutherios's grubby white apron, gave much substance to the majesty of the law. They were both anxious for a quick resolution to whatever this crisis was so that they could enter into negotiation with the tourists for some brisk business.

Ariadne regarded Georgiou with a quizzical look.

"Your turn. What's next?"

"Tell them that I am confiscating those, those things there on the dinghies. Tell them they have no permission to be lifting these things from the sea and they could be arrested for illegally moving them. That it is only from the kindness of my heart that I am not putting them in my cells. We will tow the..."

The blast from the coaster's foghorn cut through the Chief's orders, causing a uniform sense of an impending heart attack. Even Bernie glanced in Jürgen's direction with the unfair suspicion that Jürgen's digestive system was playing up again.

Georgiou glared up at the control room where Stavros was gesticulating wildly. He turned to stare in the direction of his brother-in-law's pointing arm.

With everyone's attention concentrated on the Chief's pronouncements, only Stavros had observed the fast-approaching patrol boat bearing down on the flotilla. All heads turned to watch the sleek new arrival as it throttled back, cut engines, and pulled alongside the grubby coaster, the rattle of its anchor chain inducing a mesmerized silence.

General Samuel B Hockhymer had arrived.

He was not a happy General. The sea was not his natural milieu, even a sea as calm as the Ionian. And a patrol boat was hardly a gunboat, not exactly the bristling sort of vessel which conveyed the authority of a senior ranking officer of the United States Army. Particularly when none of the god-damned multi-national crew that NATO saw fit to represent its might spoke any English. He'd had to rely on the multi-lingual Major Swit to issue commands, another little triumph for the yackety-yack upstart, another little sidelong sneer of triumph from the ladder-climbing creep.

Now, as he surveyed the motley crews packed together on the decks of the three yachts at the end of the row of pleasure crafts, he felt misled by his aide's use of the word 'flotilla'.

He eased a button loose around his midrift and turned to the rigid figure of Major Gabriel Swit. Flanking the Major were two smooth-helmeted marines, white spats gleaming, armed and imposing.

"This – this is a 'flotilla'? This ain't nothin' but a bunch of sailing boats! You said..."

"We couldn't get a 'copter, sir."

Swit was not going to take the rap for this, particularly when the rap belonged to the General's loose-living daughter.

His Raybans threw fierce glints from the declining sun into Hockhymer's eyes.

"The only 'copter available was being used by your daughter, General. Seems she had an important engagement with the Minister of the Interior. Same time every week. So we couldn't get an aerial view. Of the 'flotilla'."

He cast a sidelong glance at the General. Miss Hockhymer's liaisons with the Minister could prove to be the downfall of the General: hurried retirement on a basic pension; Major Swit in charge – good reasons for not insisting on commandeering a helicopter.

"Anyway, they're up to no good. We've got 'em cold. There's something going on, look at that guy in uniform, he's off this – this stinking crate here."

General Hockhymer sighed. The sea-sickness pills he had gulped down several hours ago were losing their effect and the unpleasant mixture of odours which assailed his nostrils made his stomach heave.

"OK, Gabriel, get me over on that there deck."

He disliked calling his aide by his christian name but the misappropriation of helicopters by his offspring was something he preferred not to see in a report.

The Major barked an incomprehensible order and the small lifeboat was lowered from its davits to the water. The General was conscious that being rowed by a gum–chewing marine for nearly a minute appeared an excessive show of pomp and zeal but NATO's honour had to be upheld even if his ample rear had to be supported by the Major as he climbed up the stern gangway of the crowded *Angela Mia*.

"Bloody 'ell," snorted Jack to the flotilla crews who, all agog and metaphorically all adrift, exchanged looks of apprehension and a collective desire to go home, "it's the 'over-sexed and over here' brigade!"

Even Steven was impressed by the display of home–grown military brass.

"Well, now," he grated to Amy, "look at where their little treasure hunt has got them. I guess our great Aussie skipper wishes he'd never been born."

It was a reasonable guess since Ted's popping eyes and hanging jaw did indicate some inner consternation, but Amy gave no response. If anything, she seemed more transfixed than Ted. The sight of the General, beribboned and bedecked with his Belgian award for traffic control, had left her speechless, her hands gripping the handrail in an effort to remain upright.

Samuel B. Hockhymer raised a hand in a cursory salute to no one in particular. Just as well to observe the preliminaries.

"Gentlemen. *Ladies* and gentlemen. Sweet Jesus, what a pong!"

The last remark was addressed as an aside to his aide who dutifully produced a handkerchief for the General to dab surreptitiously to his nose. Foreigners always seemed less sensitive to pongs.

His eyes took in the array of faces, travelled over the immediate decks, paused for an instant as they aligned with Amy's, registered a fleeting puzzlement, then fixed straight ahead on Luigi's mast. The rule book said eye confrontation was to be avoided when dealing with a mob.

"You have been boarded by a NATO patrol. I am General Hockhymer, responsible for security in this," he waved his hand to encompass the eastern hemisphere, "region. We have reason to believe that a – er – a violation has been committed in these waters."

He was conscious that it sounded as if someone had taken a leak in otherwise pure drinking water.

"Which one of you is – er..."

"Crispin St Clair.

Major Swit pronounced the name with an audible sneer. Only some British jerk would have a name like that.

There was a surprised murmur from the spectators. The Chief of Police, who felt that his authority was being diminished, was about to announce his important presence when Crispin edged Jack aside and stepped forward.

Immaculate in white ducks, he held out his hand to the General.

"Good afternoon, General. Been rather a splendid day, don't you think?"

The General looked pleased and grasped the proffered hand. The trepidation he had felt at the start of this mission receded somewhat. Though a gong awarded for bravery in the face of the enemy might have put a few more dollars in his account, he knew that at heart he was an armchair soldier.

"Sure is – ah – Crispin St Clair. That's one helluva handle. You got a given name?"

"Crispin," replied the scion of the St Clairs, "but why don't you call me Crisp? This, by the way," he indicated to Ted who returned the General's handshake like a water pump whose handle produced only a dry rasp, "is our skipper, Ted Banks."

Eric, whose attention to the events which had unfolded since his ministrations by Monika had been half-hearted, was astounded.

"Did you hear that?" he said, to no one in particular, "after all that talking about nicknames! Well, if he asks mine..."

Penny shushed him by inserting her hand in his. Eric had looked feverish ever since his attack of the bends and, though the sun had remained relentlessly hot, she felt that there was something more amiss with her agitated man than mere sunstroke.

"Crisp," began the General, "what in tarnation is goin' on here? We have, ah, information that you're leadin' some expedition to pick up...Major?"

Major Swit had no qualms about looking this Brit in the eye. Interrogation procedures emphasized the importance of eye contact. While applying contact of an even more personal nature to other sensitive areas.

The Raybans bore in on the English wimp.

"We're on to you, mister. Forget the crap. We've got you covered, you and the whole operation. We're no muts. You've been lifting that there stuff," he pointed at the mute oblongs lying on the dinghies, "and you're in the corner.

You can come clean – or you may never be able to come again."

It was crude but life, life sure is crude. That's what it is, in aces. Crude. Life. Sorta crude. Major Swit thought deeply about life.

Crispin gave him the sort of disarming smile that had persuaded natives to hand over kingdoms for a bucket of beads.

"Oh, I say old chap, you're getting yourself into a bit of a muddle. We've found some interesting boxes sitting on the jolly old sea-bed and hauled them up, that's all. We were going to hand them over at Corfu, but this Johnnie," he indicated the Chief, "wants to take them himself, so there it is. As far as we're concerned," he waved an elegant arm to embrace the flotilla, "he can have them. Or you can. We'll be glad to see the back of them."

An excited buzz arose from the flotilla crews. Crispin seemed to be taking matters into his own hands, surrendering their hard-won booty without a fight.

"Vell, Crispin, are vee sure of vot you are saying? All this vork for nozzings?"

Jürgen's objection received a murmur of approval from his crew mates.

Sally spoke up.

"I think there's something very odd going on here."

She stared fixedly at Luigi.

"The world and his wife seems to know where we are and what we've found. As if someone had been letting them know, *broadcasting* over the radio, maybe. There's been a few funny things going on, like Penny finding herself adrift. And this fat – policeman – ", she transferred her hostile gaze on to that portly official, "seemed to be expecting us."

The Chief of Police had had enough. Out-ranked by gold braid, intimidated by the business-like look of the P.T. boat and its array of ensigns, Georgiou Komoulides felt the stirrings, deep within his soul, of the spirit of Ancient Greece, a refusal to accept the dictates of wilful gods, no matter what their power.

He planted himself, legs astride, before the Major , following his innate perception of where power truly lay.

"Piss off," he said in Greek.

The Major bridled. This scruffy-looking minor official in his greasy uniform had used the familiar form to address a graduate of the Greenback Academy of Milwaukee.

He removed his shades, to give the Chief the full benefit of his colourless eyes and thin, cruel lips. His lips, in fact, were quite thick, but he practised stretching them during his morning shave to convey the right air of menace.

"You short-arsed fuck-faced prick of a bunch of degenerates," he responded, in faultless colloquial Greek, "get yourself and any arsehole you'd care to call a friend outta here, *pronto*."

Though the sun had well passed high noon, both men reached for their holsters. Georgiou's English might well have diminished since his active days in the Sixties, but the word 'prick' had a familiar ring about it, and he seemed to remember not liking it being applied to him when smacking hippies on beaches.

As, with one accord, the crowd edged back from the two protagonists, the tension was broken from a most unexpected quarter.

"Sam!"

The cry came from Amy, an Amy who scrambled over rails, who pushed through gaping onlookers, who threw herself at General B Hockhymer and clasped him to her mou-mou, who pressed her red-lipped mouth to his drooping jowl and clung to him so that he tottered, recovered – then returned her fierce embrace.

"Amy!"

"*Mein Gott!*" groaned Jürgen who had been floored by Amy in her haste to reach the General. "Vot is it that is happening?"

The answer was not apparent. It could not even be guessed at. The couple remained locked in each other's arms, the Major staring aghast as the Supremo of Baltic Operations clasped a middle-aged bottle-blond and uttered endearments of an embarrassing nature, the most emotionally–charged being 'my cuddly-bubbly', over and over again.

A smidgen of air finally inserted itself between their lips, and the couple broke apart.

"Oh, Sam," said Amy, holding him by the shoulders, "I can't believe it's you!"

The General gazed into Amy's blue-tinted contact lenses and sucked in his paunch.

"Amy," he choked, "My Amy. Why, it's what? It's near on thirty years. And you ain't changed a bit. Well, hardly a bit."

A general's reports should, at least, be plausible.

"I ain't clapped eyes on you since you were in that movie, what was it? The one where you were captured by redskins, that was it, *The Woman in the Wigwam* – I've looked out for that movie for years but never seen it."

Amy gulped back a sob.

"It was never released. The censor wanted more feathers. They couldn't paint them in. I was the star, *the* star, I was gonna be famous an' I thought..."

She faltered to a dismal halt.

"An' you thought gettin' hitched to a young soldier would hold you back. Gee, Amy, you *were* a star, my star. I had you up there, right among those bright lights."

Samuel B Hockhymer paused, his hand reaching out to touch the bright yellow tresses. It was just about the right time for the matinee: even the Chief of Police thought he could hear violins.

"I couldn't forget you, Amy. That's why my wife left me; said she couldn't compete with somethin' up there in the sky, always hoverin' above us. All those years, all those god-damned years..."

The General looked away, for fear any of the observers might see an old war horse with a tear in his eye.

"Sam, Sam."

It wasn't a long speech, and the caustically inclined might have thought of several unkind rhyming lines, but it was an emotive one, Amy's cracked tones evoking sun and youth and bubble-gum and, well, other more specific memories of Sam Hockhymer.

"Ahem," coughed Crispin, "it would seem that we have more visitors."

Crispin's cool English understatement concerning the grey, mean-looking cruiser with gun turrets that swivelled from one end of the flotilla to the other was not meant simply to impress his listeners with his *sang-froid.*

Steven Spielberg would have had to come up with something more creative than a few dinosaurs to have astounded the crews of the Ulysses Flotilla. When, in the course of a few hours, you have raised sunken treasure, been boarded by the Greek Police, and watched a NATO General blubber into the bosom of a honeymooning member of your party, you are naturally not going to turn a hair at the arrival of an Albanian gunboat.

The knife-like bow sliced silently between the flotilla and the other two boats, the crusty coaster and the spick and span P.T. boat, effectively cutting off both the NATO Forces and the Greek Police from their bases. It was a matter of some strategic interest that a gun turret was turned towards each of them.

As the engines reversed with a threatening growl, and the cruiser nudged gently but with the certainty of a nightclub bouncer between the boats, the crowd on the flotilla decks squinted into the sinking sun at the silhouette which stood at the bow.

It appeared to be an Albanian equivalent of Major Swit. With legs planted firmly apart, the peak-capped figure towered above the yachts, a halo of light, brilliant against the gathering dusk, defining its sharp outline.

"Jesus," muttered Major Gabriel Swit inaccurately, despite the almost miraculous sudden appearance, "what we *don't* want is Albanians at this party."

General Hockhymer was struck by a depressing thought.

"Swit. You're not about to inform me that we are in Albanian waters, by any chance?"

The Major shuffled uncomfortably.

"There's – er – just a chance, General. Just a chance. Could be we're kinda right on the line."

The General gave Swit the sort of look Joshua might have given his aide when he turned up in front of Jericho without a trumpet.

"Well, ain't that just dandy..."

He was about to add something sarcastic concerning resignations on the part of senior officers when he found, with a feeling of warm delight, that Amy's hand had sneaked into his own. A seraphic smile spread across his face.

For once, Major Swit was impressed by his boss. He had not expected the General to face an international incident with such equanimity.

There was a collective start as a deep voice crackled through a loud hailer from the Albanian cruiser.

With the exception of Oleg, whose studied appraisal of the cruiser had a look of fine calculation, there was only a look of puzzlement on the faces of the listeners.

"Anyone here speak Albanian?" appealed Major Swit. His fluency in several languages did not extend to Albanian.

He turned to Georgiou Komoulides who seemed to have shrunk within his uniform. The Chief's previous experiences with the Albanian authorities had not been fruitful: they had a way of dismissing international law with a careless disregard.

Major Swit was conciliatory. His Greek was exquisitely polite.

"Er – Captain – I didn't catch your name – do you want to handle this? I mean, it's probably more within your jurisdiction than ours. We wouldn't like to muscle in on your territory – we'll leave it to you, shall we?"

The Chief of Police for Thessadikios was equally polite.

"Don't worry, *Captain*, this one is all yours." He reached into his tunic pocket, pulled out a cigar and applied a light with a slightly quivering hand.

"Such situations," he added maliciously, "are rarely handled by 'pricks' when the finesse of Americans is so widely respected."

And he blew a cloud of smoke into the glaring Raybans.

The loud hailer barked again, this time with a note of impatience. The sun was fast melting into the sea and the shadows cast from the towering ships over the yachts conveyed an urgency which induced unease.

"I speak some Albanian words, some phrases for the tourist."

It was Gerhard who spoke as he edged his way to the stern of *Angela Mia*.

"I will say a phrase for welcoming."

He stood in front of the General whose fingers, under cover of the gathering dusk, played with Amy's.

Gerhard cupped his hands and bellowed his Albanian welcoming phrase towards the dark figure standing like a colossus above him.

Silence.

Suddenly the scene was bathed in white light as the cruiser's spotlights flooded the decks, blinding the upturned faces.

"Strewth," wailed Ted as they shielded their eyes from the glare, "that was one helluva welcoming phrase. Yer wouldn't like to tell us what exactly you said?"

Gerhard shrugged apologetically.

"Perhaps it was not for the best. My, uh, father was here during the war, you know. For a long time. He was, ah, an adviser to the Italians, when they are fighting with the Albanians. He told me of these people."

"Sure, I bet he did. So what did you say?"

Swit eyed the German with a prejudiced eye. Prejudice was never far from that eye.

"I said – it is difficult putting in the English – I said 'Hallo, I am hoping that you are well. There will be no – er – how do you say, ah, *reprisals* if you, ah, surrender.'"

"Brilliant," said Major Swit caustically, "diplomacy at its best."

Gerhard looked as though he had something to say to the Major but was saved the trouble by an unexpected intervention.

It was Oleg who brusqely pushed aside Steven and took his turn to yell at the top of his lungs to the cruiser.

This time there was an immediate response.

There followed a dialogue between the castaway and the Albanian officer which excluded the onlookers, now looking like so many lost extras on the wrong film set. Only Amy looked comfortable in the stark brightness.

Both Tara and Flora took advantage of the incomprehensible exchange to usher their protesting children into their respective cabins. To be excluded from such drama was naturally considered unfair, particularly as supper was taken amid whispered shushes from fraught mothers.

The high-decibel debate seemed to go on forever but was actually concluded inside ten minutes. Oleg was inspired: with the cunning that had made him the main source of supply for black-market produce, especially condoms, in his youth, he negotiated a deal which was satisfactory to both Lieutenant Ramon Manski – for such was the name and title of the silhouetted presence – and himself.

He explained how he had been harmlessly fishing when he had been run down by a particularly stupid Greek ferry captain – this easily fitted with the Lieutenant's perception of most of the Greek nation – and was eventually picked up by the flotilla. He neglected to mention any interval of time between the two events.

While he was not sure of the exact nature of the objects lifted from the sea, he had heard the word 'money' mentioned several times and it was not difficult to deduce that this probably meant money. Since the activities of the flotilla had aroused such international attention – and especially as the Greek policeman showed a determined interest in the oblongs – it was surely logical that the discoveries should be confiscated in the name of the Albanian government.

He pointed out the esteem with which the Lieutenant would be regarded for such initiative – and that he, Oleg, would be instrumental in proclaiming the efficiency and zeal displayed by the same officer.

The subtleties of the exchange were not lost on Lieutenant Ramon Manski who was no slouch when it came to a little enhancement of his career. Reading between Oleg's lines, which displayed a certain ignorance of political changes in Albania in recent months, he informed him as a matter of conversational interest that a general amnesty had been granted to all political offenders and those convicted of minor offences.

This news bit deeply into Oleg's soul and a nostalgia surfaced for his village, Sinanaj, and his deserted Katrina, the mother of what would now undoubtedly be a sturdy son. Unfortunately, Ramon had no contact with the village though he seemed to recall that, some years ago, there had been a scandal emanating from Sinanaj which had resulted in a national hue-and-cry for an absconding bridegroom. He was sure, though, that under the present conditions, if such a person was to return, he would be welcomed with open arms, particularly if he was the source of some useful booty.

That did it. Oleg secured the services of Eric, the first of the flotilla crews to extend a welcoming hand. Puzzled yet pleased by his new role of negotiator extraordinary, Eric interpreted the gestures and guttural ourpourings of the Albanian stowaway with an aplomb that astonished both himself and his fellow crew members.

Ignoring the brass from NATO and the Greek Police, he explained the choices to his totally perplexed skipper, the mighty Ted Banks.

"We've got to hand it over – the stuff we picked up. Otherwise," he imitated the gestures made by Oleg, " 'poof, poof'. I mean 'bang, bang'. I'm pretty sure he means 'bang, bang'. Maybe their guns go 'poof, poof'."

Major Swit gave way to a little exasperation.

"Whaddya mean 'poof, poof'? They're a bunch of bandits, are you suggesting we just give in to them?"

His Raybans glared up into the spotlight, blindingly trained on Lieutenant Manski. The latter, aware that the sunglasses which he wore were a poor imitation of the Major's, imported from the People's Republic, with lenses held in place by an even poorer imitation of Sellotape, glared back. The forward gun turret on the cruiser lowered its sights a little, just enough to line up directly with General Hockhymer.

"Major Swit," intoned the General hurriedly, "you've already made one pig's arse out of this whole affair. Give 'em whatever they want and let's get the hell outa here. I take it you've no objection, er – skipper?"

Ted had no objection. He had no power of speech, either. He grinned idiotically at the General and nodded his head vigorously. There were no objections from the rest of the crews. It mattered not if the guns went 'poof, poof' or 'bang, bang': it was preferable for the guns not to go at all.

The dinghies bearing the metal cases were, without further ado, towed by Luigi to the Albanian cruiser. The Italian had remained uncustomarily silent throughout the succession of events. When you're on to a loser, the best way forward is to say nothing and be obliging. Luigi was unctuously obliging.

As the Albanian cruiser rumbled into life, with Oleg on board preparing his excuses for Katrina and hoping that her father was no longer superintendent of the jam factory and thereby rendered somewhat impotent, Ted came to terms with the loss of three dinghies.

The cruiser swept away into the dark and starry night, the 'treasure' in tow behind her. With the spotlights extinguished, the yachts bobbed in the softer radiance of the stars and the cabin lights.

"I suppose," said Ted gloomily to Sally, "we ought to be thankful that three dinghies is all we've lost."

The General put his arm around Ted's shoulders. Amy still held his free hand in an intimate clasp. Perhaps there *was* a little disappointment that Oleg had departed without even a backward glance, but that weighed little in present circumstances.

"Son, you did OK. That could have been real nasty. You took the right decision. It takes a real man to do that."

Ted looked at Sally. Sally looked at Ted.

"You hear that?" he husked.

Ted possessed the average Aussie scorn for authority but to be praised by an American general when you are only wearing shorts was something to be proud of.

Sally recognized that husk. She turned to the General.

"Well, General, that's it, isn't it? I mean you're welcome to stay but, really, there's not much point is there? Or, for that matter, this gentleman?"

She addressed the Police Chief who only returned a discontented scowl. The whole episode had been a waste of time.

He flapped his arm at his deputies who were reckoning up the loss of business which had been sacrificed to the whims of Georgiou Komoulides. When it came to election time, the Chief was going to find himself short of a few votes.

"Let's get out of here," he said to his unwilling support. "Give me a hand up that gangway."

His eyes sought Ariadne's.

"Tell that – ", he sought for the appropriate word and came up with a recent reminder, "tell that 'prick' Luigi that he can find some other waters to sail his boat in. Tell him he's finished. If I catch Luigi anywhere in my area..."

He abandoned the threat in mid-air and, hoisting himself onto the coaster's gangway by clamping his boots on his deputies's shoulders then leaving them to fend for themselves, he left *Angela Mia*'s deck for ever.

As the coaster got underway, its engines once again causing the entire flotilla to rock erratically, General Samuel B Hockhymer extended his hand to Ted.

"Skipper, I just want to thank you, in the name of NATO Operations for the Eastern Hemisphere, for the initiative and courage you and your crews have displayed in the face of – ahem – adversity. You can be sure of an honourable mention in the report on this incident when faced with hostility by an unidentified Albanian warship. I will personally make sure that you get a copy."

Major Swit, bouncing from foot to foot with irritation, interrupted.

"That was no warship, that was a small cruiser and we let the bastards walk off with whatever these idiots had yanked up from down there. If you think..."

The General faced his Raybanned subordinate.

"Major Swit," he said firmly, "when it comes to idiots, you take the prize. And take of those damned sunglasses, it's too dark, you look a first-rate asshole."

"Sorry," he apologized to Amy who pressed warmly against his shoulder, "I'm slippin' into the vernacular. You," he poked Swit in the chest with an unnecessary firm poke, "have nearly brought about a major confrontation with an unaligned State. You have brought me here on a wild goose chase. And when my report goes in, Major, you'll be lookin' for another berth. And *not* one with me."

He signalled to one of the laconic marines who had seen brass-hats fall out before.

"Can that little tub down there take one extra passenger?"

The marine's chewing-gum hit the deck with a dull splat.

"Sure can, General," he grinned. "Like one lady passenger?"

The General took Amy's hands in his.

"Well, how about it, Amy? If the stars above haven't brought back my own little star this night, there ain't nothin' to believe in no more!

Amy looked across the dimly-lit sterns to where Steven stood on the *Discovery*. Her contact lenses being more suitable for close range, she actually addressed her words to a surprised Hamish.

"Steve, honey."

Her voice tremblingly tinged with a mixture of sorrow and joy, she missed the wince Steven gave at this diminutive.

"Steve, honey, it jest didn't work out. I cain't remember a time when I was more miserable 'cept for the time when Vincent Price's stand-in bit me in *Dracula's Last Supper* an' I got septicaemia."

She grasped Samuel's hand and pressed it to her lips. It was a happy hand.

"We loved each other a long time ago. Well, *quite* a long time ago. And our paths parted. But now," she raised her arm theatrically to the bejewelled night, her voice dropping into a *Wizard of Oz* mode, "we've jest got to follow that starry path to our own little heaven. Will – will you ever forget me, honey?"

Hamish shuffled with embarrassment. He'd had no idea that Amy had been so smitten. He wished Flora was on deck to hear this thought-provoking declaration.

Before he could reply, Steven leant forward so that the stern light of *Discovery* could fully illuminate his scathing countenance.

"Oh, pass me the sick bag. Take off with your soldier, *baby*, I figure you deserve him. I'll send you the papers when I get home."

And Steven disappeared into the blackness, to open a bottle of bourbon alone aboard *The Bounty*.

The General pressed his lips to those of Amy Clawrer, née Blashdip, née Shufflebottom, née...

There were to be no more 'nées' for Amy. Planting a kiss on Ted's cheek, she whispered tearfully "you're a real sugar, Ted, just like Erroll. Flynn," she added, noting Ted's mystification. "I'll get Sam to pick up my things. Goodbye, Ted, you take care of that sweet Sally now."

With a wave to her former shipmates, and a last parting look at the empty sternrail of *The Bounty*, she allowed the General to help her unsteadily over the side into the supporting arms of the waiting marine.

As the Americans departed for their P.T. boat, the flotilla crews crowded the rails and spread their good wishes across the still-warm Ionian.

"Oh, Jack," sobbed Rosie, laying her head on his goose-pimpled but well-oiled chest, "it's just like a fillum."

Many's a true word spoken in chest.

CHAPTER TWELVE

Steven clears the decks. The Flotilla Race. Tactical manoeuvres in the wind. Surprises, prizes and tears in Ted's eyes. Oleg, the National Hero, unveils his monument and gets out of a jam.

The customary flotilla race for the home port, Mengalissi, on the last day of the holiday, was to prove a great success.

Though the treasure hunt had resulted in such an unsatisfactory conclusion, with the 'artefacts' having been nabbed by the Albanians, the relief from tension and worry had been tangible.

Ted, in particular, had felt a great weight lift from his shoulders with the departure of both the enigmatic oblongs and the exiled Oleg. The generosity of the General's praise, if somewhat over the top since Ted had done little more that drop his jaw as the succession of events unfolded, had buoyed his spirits to the point where he husked continuously.

But even more pleasing, though he had tried to hide his sense of inner triumph, was the obvious discomfiture of Luigi. That there had been a informer in their midst was obvious to all the flotilla crews and suspicion had become certainty when the Chief of Police had referred twice, with a display of unalloyed venom, to Luigi's name.

Ariadne had seemed to share the Chief's sentiments, rounding on the subdued Italian as the crews silently deserted the deck of *Angela Mia* to return to their individual yachts. In the noisy bustle and the concentration on supper preparations followed by bed created by the rest of the flotilla, *Angela Mia* weighed anchor and stole off into the balmy night, harsh words from Ariadne still trailing across the unheeding sea. Only Gerhard, standing in the darkness at the bow of *Becker*, was a witness to their departure, those sinister silvery eyes following their wake.

Exhausted by the day's trials and tribulations, the crews kept to their own individual yachts, until the turning off of cabin lights extinguished the murmured discussions and analysis of who had done what to whom. Gradually, only the lapping of the water against hulls, the metallic whispering of the shrouds, and the red and green winking of the stern lights betrayed the flotilla's presence in the Ionian. *Ulysses X* was the last yacht to indicate any signs of life, as befits a responsible skipper. The return of the husk was cause for celebration.

The next morning, predictably blessed by a smiling sun and peerless blue sky, was marked by a communal spirit both relaxed and companionable.

Oddly, even Steven appeared to be as amicable as his nature would allow, whether because of the medicinal properties of bourbon or perhaps some newly-found sense of freedom, it was hard to tell. He certainly wasn't telling, but it was strange to hear the sound of cheerful whistling coming from his cabin.

There were frequent splashes from the vicinity of *The Bounty*, as though some unwanted mementoes were being ditched overboard, but nobody felt like enquiring if any help was needed. If anyone noticed the large pink bra which refused to sink clinging to Steven's dinghy, not a single person passed any remark.

The condition of Sidney Chippendale, now unilaterally accepted as 'Chippers', aroused much sympathy and discussion but the nurses proved equal to the task of restoring Sidney to the perpendicular. The diagnosis was a slipped disc, not quite as drastic as Bernie's opinion that Chippers' bones had been reduced to marrowbone jelly.

Stuffed with pain-killers, and propped up by a whaleboned corset produced with a flourish from the resourceful Lorraine's medicine chest, Sidney had insisted that he was fit to take part in the race. The restriction of the corset *did* give him the appearance of having a waist, something he had lost sight of for many years, and he sat in the cockpit of *Discovery* holding the hand of his repentant Clara whilst being tended with solicitous care by the three nurses.

The boats had to be cleaned up before the race could start since, once into port, crews had been known to bolt for home leaving the debris of two weeks' holiday behind them. Sharon was particularly pleased: while she stretched out on the foredeck of *Moby Dick* to make the most of the last few hours of sun, her heels drumming to the sound of INXS in her headphones, and Arnold dutifully applying suntan oil to the most exciting bits, her mother industriously mucked out the lower decks.

Rosie's scream brought Jack down the ladder, there to fall back in astonishment at the sight of his wife's buttocks winking at him. With delicacy and precision, he pulled Snubsy's missing eye from Rosie's tender rear, ruining her appreciation by remarking wrily that she would do anything to keep an eye on him. With sight restored to Snubsie's empty socket, the pink and white panda sat in a pool of oil above Sharon's navel, there to receive affectionate strokes and pats from Arnold, keenly aware of Jack's own beady and watchful eye.

By midday there was sufficient breeze to get under way. Mainsails were hoisted, jibs unfurled, cruising shutes – for the likes of Crispin, Ted and Gerhard who knew what to do with them – unpacked in readiness. With *Ulysses X* in the lead, the flotilla fanned out in an arrow formation, stark-white sails taking up the freshening wind, a sight for any skipper to be proud of.

Ted *was* a proud skipper: two weeks ago, nine yachts had been filled with a miscellaneous bunch of sailing tourists plus a sense of foreboding. Now they were all returning safely (Jack wasn't *yet* in port but at least Ted knew what to watch out for), healthy (Sidney could be described as painfully healthy), bronzed (the Gillicuddys could be described as brownish) and complete.

Well, almost complete, thought Ted as he winched in the mainsail. At least Amy was lost to love and not to the sea. He must remember to get her things from Steven, particularly her passport, as long as it was not included among the objects that had been dropped into the Ionian.

"I think we're about ready, Ted."

Sally stood at the helm, the wind curling her hair in soft caresses about her face. She felt a tangible happiness, the sort that made you fearful of its loss. Her mood was influenced by her joy in actually *sailing*, flying before the wind, a glorious freedom of unhindered motion and lightness of spirit.

"Always ready, Sal," grinned her ruffle-haired Adonis.

That was Ted, down to earth even at sea.

He reached down the companionway and yanked up the microphone.

"Alright. This is *Ulysses X* callin' all flotilla boats. We're goin' to do something that's not strictly pucker, eh? We're going to sound our foghorns. All of you, stand by an' when I say 'now', stick yer digits on yer buttons."

He paused to allow for the necessary digit selection, scanning the glinting sea for any sign of other boats. It remained deserted, as though the Ionian was Ted's own personal playground.

"Now," he yelled, and was rewarded with nine echoing blasts, almost simultaneously, that sounded to the crews like a trumpet call from the heavens.

"Stop, stop," he roared, and the last echo dropped into the sea. "I'll be up to my neck in sheepdip if I get reported."

"Okay, folks, it's time for the Big Race back to Mengalissi. Remember what I said about keepin' a sharp eye out for other boats, particularly as we get near the port. No arguments with tankers, please. And, NO ENGINES. Now, get into position, line up with me."

It took another ten minutes for the yachts to form an approximate line, some losing wind, some – predictably – not knowing how to find it. Bernie, on board *Discovery* in order to generously help out the Chippendales, was busy bawling unheeded instructions to Liz, Lorraine and Julie who handled *Siren* without any need of his help whatsoever.

At last even *Moby Dick* was at least facing in the right direction though Jack had been caught a mighty swipe with the boom – which he naturally blamed on Darren.

All eyes concentrated on *Ulysses X* which had motored half-a-mile ahead and gone about to face them. A rocket whooshed into the air pulling a red smoke trail, and the flotilla was off.

Exhilaration and excitement caught the crews as the flying boats eased into the wind, sails taut, hulls leaning to the water. Ted, under full sail and throbbing power from his diesel, used both wind and engine to speed ahead, to await the flotilla at the finishing line.

The experienced crews immediately went into the lead, neck and neck, the St Clairs slightly easing ahead, Crispin having had the foresight to lift his dinghy out of the water and rope it to the stern rail to prevent unnecessary drag.

There was just sufficient wind to make it a race, but not quite enough for the leaders to leave the stragglers too far behind.

Steven edged up on *Annus Mirabilis* and took Crispin's wind, much to the indignation of Tara whose strident remarks were lost among the shrouds. But it was *Becker* who played cunning, steering leeward and tacking expertedly to put Monika and Gerhard out front.

"Dad," bawled Darren, "follow him, whatsisname, Octopus Paws."

The Armitages clung to their locker seats as *Moby Dick* heeled over and the boom swung in answer to Jack's lunge at the tiller.

"Winch in, winch in," shouted Darren as the mainsail flapped erratically, and for once Sharon responded to her brother, she and Rosie hauling on the winch handle while Darren tugged at the mainsheet.

"Ye're supposed to say 'ready about'," said Jack smugly. He was feeling distinctly salty, this doughty man at the helm. He was *sailing*, hauling close to the wind, a man with the sea in his veins.

"Yeh, yeh, Dad, say what yer like but *follow* 'im. If we do wot 'ee does, we'll go faster."

Darren was keeping a weather-eye out for Trudy on the *Nemesis* where the Warbelows were fast gaining ground on the leaders. Mark and Alan were working on the principle of doing the exact opposite to what their heated father commanded and were thus making steady progress.

Except for Steven and Crispin, still almost jostling each other for the lead, the yachts were now spread out over a wide area, each tacking and gybing to the wind according to the expertise of their crews.

Jürgen, to gain the most from trimming his sails, had

taken *De Profundis* considerably off course and was now having to tack endlessly to get back into the race. This unfortunately brought him across the bows of *Thistle*, eliciting a string of vituperative comments from the newly confident Hamish. Flora told her children to cover their ears. It would be some time before Hamish would be allowed another haggis.

They were more than half-way through the race when *The Bounty* unaccountably slewed to starboard and collided with *Annus Mirabilis*. Steven, sailing single–handed, had genuinely made a mistake, giving a luff too many after the sail had filled and desperately over-correcting.

There was little impact between the yachts, just enough to cause consternation and a drop in concentration, the boats falling back as they veered off, effectively knocking them out of the race.

The coastline of Corfu now in sight, the flotilla sped on towards *Ulysses X*, less than a mile distant. *Discovery* had given up the chase, Sidney's back causing him to wince out aloud at each abrupt turn, until Clara bellowed for respite into Bernie's ear. The three nurses, ever mindful of their charge and despite Bernie's frantic signals to carry on regardless, hove to and lost the wind from their sails.

Becker was now confidently in the lead, pursued by the whooping crews of *Nemesis* and *Moby Dick*, the latter imitating every action of Gerhard closely observed through binoculars by Darren.

With less than a quarter-of-a-mile to go, a jaunty little speedboat, cutting carelessly across the sea as its two occupants waved champagne bottles, swerved in front of a bulging-eyed Gerhard. If it had not been for Monika's firm hand on his, Gerhard would not have swung the tiller – and, in consequence, lost the race.

Which left *Nemesis* and *Moby Dick* fighting for the lead, bearing down on Ted at eight knots, their crews shouting, waving, shrieking. Even Snubsie looked rigid with excitement.

As they passed *Ulysses X*, the flotilla's radios crackled on to the air.

"*Ulysses X* to flotilla. *Ulysses X* to flotilla. This is Ted Banks announcing the result of the race. We have TWO WINNERS, not a duck's arse between 'em. Congratulations, *Nemesis* an' – an' *Moby Dick!* Cripes, Sally, *Moby–bleedin'–Dick* can ye believe it? I thought he'd be on his way to Turkey by now..."

And Sally's hand tactfully switched off the radio before Ted could offer any further opinions of Jack's seamanship.

*   *   *

It was almost with a feeling of surprise that the Ulysses Flotilla crews found themselves sitting under the same umbrellas in the Mengalissi café, the scene of their departure two weeks ago. They were experiencing that feeling so familiar to holidaymakers: at the beginning, there is so much time, so much to be experienced, so many things to look forward to, time seems to stretch out endlessly in front of them. Then – it's over. The last hours of the last day.

Steven had already left, by taxi to Corfu town. He had moored up with the rest of the yachts, but had avoided talking to the others, piling his luggage on the quayside for the taxi which would take him to his evening flight.

While the rest of the boats had their decks swabbed, their rubbish sealed into plastic bags, Steven had sought out Ted who, with Sally, was busy at a café table filling in the log books of his departing crews.

He explained to Ted that, despite appearances to the contrary, he had not intended to deliberately take the St Clairs out of the race, but he knew what suspicions were harboured in the minds of the rest of the crews.

There was an air of genuine apology about Steven, and Ted was never one to harbour grudges for long. Though he and Sally tried to persuade the *angst*-ridden American to join the crews in a last drink, he shied away from the possibility of putting a damper on the Happy Hour, and took off in his taxi.

True to form, his last remarks implied criticism of Greek hygiene and island toilets in particular. Sally forebore from making acid comments on how, if he and his ilk would have their way, a homogenized Disneyland would turn the whole world into a Mickey Mouse play area for glazed-eyes tourists with enormous bums scoffing buckets of popcorn. Steven would not have understood, anyway.

Now, with a quayside littered with an odd assortment of belongings stacked to await the coach which would dump them at Corfu airport, the members of the treasure-hunting flotilla sat, drinks in hand (a microwaved pizza in mouth, for Clara), watching the dying Greek sun spread its farewell rays on the row of white yachts that had once been their homes.

Ted and Sally stood before a table spread with log books, medals – and two ashtrays each inset with a shiny medallion representing a yacht under full sail.

"This has been," muttered Ted, swallowing an emotional lump which rode up and down his neck like a snail on an escalator, "the best flotilla I've ever skippered. The best."

"I'm not brown-nosin', we've been a *team*. One helluva team."

He paused to allow himself time to control a manly husk. Flora was about to ask the meaning of 'brown-nosin' then changed her mind. It was better not to know. The children had picked up enough coarse expressions on this holiday without adding another to their collection.

Picking up the ashtrays, Ted held them up, one in each hand.

"These – er – prizes are for the two winners. But ye're all winners in my book, there's no wood ducks here."

There was a pleased murmur at the lack of wood ducks.

"Right," said Ted, prompted by Sally's nudge to get on with it, "this one goes to the crew of *Nemesis*. Cop that, Eric, an' well done. Yer showed plenty of spunk, mate."

Eric copped the trophy, a ripple of applause acknowledging his show of spunk. It was Monika's hands which continued clapping after the rest of the applause had died away, and Eric's face flushed crimson as he hurried to seat himself amidst his family.

In their humid cabin the night before, Eric had seemed to want to unburden himself of some deep thoughts, but Penny had remained obstinately detached while he wriggled in the throes of explanation.

She had finally silenced him by leaning on her elbows and turning his face so that, in the dim cabin light, he had looked deep into her knowing eyes.

"Eric," she had said, "how long have we known each other? Over twenty years? There's nothing you can say to me that I don't already know. Including the fact that I love you, and," she bent her head to kiss his sun-scorched lips, "that you love me. So go to sleep. It's been a marvellous holiday, for us all."

And she had clicked out the light before he could get up and check that the taps had been turned off, or whether the freezer box had been left open.

So Eric now felt shrived, without the necessity of being shriven, and sat contented with his lot, a man who could face being fifty years with equanimity.

"And the other one," continued Ted, "goes to the crew of *Moby Dick!*"

Jack's brow creased with a slight frown at the amazement in Ted's voice. Rosie squeezed his thigh warningly before he could respond.

Ted rubbed his hand through his blond-streaked thatch.

"If anyone 'ud asked me what Jack knew about sailin', I would have said my mate Jack wouldn't know if a band were up 'im until he got the drum, but there it is, ye can't get it right all the time and Jack sure showed us what your Yorkshire terriers can do when they try. So an ashtray to you, Jack, for a brilliant bit of sailin'."

It was Darren, however, who went up amid applause to collect the trophy, Jack for some reason unknown to Ted being in the grip of some strong emotion.

Darren stood with the ashtray in his hands, seemingly controlling an unwelcome spasm, a tanned, clean–cut Leeds fan whose support on the terraces had given way to a new passion.

"It's been great. Great. Our Sharon an' me, we didn't really fancy it, poncin' around on sailin' boats, did we, Sharon?"

But his eyes fell on an empty seat. Sharon had taken advantage of the growing shadows to slip away with Arnold to a more deserted spot, under the olive trees behind the café. Swapping addresses and embraces was much more exciting than watching her brother making a right dick of himself.

Used to his sister's desertion, Darren stumbled on.

"So, anyway, now we're gonna do it again if Dad comes up on the pools, an' – an' – an' Trudy an' me are gonna see each other 'cos we've got our addresses an' it's not all that far away an'," he grinned shyly, "she ain't even been to a football match, 'ave yer, Trudy?"

Penny laughed and patted her daughter's hand while Darren loped back to his father's side, the latter looking as stricken as Eric at the news of this continuing liaison.

Rosie and Penny exchanged a smile, a smile that spoke for the insight of women as opposed to the obtuseness of men.

Sally picked up a cluster of medals.

"These are mementoes for everyone from us, Ted and me. So that you'll remember us when you're back at home while we're..."

She was going to add that she and Ted would be preparing barbies on the beach for the next flotilla but Ted interrupted.

"While we're settin' up ourselves, eh Sally, back home with a boat of our own?"

Sally didn't argue. Ted's dream was something she could share in, even if the reality was to remain far beyond his grasp.

Chippers chimed in, sitting rigidly to attention, Lorraine's corset holding him stiffly erect.

"That's the right spirit. Set up for yourself. That's right, isn't it, Bernard?"

Bernie remained preoccupied with adding water to his ouzo, wondering if his stomach would ever take another onslaught of spiced meatballs.

"Bernard and the – ah – girls are setting up in private practice. The Flying Nurses. With, uhm, Bernie as the manager and, er, financed by us. Myself and Clara. The Chippendale Flying Nurses. Rather impressive, don't you think?"

The nurses looked suitably gratified by the chorus of approval. Bernie decided he could, after all, handle another round of meatballs.

Crispin pushed back his chair, raised his last glass of Domestica – something he wouldn't miss back home – and addressed the home-bound gathering.

The glass caught a last red ray of sun, a handful of sparkling light bidding goodbye from the Ionian.

"To Ted and Sally. I never thought we would enjoy it so much. All of us. It's been jolly nice."

It was only when the crews stood up to raise their glasses that they became aware of an increase in their numbers.

Between Gerhard and Monika, in the deep shadow beneath the café's straw roof, stood the tall and statuesque figure of Ariadne.

Gerhard had found his woman after all.

*   *   *

The brass band of Sinanaj could have done with a few more rehearsals, but without the stimulus of competition it was to be expected that the norm should be something of a cacophony. Besides, despite the spirit of free enterprise that was now official government policy, the workers in the jam factory still spent more time in canning raspberries than in blowing them.

Never had the village been so bedecked with bunting, so flamboyant with flags. The brass–hats and big–noises had arived that morning from Tirana, all anxious to shake hands and kiss babies now that democracy – or a kind of democracy sufficiently recognizable to the West to qualify for a few subsidies – was beckoning on the horizon.

Getting everything ready in time for the ceremony had been a touch-and-go affair, with desperate last-minute activity behind the scenes. Lieutenant Ramon Manski had persuaded the authorities that, as Oleg was a son of Sinanaj, the village should have the honour of opening up the rusting metal cases and revealing their contents to the world. Or at least to the authorities who might have other plans.

It had taken nearly a month to clean up the flotilla treasure. True, there had been an initial feeling of disappointment that the crustaceous containers had not concealed bars of gold, silver chalices or even straightforward piratical pieces-of-eight.

The acetylene torches applied by the Lieutenant's troop had zipped through the metal of the first of the larger boxes to reveal – a pedestal. Though sea water had seeped into the container and with it those persistent creatures, molluscs and barnacles, what lay on its side was undoubtedly the pedestal of a sizeable statue. A rounded base, with patches of white marble peeping through a clinging patina of marine life, merged into a fluted column, ending abruptly in a flat surface with a hole in it.

Predictably, the next box contained an extension of the column, similarly holed for the metal support that would keep the two pieces in place when hauled into position, one on top of the other.

The third and smaller box encased the head, pillowed on its side, a head the size of a slumbering man, its features blurred beneath a fuzz of brown-black seaweed and a coating of shells. Male or female, god or mortal, there was no telling. But the hand or hands that had sculpted the marble had obviously been commemorating a being of great importance, an image that would inspire awe in its beholders.

It had fallen to the lot of the village carpenter, one Josef Tsenyetska, to restore the statue to its original splendour. Not over-endowed with skill, patience or an education that enabled him to read let alone harbour any knowledge of classical antiquities, he had nonetheless set to with a will. It made a change from banging wooden crates together to hold tins of jam.

The pedestal and column were easy enough. Scraping here, chiselling there, even Josef could follow the lines and curves originally determined by the unknown hand.

The head, though, presented problems. For one thing, it wore a hat, a sort of round helmet with a flat top and a crest at the front. Expecting to find petrified locks of hair, Josef became convinced that he was working on a statue of a famous footballer from the Albanian national team whose premature demise after head-butting the opponent's goalpost instead of the goalkeeper had been the occasion for national mourning.

But it was the nose that gave Josef a honker of a headache. Chiselling clean the nostrils of a beezer the size of a settee requires more skill and muscle power than the shifty pick by the finger of a car driver in a motorway jam. For one thing, you have to sit on a conk that big: Josef had to find secure purchase with a leg each side of the bridge as he hunkered off tangled collections of clinging debris from what Crispin would have recognized as a *probiscus Romanus*.

It was in an effort to remove a particularly persistent mollusc that Josef too firmly applied mallet to chisel and – CLUMP! – or more linguistically – CRUUMPTA! – both snoot and snoot cleaner hit the dusty deck.

Though uninjured, the carpenter was dismayed by the faceless nose, and none too happy about the noseless face. Despite never having travelled beyond the vicinity of Sinanaj, Josef Tsenyetska was aware that statues depicting faces possessed, in general, some sort of snozzle. When the statue is important to the government, and it is your job to restore it to prime condition, the loss of its nose is quite likely to lead to the loss of your own.

Thus it was that, on the eve of the unveiling, the entire Tsenyetska family applied itself to repairing the damage by applying the nose to the face. Josef's wife, five of his older children, his aunty Benitska and mad cousin Piotr held the nose in position beneath the outraged eyes while Josef drilled in metal rods, mixed buckets of cement and rubbed dust around the join so that the face wouldn't look as though it had met its nose under colossal impact.

As dawn spilled into the decorated streets of Sinanaj, the head was finally being lowered into place on its column, possibly for the first time since it had been carved from a marble block. Concealed by its silk shroud, the statue stood rigidly ready to play blind-man's-buff, and the square began to fill with the participants in the new day's game.

Oleg stood to attention next to his father-in-law while the strains of the national anthem wheezed uncertainly into the ears of the crowd assembled in the town square. By his side stood a matronly Katrina, her hand ready to deliver a sharp smack to any of her three children who might give a sly pinch to one of their siblings.

He shifted uncomfortably in his ill-fitting suit, the sort of baggy-crotched ensemble that some Englishmen still take pride in. His eye swept the audience beneath the flag-bedecked dignitaries' stand, searching for clues which might indicate the paternity of two of the children who were now to regard him as their father.

Better not to know. Let sleeping Albanians lie. The superintendent of the factory and the Police Commissar were like *that*: life could be made extremely unpleasant if he was to prove troublesome yet again.

He winced involuntarily as a trombonist tromboned a pronounced miss-hit. For a moment, he allowed himself to recall the murmuring breezes of his Crusoe existence, the smell of rosemary and burning olive branches.

But only for a moment. He was, after all, now assistant superintendent and would take over the entire factory in a year. A car was a distinct possibility if output was doubled over the next two years.

With a final discordant burst, the band blew itself out.

There was an expectant hush.

Oleg walked forward, shoulders squared, past the assembled suits.

He mounted the podium steps.

His hand reached for the cord and, with a jerk, the red

silk of the national flag, appropriately adorned with a black double-headed eagle, billowed out and fluttered skywards, the eagle at last spreading its wings.

The handclaps, the exuberant shouts, the bustle of anticipation broke off abruptly. A few children, scattered among the crowd, cheered mechanically and whirled their wooden rattles, the noise echoing hollowly from the houses bordering the square.

The big-wigs and the brass-hats held their hands frozen in mid clap, like a team formed to catch a fly. The President was in danger of swallowing one. His eyes yo-yoed in their sockets. His tongue dried out on his fillings.

From where Oleg stood, at the foot of the column, it was difficult to make out the statue's features. Peering up its nostrils was of no help. But he could make out the inscription, carefully restored but not understood by Josef Tsenyetska.

It read

Il Duce
Benito Mussolini
Vincitore di Albania
1942

"That probably means," mused Oleg, "Conqueror of Albania."

Benito Mussolini, all lip-curl and square-jawed, gazed out whitely above the roofline of the surrounding buildings. The double-headed eagle sculpted on his hat looked stolen from the Albanian flag. The Roman nose sniffed imperiously, twitching for its lost empire.

The President's gaze transferred to Oleg as he walked slowly back to his place, his footsteps echoing questioningly around the square amid the stunned silence. This man, thought the President bitterly, this man told us that we had taken possession of a pure example of Ancient Greek or Roman art. Maybe a part of our heritage. The Albanians could, after all, trace themselves back to the Thracians.

The President's thoughts slid between grinding teeth. If

241

nothing else, the statue could have been bartered in negotiations with Greece or Italy, used as a gesture of friendliness – or an instrument of blackmail.

What they *had*, here in Sinanaj, was – was Benito Mussolini! The swine who had invaded Albania thinking it would be a walkover – and whose defeat ultimately led to his personal downfall. *Il Duce.* They had erected a statue to the Italian fascist.

From somewhere in the crowd, a stone flew. Then another. And another. A low growl of recognition and fury swelled into a concerted hymn of hate and outrage.

The missiles aimed at Il Duce were joined by more, aimed at the platform of dignitaries. Stones were scarce, but a crowd can always find something to throw and mules were still a common form of transport: there was plenty of mule shit.

Suddenly, abruptly, there were cries of "look, look" and a shocked and frightened "aaahhh" fell from the mouths of the frozen spectators.

Mussolini was moving.

Catholics crossed themselves, muslims bent their heads, gypsies warded off the evil eye and ex-Marxists – very few these days – tried to remember one of Chairman Mao's maxims.

Benito was breathing.

Il Duce's face was changing expression. It seemed to become cross-eyed, then macaw-like as the nose tilted forward with an audible crack. For a moment it balanced trembling on Benito's petulant upper lip, as though he was testing his own breath for halitosis.

Then the loosening metal rods detached themselves from the rest of Il Duce's visage, the cement slapped to the ground, and half-a-ton of Mussolini's marble hooter landed on, then in, the President's car.

The statue was, in truth, a bust. And it was busted.

*　　*　　*

If that car had not been so important to the President, mused Oleg as he gnawed the leg of one of Andreas's chickens, he might not have reacted so badly.

Trouble was, the car was a Zill, a big, black Russian limo, sinister and imposing. And the Russians weren't giving them away anymore – weren't *repairing* them anymore. So the President was down to a Strada.

And Oleg was back in Abeliki. Ironic. They'd deported him, at dead of night, to the place he'd escaped to all those years ago. They'd offered him a compromise of sorts: a firing squad or the late-night pleasure cruise, single ticket, to an accessible island of his own choice, outside Albanian waters.

It was an amazing indication of how liberal the government had become. And if the Greeks didn't like it, they knew what they could do.

The statue remained noseless in Sinanaj. The inscription had been altered to read, somewhat laboriously, that Mussolini's victory was as plain as the nose on his face. Heavily sarcastic, but in the tradition of Albanian literature.

Oleg tore the other leg off the chicken and offered it to Ramon Manski. The offer was curtly refused. Ramon was still sulking.

Oh well, thought Oleg, he'll get used to it in time. Couldn't be any worse than the army. Or being shot by the army.

From the height of their olive-fringed knoll, they could see across the sparkling azure sea to where a group of yachts sailed purposefully towards Abeliki Bay.

Oleg smiled comfortably to himself. He threw his chicken bone at a slumbering lizard and missed. The lizard smiled conspiratorially. What was the jam factory, what was a wife and three suspect children, compared to the pleasure of living by one's own wits, the thrill of anticipation at the arrival of each new flotilla?

He rubbed his hands, slapped Ramon on the thigh with an unrewarded gesture of camaraderie and light-heartedness, and settled down to wait.

Out at sea, a radio crackled into life.

"This is it, folks, get set for the barbie. Everyone anchors up in line next to me. OK? Cripes, Sally, that piker with those three stupid ankle-biters ought to fetch them one, I'll drown one of them kids if..."

And the radio was abruptly turned off.

THE END